NAME THIS INSECT

NAME THIS INSECT

BY

ERIC FITCH DAGLISH

*Illustrated with
16 pages of colour plates,
48 pages of black-and-white half-tones,
and many diagrams in the text*

LONDON
J. M. DENT & SONS LTD

© Revisions, Eric Fitch Daglish, 1960

All rights reserved
Printed in Great Britain
by
Lowe & Brydone (Printers) Ltd
London N.W.10
for
J. M. DENT & SONS LTD
Aldine House · Bedford Street · London
First published 1952
Revised edition 1960

CONTENTS

ILLUSTRATIONS

Between pages 6 and 7

COLOUR

BLACK AND WHITE

Full reference to the contents of the plates is made in the index (page 283).

vii

FOREWORD

OF the various types of animal life found in the British Isles insects are by far the most numerous. They may be seen in all parts of the country at all seasons and, because of their universal abundance, are particularly favourable subjects for study by all for whom nature observation holds an appeal. On sunny days in spring and summer one can hardly fail to notice some, at least, of the myriad forms which fill the air with the buzz of wings, but, unlike some other members of our native fauna, they do not disappear with the advent of winter's frosts. Even on the coldest day a goodly collection of insects may be made by turning over a heap of dead leaves, exploring the withered herbage of a hedgerow bank, probing beneath bushes, under sods, stones, loose bark, and similar hiding-places. Neither is it necessary to make special excursions in order to pursue their study. A garden, a clump of nettles on a piece of waste ground, the grass verge of a roadway, a ditch or a pond almost anywhere will afford a variety of species sufficient to keep the student occupied for many hours. In large cities public parks and bombed sites will often prove fertile hunting-grounds, or a water-butt or forgotten static water-tank may reveal a surprising variety of aquatic insects in all stages of their life cycles. The country rambler, however little attention he may previously have given to the tribe of insects, cannot for long remain unconscious of their number and diversity through whatever kind of country his way may lie; whether by field path, woodland glade, hillside, river bank, or seashore. Butterflies, dragonflies, or other less conspicuous winged forms may flit above his head; while creeping, running, or jumping beetles, bugs, earwigs, grasshoppers, and the like, as well as the immature young of the flying types, may be seen on the ground or on the foliage of grass, hedges, and trees. Yet should he, from awakened interest, wish to name and find out something of the life stories of the insects which he has noticed he may be discouraged by unexpected difficulties. Apart from butterflies and moths, the great majority of British insects have no generally recognized English names, and the details of their structure and habits are to be discovered only by patient delving into a number of separate works, each devoted to one of the several orders into which the class is divided. The main purpose of the present volume is to provide such information in a form calculated to appeal to the non-technical reader. The aim is not only to enable the rambler to identify all the insects commonly met with in this country whose appearance is likely to arrest attention but also to give in brief the salient facts of their life stories. The key sections are based on those character-istics which, it is thought, will be most easily recognized by the non-specialist. The primary divisions depend on the number of wings present; the subdivisions on the texture of the wings, the general body shape, colour, and size. As the book is intended to serve as a companion during rambles, all technicalities have, as far as possible, been avoided. Where, in the interest of accuracy or clarity, it has been necessary to introduce technical terms a simple explanation of each is given.

As there are approximately 20,000 species of British insects, a selection of those to be included in the descrip-tive sections has had to be made. The rare, very local, or minute have been passed over in favour of species more likely to be seen or to attract notice. Insects less than a quarter of an inch in length are not, with a few excep-tions, included, for it is felt that to identify such tiny forms involves the use of a lens, microscope, or equipment of a kind not usually available outside the specialists' work-room. Because so many British insects have no generally recognized English names, the scientific names of all the species dealt with are given. Even when an insect is well known by a popular name in one locality it may be called by an entirely different one elsewhere, or have been referred to under various titles by older writers. The inclusion of scientific names will enable a reader who wishes further to pursue the study of a particular order to refer to the larger works devoted to the special type of insects about which fuller information is desired. Butterflies and moths have received so much more popular attention than other insects that all the British species have well-established English names. For this reason their scientific nomenclature has been omitted from the descriptive text but is given in appendices to the sections dealing with the Lepidoptera.

Weather conditions or lack of time may sometimes make identification in the field difficult. In such circumstances specimens may be captured and carried home for later examination, and a few hints on the equipment necessary for collecting insects may be useful. The rambler will not wish to be encumbered with heavy or unwieldy apparatus and the essential appliances are few and easily carried. A large, strong net is useful both for taking insects in the air and for sweeping over low-growing herbage to collect the many species which frequent such places. The bag of the net may be attached to a metal rim with a screw attachment, so that it may be removed from the handle when not in use. A sheet of white or light-coloured material is another valuable aid. It may be spread under trees and tall bushes while the branches are shaken to dislodge some of the innumerable insects which hide among the foliage and twigs. It will also serve to receive the contents of

the sweeping net; its light colour making the sorting
of the catch easy. Sheets of white paper may be used but
are liable to be torn and soon become sodden if the ground
is damp. For killing the captured insects a wide-
mouthed glass jar or bottle, with a tight-fitting cork or
screw top, may be about half filled with fresh laurel
shoots or young leaves which have been crushed, bruised,
or finely chopped. This will prove lethal to all but the
toughest captives. Another effective method is to put a
piece of blotting-paper saturated in benzene in a well-
corked bottle. It is advisable to carry two killing
bottles, one small, the other larger. In the smaller one
a few pieces of soft crumpled paper should be laid on the
top of the killing ingredients. This is reserved for small
insects which might be damaged by being knocked about
in the larger bottle. The crumpled paper affords chinks
and crannies into which the captives may creep and from
which they may be carefully shaken on reaching home.
Large, hard-cased beetles and similar insects may survive
incarceration in the laurel bottle for some time. These
may be killed instantly by dropping them in boiling
water. Before being placed in a permanent collection
insects must be set. Butterflies, moths, and many other
winged insects are usually arranged with the wings
outspread. This is done by fixing the body to a flat
board by a small pin through the thorax, spreading the
wings by the aid of fine needles, and securing them in
position by threads of cotton or by slips of paper or thin
card. The legs should be arranged and held in place by
supporting pins. Beetles, bugs, grasshoppers, etc., may be
set in their natural attitudes, with wings folded along the
back. The legs should be set in the manner already
described. When the limbs are firmly set in the desired
positions, the insects may be fixed to small cards by
gum smeared on the foot joints. In the case of large,
heavy specimens a little gum may also be placed on the

side of the body to keep the subject firmly attached.
isects are not set soon after death they will be found
be too rigid for the legs and wings to be manipulated.
Such specimens may be relaxed by placing them in a
metal box lined with cork. The cork must be damp
when the insect is put in the box and the lid kept closed.
After some hours in such a relaxing chamber the legs and
wings will be as easy to arrange as are those of fresh-killed
specimens. A well-arranged collection may be of great
value in the study of insects. It is, indeed, almost
indispensable if any serious work on classification is
undertaken. But mere collecting should not be allowed
to become the chief object of the rambler. The living
insect in its natural haunts holds more fascination, and is
of greater interest to the nature-lover, than its corpse,
however well set and mounted. Much is known in
minute detail of the structure of insects as seen in
museum cabinets. A very great deal remains to be
discovered of the inner secrets of the lives of many of
our most common and widely distributed species. The
unravelling of the mysteries of insect life can be an
absorbing occupation, and is one which may be followed
by any one possessed of a seeing eye, patience, and a
zealous love of the open air.

INSECTS IN GENERAL

INSECTS form the most numerous of the classes into which the various types of animal life are divided. Approximately a million species have been described and named and doubtless very many more have yet to be discovered. In the British Isles some 20,000 species occur, ranging in size from the Death's - head moth, which may have a wing-span of over five inches, to minute forms almost invisible to the unaided eye.

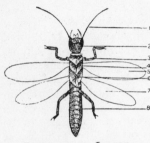

PARTS OF AN INSECT

1. Antennae. 2. Head. 3. Prothorax. 4. Mesothorax. 5. Forewings arising from mesothorax. 6. Metathorax. 7. Hind-wings arising from metathorax. 8. Abdomen.

The middle pair of legs is not shown.

The salient peculiarities of insects are that in the typical adult condition there are three pairs of legs, the body is divided into three distinct parts, the head, thorax, and abdomen, and all the parts are covered with a hard coat of a substance called chitin. These characteristics clearly exclude from the class such creatures as spiders, harvestmen, millepedes, and centipedes, which are frequently vaguely referred to as insects. The head bears a pair of large eye masses, each consisting of many thousand small, separate eyes, which may occupy almost the entire surface of the head. In addition to these compound eyes many, though not all, insects have a few simple eyes, or ocelli, situated near the top of the head in the space between the globular eye masses. This complex visual apparatus enables an insect to see sideways and to the rear as well as in front. The mouth parts in the more generalized types consist of an upper and

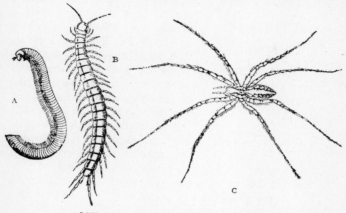

A. Millepede.   **B.** Centipede.   **c.** Spider.

lower lip, the labrum and labium, a pair of strong biting jaws or mandibles, with toothed edges, which move horizontally, not vertically as in vertebrates, and a pair of secondary jaws which are smaller than the mandibles, though sharp and serrated, called maxillae. The last-named parts bear lateral processes, the palps, which may be clearly seen in some insects, projecting below the head. Beetles and earwigs are among the insects showing mouth parts conforming to this typical pattern.

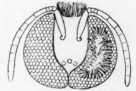

Head of bee, showing large compound eyes, each composed of numerous simple eyes.

But in many other types the mouth is specialized for sucking or for sucking and piercing combined, resulting in remarkable changes in the shape and relationship of

xv

the parts. In the butterflies and moths all but lished maxillae are reduced to minute vestiges, and tho to

MOUTH PARTS OF BEETLE

a. Antennae.
b. Mandibles.
c. Maxillae.
d and e. Palps.

secondary jaws are transformed into a long, tubular proboscis which lies coiled in a spiral below the head when not in use. The long tongue of some bees represents the greatly elongated labium or lower lip ensheathed in the modified maxillae; while the sharp, horny beak of the bugs is made up of the lengthened and flattened labrum with its margins turned inwards to form a tube, enclosing four sharp, bristle-like stylets which are the mandibles and maxillae.

The antennae are sensory organs which, because in many insects they are in almost constant motion and appear to be used as organs of touch, are often referred to as feelers. They vary widely in size and shape, not only in different orders but in closely related species and even in different sexes of the same insect. The thorax is made up of three parts, the fore or prothorax, the middle or mesothorax, and the hind or metathorax. In most insects these parts are more or less fused together but in some, like the stone-flies, each segment is quite distinct.

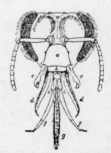

MOUTH PARTS OF BEE

a. Clypeus.
b. Labrum.
c. Mandibles.
d. Maxillae.
e. Labium.
f. Labial palps.
g. Lingula or tongue.

Each of the thoracic segments bears a pair of legs. When wings are developed the fore pair springs from

mesothorax and the hind pair from the metathorax. The legs are often modified to suit the habits of
particular insects. The fore pair may be specialized as
digging implements, weapons of defence or offence, for
the capture of prey, or in
various other directions. In
some water insects the
hind legs are elongated and
flattened to act as paddles
or oars; in crickets and
grasshoppers they are
lengthened and strengthened
for jumping or leaping. Each
leg consists of five parts.
The first or basal joint is
the coxa, or hip, and at-
taches the limb to the underside of the thorax. Next
comes a small ring-like or
triangular joint, the trochanter, which articulates with
the longer thigh or femur,
usually the largest portion
of the leg. Following this
is the tibia or shank, another long joint which often
bears stiff hairs or spines
on its edges. Finally there
are from three to five joints,
usually short and small,
which form the tarsus or foot.

DISARTICULATED INSECT

a. Head.
b. Prothorax with fore-legs.
c. Mesothorax bearing middle
   legs and fore-wings.
d. Metathorax bearing hind-
   legs and hind-wings.
e. Thigh or Femur.
f. Shank or Tibia.
g. Foot or Tarsus.
h. Abdomen.
i. Ovipositor.

The last of the tarsal joints usually ends in a pair of claws
which in some kinds of insects is associated with a pair of
soft, membranous pads, called pulvilli. These may be
seen under a microscope on the feet of the house-fly,
blow-fly, or dung-fly, and enable these insects to walk

back-downwards on ceilings or crawl up the po
glass of windows. The fore-wings may be hardened

PARTS OF AN INSECT'S LEG
1. Coxa. 2. Trochanter.
3. Femur. 4. Tibia.
5. Tarsus.

form horny or leathery cases
beneath which the more
delicate hind-wings are folded
when not in use, as in
beetles and bugs. Many insects have lost the power of
flight and are wingless. In
others wings are developed
in one sex only ; while in
such forms as the aphids or
green-fly the males are always winged but the females
may be either winged or wingless.

That butterflies and moths begin life in forms start-
lingly different from that
which they finally assume, is
among the most generally
known facts connected with
insects. The life cycle begins
with the egg, from which
in due course a caterpillar
emerges. This caterpillar
feeds voraciously and grows
quickly, eventually changing
into a chrysalis which after
a longer or shorter period is
transformed into the flying insect. A similar *complete* metamorphosis occurs in beetles,
bees, wasps, and flies, but it
is not universal among
insects. In some cases the

Foot of fly showing pulvilli
between the claws.

young leave the egg differing very little in appearance
from their parents, except that they are without wings.
Such *incomplete* metamorphosis is characteristic of bugs,

earwigs, crickets and grasshoppers, and several other orders. The creeping, leaf-eating, worm-like caterpillar is adapted for a mode of life wholly different from that

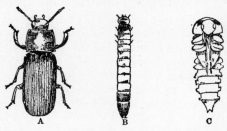

STAGES IN THE LIFE CYCLE OF A BEETLE
A. Perfect insect.   B. Larva.   C. Pupa.

of the winged, nectar-sipping butterfly or moth. The quiescent chrysalis or pupal phase represents the intermediate stage, during which the body of the caterpillar or larva is, as it were, reorganized to conform with the needs of the butterfly or moth which it is destined to become. The larvae of insects in which metamorphosis is incomplete are called nymphs. Since the young differ from the adult condition only in minor directions there is no need for the quiescent pupal stage

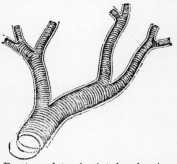

Portion of tracheal tube showing supporting bands of chitin.

in their development and they remain active throughout their lives.

All adult insects need access to atmospheric air for purposes of respiration. Air is taken into the body through small breathing pores, or spiracles, situated on the sides of certain of the thoracic and abdominal segments. The spiracles are the external openings to a system of tracheal tubes which ramify through all parts of the body. These air tubes are kept distended by spiral bands of chitin which, when greatly magnified, look like the metal coils sometimes inserted into rubber hosepipes to keep them from collapsing. The spiracles of many insects are provided with lips or valves, which enable the pores to be closed or opened according to whether the needs of the body demand the air supply to be renewed or the air already taken in to be conserved. In insects which pass the early stages of their development in water the immature forms may possess gills instead of, or in addition to, spiracles. They are, therefore, able to remain permanently submerged, without having periodically to rise to the surface to take in fresh supplies of air.

AN EASY WAY TO NAME INSECTS

HAVING found an insect the identity of which is in doubt, the reader should turn to the primary key on pages xxv and xxvi. This will direct him to one of the twelve sections into which the body of the book is divided. Each of these sections is prefaced by a general introduction to the insects which it deals with; explaining their salient characteristics, mode of life, development, and how they differ from the insects described in other sections. Having found the appropriate section, the sectional key there given should be consulted. This will lead the reader by a number of alternatives to a description of the species in question, giving both its popular and scientific name, except in the case of insects which have no recognized English cognomen, with particulars of its distribution, haunts, and habits. To make the correct interpretation of the alternatives more certain text figures are given to illustrate the main divisions of the keys. Where there is likely to be uncertainty as to which of two alternative descriptions apply to a species, the insect is included in each division of the text to which the alternatives lead, so that the same goal may be reached by two or more routes. Similarly, in insects which vary in colour or form in the same or opposite sexes, or in which colour or shape may be differently regarded by different observers, alternative means of identifying them have been arranged. For this reason the name of some species may occur several times in various divisions of the key. The keys are based on easily seen external features, such as number of wings, shape of body, length of legs, colour, and size, which the ordinary reader with no previous knowledge of insect structure should have no difficulty in recognizing. The system has been built up on characteristics chosen solely with the object of making identification easy and rapid, without regard for entomological classification. But with the exception of X and XII all the sections cover one of the orders or main divisions of the insect tribe. Section X includes a varied assortment of four-winged insects which are not closely related. They have been grouped together here because they show certain superficial resemblances which are more likely to be apparent to the non-specialist than are the distinctions on which their positions in scientific classification rest.

For those who are making their first acquaintance with the study of insects the brief introduction to the class given on pages xiv–xx will serve to explain the terms used in the descriptive parts of the text. That introduction and the sectional prefaces will enable any reader clearly to understand the few technicalities which it has been found necessary to employ.

As an example of how the key system works let us suppose we have seen an insect sunning itself on a post or fence in a garden. We notice that it bears a general resemblance to the common blow-fly, or bluebottle, in shape and size, but that the body is shining black with bright orange wing bases. The insect has only two wings, so on turning to the primary key on page xxvi we are directed to Section XI. Turning to page 260 we find that, as the fly is not long and narrow, we must go on to No. 7. Here we are asked whether the body is hairy or smooth. As we particularly noticed the glistening black of the body we know that the insect is not hairy, so we pass on as directed to No. 20. As the abdomen is not long and narrow we go to No. 22. The insect is neither bee-like nor wasp-like so that our next reference is No. 28. As the insect is about the size of a blow-fly we pass to No. 29. Here we find that the first alternative offered seems appropriate. This leads us to

No. 30, where we come on a description which fits exactly, identifying our fly as the Noon-fly, the scientific name of which is *Mesembrina meridiana*, and find a brief account of its habits, distribution, and mode of reproduction. Thus in a few minutes we have succeeded in identifying an insect which, though by no means uncommon, is not generally known by name and of which many works on insects make no mention. To achieve the same result by searching at random through the pages of entomological books of reference might have involved several hours of patient delving. By the method adopted in this book the majority of the insects the reader is likely to encounter may be named even more quickly and by fewer steps than in the example chosen.

KEY TO SECTIONS

1 ⎧ Insects with four wings.　　　　　　　2
　⎨ Insects with two wings.　　　　　　　11
　⎩ Wingless insects.　　　　　　　　　12

2 ⎧ Wings large, covered with feather-like scales.
　⎨ 　　　　　　　**Butterflies and Moths.**　3
　⎩ Wings not covered with scales.　　　　4

3 ⎧ Antennae clubbed.　　　　　　　**Butterflies.**
　⎪ 　　　　　　　Section I, page 7.
　⎨ Antennae of various shapes but not clubbed.
　⎪ 　　　　　　　　　　　**Moths.**
　⎩ 　　　　　　　Section II, page 33.

4 ⎧ Fore-wings hard and horny.　　　　**Beetles.**
　⎨ 　　　　　　　Section III, page 112.
　⎩ Fore-wings not horny.　　　　　　　5

5 ⎧ Mouth parts forming a piercing and sucking pro-
　⎪ boscis.　　　　**Bugs, Plant-lice, White-**
　⎪ 　　　　　**flies, Scale Insects.**
　⎨ 　　　　　　Section IV, page 166.
　⎪ Mouth parts not forming a piercing and sucking
　⎩ proboscis.　　　　　　　　　　6

6 ⎧ Fore-wings leathery.　　　　　　　7
　⎨ Fore-wings not leathery.　　　　　9

7
{
Abdomen bearing a pair of terminal forceps. Fore-wings very short. **Earwigs.**
Section V, page 187.
Abdomen without terminal forceps. **8**
}

8
{
Hind-legs much longer than the others; specialized for jumping. **Crickets and Grasshoppers.**
Section VI, page 191.

Hind-legs not much longer than others; not specialized for jumping. **Cockroaches.**
Section VII, page 201.
}

9
{
Wings membranous, narrow, with few veins. Fore- and hind-wing on each side connected by minute hooks when in flight.
Bees, Wasps, Sawflies, Ants, Ichneumon-flies.
Section VIII, page 214.

Wings membranous with fine, close network of veins. Fore- and hind-wing on each side not connected by hooklets when in flight. **10**
}

10
{
Head large, antennae minute, bristle-like, body very long and narrow. Wings long; fore- and hind-wings of equal length. **Dragonflies.**
Section IX, page 239.

Not as above described.
Mayflies, Alder-flies, Caddis-flies, Stone-flies, Snake-flies, Lacewing-flies.
Section X, page 249.
}

11. Two-winged flies. Section XI, page 260.

12. Wingless insects. Section XII, page 280.

BUTTERFLIES AND MOTHS

BUTTERFLIES and moths constitute the order Lepidoptera or scaly-winged insects, so named because the wings are covered with feather-like scales, the broad ends of which overlap like tiles on a roof. It is to these scales that the numerous colours shown by the wings of such insects are due, arising either from contained pigment or from prismatic effects produced by surface markings.

Scales from butterflies' wings.

If a butterfly or moth is handled small patches of what appears to be dust-like powder are usually left on the fingers. Under a microscope each grain of this powder is revealed as a tiny stalked scale. The shape and markings differ with the species of butterfly or moth from which it came. It may be long and comparatively narrow, or short and broad. Its upper edge may be serrated or smooth. Markings on its broader portion may be in the form of fine striations, pits, or a combination of the two. Similar scales occur on a few other kinds of insects but never in such abundance. In no other order are the wings completely covered with these outgrowths.

Apart from their scaly wing covering there is little difficulty in distinguishing a butterfly or moth from any other kind of insect. The large, opaque wings, as well as the formation of the body, head, and antennae, are in all

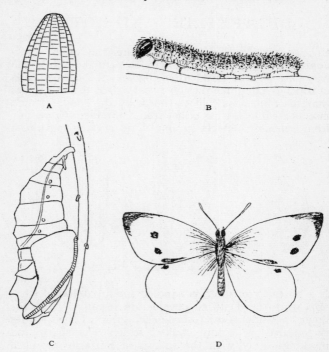

DEVELOPMENT OF A BUTTERFLY
A. Egg.   B. Caterpillar.   C. Chrysalis.   D. Imago.

but a few species sufficient to make recognition very easy. The exceptions are the females of certain moths, like the Mottled Umber and Vapourer, in which the wings are vestigial, so that the insects are flightless and spidery in appearance. Such aberrant forms are, however, rarely seen unless searched for and when found examination with a lens or low-power microscope will serve quickly to reveal the insect's relationship.

As is generally known, the life-history of butterflies and moths is divided into four well-marked stages. These are egg, active larva or caterpillar, quiescent pupa or chrysalis, and imago or perfect flying insect.

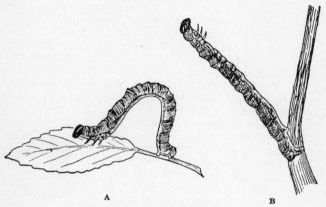

A   B

LOOPER CATERPILLAR
Showing (A) method of walking; (B) concealing attitude.

The eggs vary widely in shape. They may be round, elliptical, or oval, with or without flattened tops, bases, or both. The shell surface may be ribbed, fluted, pitted, or more elaborately ornamented with a raised network or other pattern. They are attached, usually in batches, to the leaves or stems of the plants on which the caterpillars are destined to feed.

Little need be said here about the second stage, since caterpillars of various kinds are familiar to every one. The body is soft and usually cylindrical, with large, horny head. The first three segments bear each a pair of rather slender legs. The hind segments have four pairs of short, sucker-like organs called prolegs. The last

3

body segment also bears a pair of similar processes called claspers. The prolegs are used for walking and for holding on to a leaf or other support while the caterpillar feeds, for which purpose their lower surfaces are provided with series of tiny hooklets. In caterpillars of certain moths the prolegs are reduced to a single pair and there is one pair of claspers. Such caterpillars are often called loopers from the curious manner in which they move, by pushing the head and fore-body forward, then drawing up the hind part of the body by arching the abdomen in a high hump or loop to enable the prolegs and claspers to secure a fresh hold. The body may

Pupa of moth.

be smooth, spiny, or thickly covered with hairs. The jaws are short, strong, and suited to biting. The eyes consist of clusters of simple ocelli, placed on the sides of the head. The antennae are so minute as to be visible only by the aid of a lens. Each of the body segments, with the exception of the second, bears a breathing pore, or spiracle, on either side; the position of this pore being shown by a dark, more or less circular, spot. From the mouth parts arises a special organ, the spinneret, through which a fluid, which on contact with air hardens into a silken thread, is exuded as required. As the young caterpillar feeds and grows its non-elastic skin becomes too tight for its enlarged body and splits, the larva emerging from its outgrown cuticle clad in a bright new coat. In the course of its development a caterpillar undergoes four or five such moults before passing on to the next stage in its life-history and becoming a chrysalis or pupa.

COCOON OF SILK MOTH
L. Lid raised to allow moth to emerge.

4

BUTTERFLIES AND MOTHS

Butterfly chrysalises are usually angular in shape and suspended by a pad of silk to a plant, post, wall, or other support. The pupae of moths are smoother and more cylindrical. The caterpillars of many moths spin cocoons, in the fabric of which fragments of wood, dead leaves, or earth may be intermixed, in which to pupate. These are often secreted in crevices in trees or hidden beneath the soil. The chrysalis of a butterfly or moth neither moves nor feeds. The only motion of which it is capable is a slight, jerking movement of the hind part of the abdomen. Its general appearance is that of a mummy, the developing wings and legs being dimly visible beneath the firm outer covering. During this resting phase the organic changes necessary to transfer the creeping, leaf-gnawing caterpillar, with its small, simple ocelli, to the flying, nectar-sipping imago with large, globular, compound eyes, are completed. When all is ready the pupal skin bursts and the perfect insect emerges to carry out the primary purpose of its transformation—to mate—and then to die.

Except for the large, scale-covered wings, the most characteristic feature of butterflies and moths is the long sucking proboscis which, when not in use, is curled in a flat spiral like a watch spring beneath the head. When feeding this double tube is uncoiled and inserted into blossoms offering a supply of nectar. All insects of this order feed on nectar and similar syrups, except a few moths like the Eggar, Goat, and Swift moths, in which the mouth parts are atrophied so that the flying insects are incapable of feeding at all. A few other species appear occasionally to vary the normal diet by imbibing stronger liquor in the form of the juices produced by decaying animal matter.

Sucking proboscis of butterfly.

If asked to define the difference between butterflies and moths many readers would perhaps suggest that whereas butterflies fly by day, moths are on the wing after sundown. But a number of common moths, like

5

the burnets, are as typically diurnal as are butterflies. Another generally held view is that a butterfly rests with the wings held vertically above the body with the upper surfaces in contact but a moth holds the wings flat along the back or spread horizontally. Again there are many exceptions to this generality. Such butterflies as the tortoiseshells, Peacock, and Red Admiral may often be seen resting on flowers or paths with outspread wings, and several other species which usually hold their wings vertically as they settle may occasionally keep them expanded. In moths the body is usually much thicker at the waist than in the more slenderly built butterflies, but the skipper butterflies are very moth-like in this respect. The only satisfactory means of determining whether an insect is a butterfly or a moth is to examine the antennae.

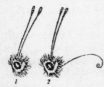

HEAD OF BUTTERFLY
Showing (1) clubbed antennae and (2) proboscis uncoiled.

All British butterflies have long antennae with knobs at the ends, giving these organs a clubbed shape. The antennae of moths vary very widely in form, some being thread-like, others feathered, comb-like, bristly, of uniform width from base almost to tip, or strongly tapered. But they never show the clubbed form seen in our butterflies. A feature peculiar to moths may be seen by examining the underside of the wing bases, when in some species each hind-wing will be found to bear a long bristle which, when the wings are spread in flight, engages in a small catch-like structure on the opposite fore-wing. No butterfly shows this bristle and catch arrangement. Though absent in some moths it occurs in all the British species which are at all likely to be mistaken for butterflies. The form of the antennae is, however, much the simplest means of distinguishing a butterfly from a moth.

1. Clouded Yellow   2. Marbled White
3. Brimstone

[1]

1. High Brown Fritillary
2. Glanville Fritillary
3. Glanville Fritillary (underside)
4. Dark Green Fritillary

[2]

1. White Admiral   2. Comma
3. Red Admiral

[3]

1. Adonis Blue (male)
2. Adonis Blue (underside)
3. Common Blue (underside)
4. Chalk Hill Blue (male)
5. Holly Blue (male)
6. Holly Blue (female)
7. Holly Blue (underside)

[4]

1. Death's-head Moth
2. Elephant Hawk
3. Small Elephant Hawk
4. Convolvulus Hawk

[5]

1. Large Emerald
2. Magpie

3. Beautiful Carpet
4. Clouded Border

5. Orange Moth

[6]

1. Garden Tiger
2. Ruby Tiger

3. Cinnabar
4. Emperor Moth (male)

[7]

1. Scarlet Tiger   3. Forester
2. Herald   4. Five-spot Burnet
          5. Burnished Brass

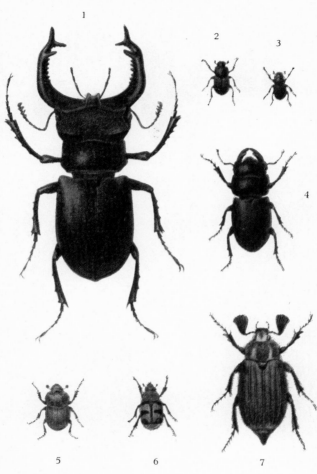

1. Stag Beetle (male)
2. Erratic Aphodius
3. Dung Aphodius

4. Little Stag
5. Cow Onthophagus
6. Bee Chafer

7. Cockchafer

[9]

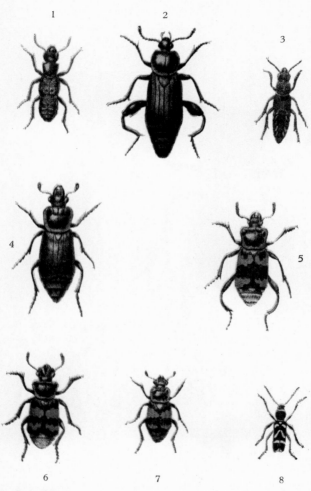

1. Creophilus maxullosus
2. Shore Sexton
3. Staphylinus caesareus
4. Black Burying Beetle
5. Common Burying Beetle
6. Searcher Burying Beetle
7. Undertaker Beetle
8. Wasp Beetle

[10]

1. Margined Dytiscus
2. Black-bellied Dytiscus
3. Grooved Acilius
4. Colymbetes fuscus

5. Two-spotted Agabus
6. Nut Apoderus
7. Dusky Ilybius
8. Spurred Phyllobius

1. Lygaeus equestris
2. Black-and-red Frog-hopper
3. Pond Skater
4. Water Boatman
5. Red-legged Bug
(All enlarged)

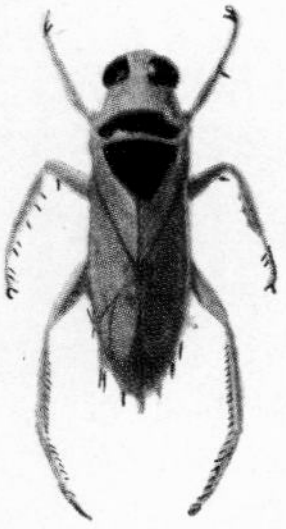

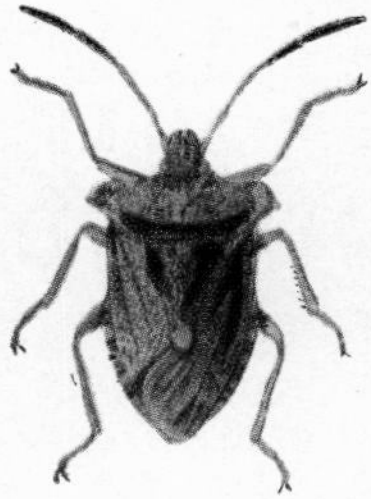

[12]

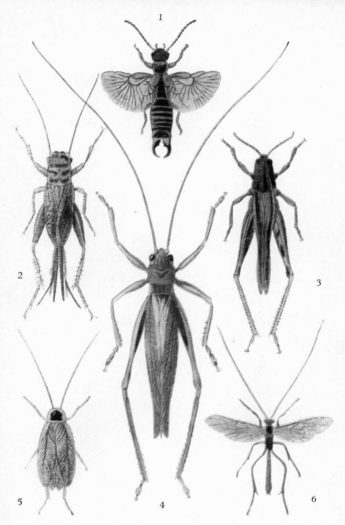

1. Earwig (with wings spread)
2. House Cricket
3. Short-horned Grasshopper
4. Long-horned Grasshopper
5. Cockroach (*Ectobius lapponicus*)
6. Yellow Ophion

(All enlarged)

[13]

1. Large Garden Humble Bee
2. Red-tailed Cuckoo Bee (male)
3. Red-tailed Cuckoo Bee (female)
4. Vestal Cuckoo Bee
5. Field Cuckoo Bee
(All enlarged)

[14]

1

2

3

4

5

6

1. Gooden's Nomad Bee
2. Golden-rod Nomad Bee
3. Lesser Red-and-black Spider-
   hunting Wasp
4. Red-banded Sand Wasp
5. Priocnemus exaltatus
6. Melancholy Black Wasp

(All enlarged)

[15]

1. Horse-fly (*Tabanus sudeticus*)
2. Hover-fly (*Catabomba Pyrastri*)

3. Great Robber-fly
4. Chameleon-fly

5. Snipe-fly
(All enlarged)

[16]

1. Black-veined White
2. Green-veined White
3. Orange-tip
4. Small White

1. Swallow-tail   2. Large White

1. Peacock   2. Painted Lady
3. Small Tortoiseshell

1. Wall Butterfly   2. Large Tortoiseshell
3. Speckled Wood

1. Silver-washed Fritillary
2. Marsh Fritillary
3. Silver-washed Fritillary
   (underside)
4. Small Pearl-bordered
   Fritillary (underside)
5. Small Pearl-bordered
   Fritillary

[21]

1. Camberwell Beauty
2. Pearl-bordered Fritillary
3. Pearl-bordered Fritillary
   (underside)
4. Duke of Burgundy Fritillary
5. Duke of Burgundy Fritillary
   (underside)

[22]

1. Gatekeeper (male)
2. Large Skipper (male)
3. Small Heath

4. Small Skipper (male)
5. Small Mountain Ringlet
6. Small Copper

1. Purple Emperor (male)
2. Purple Emperor (female—underside)

1. Meadow Brown (male)   2. Scotch Argus (underside)
3. Meadow Brown (female)

[25]

1. Chalk Hill Blue (female)
2. Chalk Hill Blue (underside)
3. Small Blue
4. Small Blue (underside)

5. Chequered Skipper
6. White-letter Hairstreak
7. White-letter Hairstreak
   (underside)

[26]

1. Brown Argus
2. Adonis Blue (female)
3. Brown Argus (Scottish variety)
4. Brown Argus (Scottish variety
   —underside)
5. Silver-studded Blue
6. Silver-studded Blue
   (underside)
7. Purple Hairstreak

[27]

1. Privet Hawk   2. Poplar Hawk   3. Eyed Hawk

[28]

1. Lime Hawk
2. Humming Bird Hawk
3. Narrow-bordered Bee Hawk
4. Pine Hawk

1. Ghost Moth (female)   3. White Ermine
2. Yellow-tail   4. Muslin Moth (female)
              5. White Satin

1. Miller Moth
2. Brimstone Moth

3. Wood Leopard
4. Swallow-tail

1. Peppered Moth
2. Speckled Yellow
3. Poplar Kitten
4. Pretty Chalk Carpet
5. Drinker

[32]

1. Goat Moth
2. Purple-bar Carpet
3. Wood Tiger
4. Blood-vein
5. Lackey
6. Scalloped Oak

[33]

1. Old Lady   2. Lappet Moth

1. Oak Eggar
2. Mother Shipton

3. Vapourer
4. Small Oak Eggar

5. Pale Tussock

1. Gothic Moth   3. Four-spotted Footman
2. Pebble Hook-tip   4. Frosted Orange
5. Yellow Underwing

1. Broad-bordered Yellow
   Underwing
2. Copper Underwing

3. Lesser Broad-bordered
   Underwing
4. Cream-spot Tiger

1. Kentish Glory (female)
2. Dot Moth

3. Bright-line Brown-eye
4. Emperor Moth (female)

1. Heart and Dart   3. Dark Arches
2. Peach Blossom   4. Ear Moth
              5. Cabbage Moth

1. Buff-tip
2. Figure of Eight

3. Buff Arches
4. Angle Shades

5. Flame Shoulder

[40]

1. Puss Moth
2. Turnip Moth

3. Pebble Prominent
4. Coxcomb Prominent

1. Red Underwing   3. Common Footman
2. Oak Beauty   4. Black Arches

1. Shark
2. Sycamore Moth

3. Knot-grass
4. Grey Dagger

5. Lobster Moth

[43]

1. Broad-bordered Bee Hawk
2. Hornet Clearwing

3. Large Red-belted Clearwing
4. Currant Clearwing

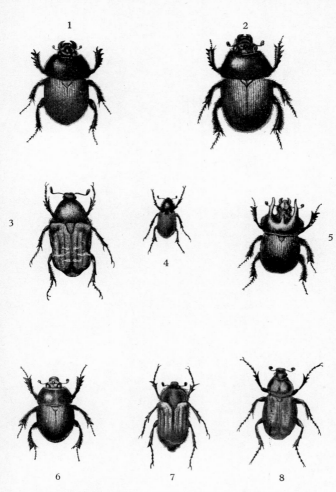

1. Greenish Dor Beetle
2. Lousy Watchman
3. Rose Chafer
4. Garden Chafer
5. Three-horned Dor Beetle
6. Spring Dor Beetle
7. Summer Chafer
8. Beautiful Gnorimus

[45]

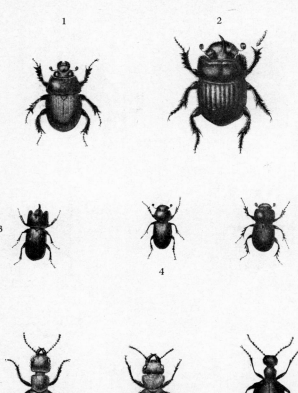

1. Wood Dor Beetle
2. Copris lunaris
3. Cylindrical Sinodendron
4. Red-legged Aphodius
5. Black Aphodius
6. Devil's Coach-horse
7. Hairy Emus
8. Oil Beetle (female)

[46]

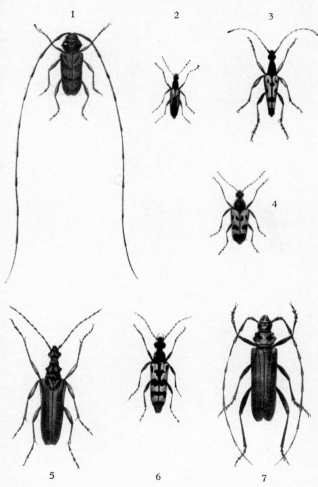

1. Timberman
2. Black-tailed Strangalia
3. Strangalia armata

4. Pachyta octomaculata
5. Toxotus meridionalis
6. Four-banded Strangalia

7. Musk Beetle

[47]

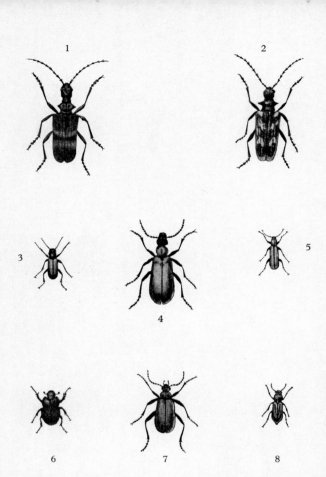

1. Searcher Rhagium
2. Two-banded Rhagium
3. Black-tailed Nacerdes
4. Black-headed Cardinal
5. Soldier Beetle
6. One-banded Nuchicornis
7. Cardinal
8. Shining Malachius

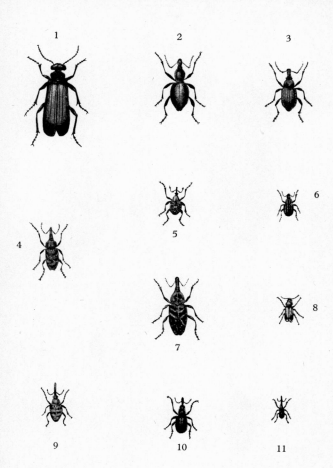

1. Blister Beetle
2. Black Otiorhynchus
3. Obscure Barynotus
4. Pine Pissodes
5. Figwort Cionus
6. Nut Strophosomus
7. Pine Weevil
8. Two-spotted Malachius
9. Nut Weevil
10. Downy Rhynchites
11. Apion pomonae

1. Great or Black Water Beetle
2. Margined Dytiscus (female)
3. Red-legged Water Beetle
4. Lesser Black Water Beetle
5. Whirligig Beetle
6. Aquatic Helophorus

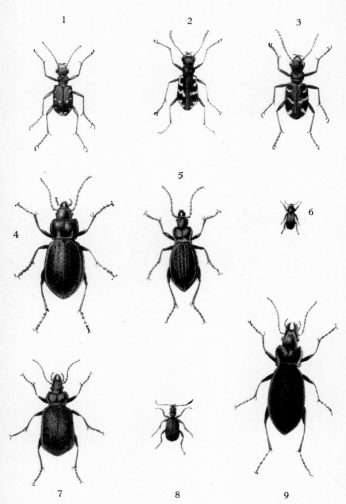

1. Tiger Beetle
2. Hybrid Tiger Beetle
3. Wood Tiger Beetle
4. Carabus nemoralis
5. Field Ground Beetle
6. Blue Corynetes
7. Beautiful Searcher
8. Bombardier Beetle
9. Violet Ground Beetle

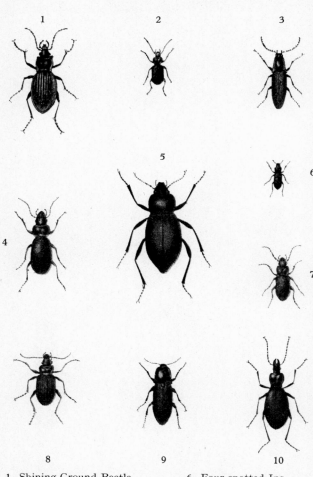

1. Shining Ground Beetle
2. Six-pitted Anchomenus
3. Copper Corymbites
4. Steropus modidus
5. Cellar Beetle
6. Four-spotted Ips
7. Bronze Harpalus
8. Short-collared Nebria
9. Bronze Corymbites
10. Beaked Cychrus

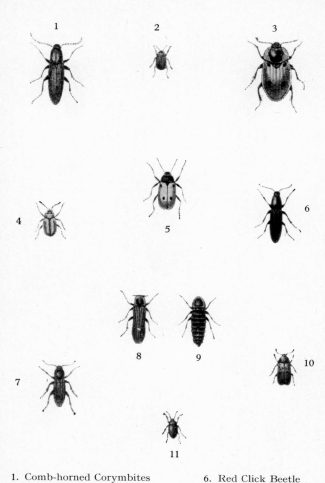

1. Comb-horned Corymbites
2. Knot-grass Beetle
3. Four-spotted Silpha
4. Golden Apple Beetle
5. Four-spotted Clythra
6. Red Click Beetle
7. Lined Click Beetle
8. Glow-worm (male)
9. Glow-worm (female)
10. Bacon Beetle
11. Two-spotted Sphaeridium

1. Red-and-black Carrion Beetle
2. Meal Beetle
3. Bloody-nosed Beetle

4. Lesser Bloody-nosed Beetle
5. Black Carrion Beetle
6. Pill Beetle

1

2

3

4

5

6

7   8   9

1. Two-spot Ladybird
2. Two-spot Ladybird (dark form)
3. Seven-spot Ladybird
4. Ten-spot Ladybird

5. Eyed Ladybird
6. Sixteen-spot Ladybird
7, 8. Tortoise Beetles
9. Shining Niptus

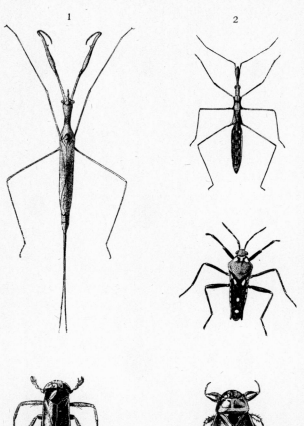

1. Water Stick-insect   3. Water Cricket
2. Water Gnat   4. Lesser Water Boatman
      5. Lesser Water Scorpion
       (All enlarged)

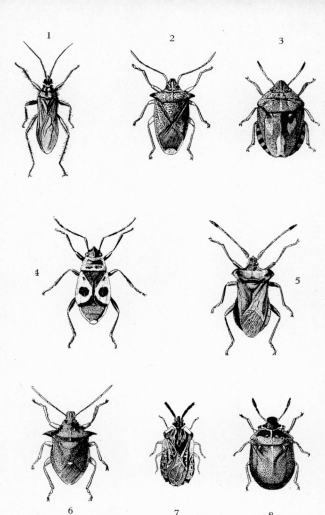

1. Fly Bug
2. Bloody Acanthosma
3. Hottentot Bug
4. Red Bug
5. Margined Syromastes
6. Two-pointed Picromerus
7. Flat Aradus
8. Podops inunctus

1. Frog Hopper
2. Horned Tree Hopper
3. Water Scorpion
4. Aphis (winged female)
5. White-fly
(All enlarged)

1. Yellow Ant—worker
   (enlarged)
2. Great Horntail
3. Large Larch Sawfly (enlarged)

4. Great Yellow Humble-bee
5. Buff-tailed Humble-bee
6. Knapweed Carder Bee
   (enlarged)

[59]

1. Two-coloured Osmia (female)
2. Two-coloured Osmia (male)
3. Silvery Leaf-cutter (female)
4. Silvery Leaf-cutter (male)
5. Belted Andrena
6. Tawny Burrowing Bee (female)
7. Davies's Colletes
(All enlarged)

1. Wool-carder Bee
2. Common Wasp
3. Norwegian Wasp
4. Heath Potter Wasp
5. Big-headed Digger Wasp
6. Field Digger Wasp

(All enlarged)

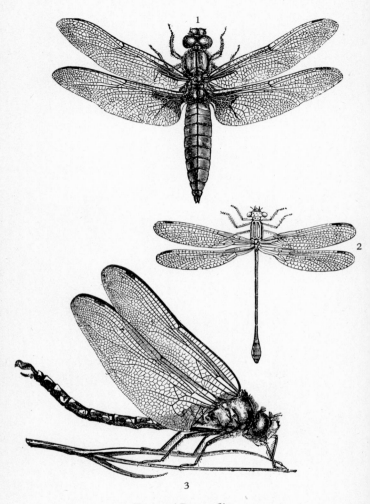

Types of Dragonflies:
1. Broad-bodied Dragonfly   2. Demoiselle-fly
3. Yellow-and-black Dragonfly

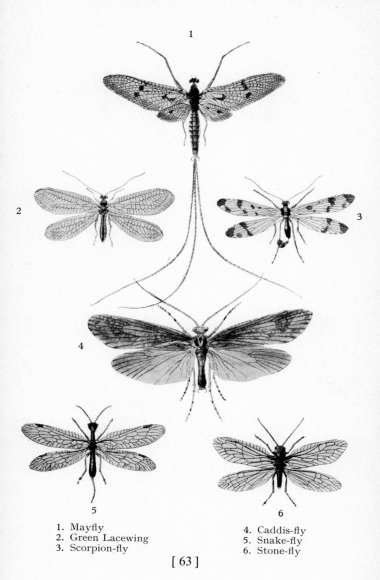

1. Mayfly
2. Green Lacewing
3. Scorpion-fly

4. Caddis-fly
5. Snake-fly
6. Stone-fly

1. Drone-fly
2. Sharp-nosed fly
3. Tesselated Empis

4. Sheep Bot-fly
5. Sheep-ked or tick
6. Bee-fly

SECTION I

BUTTERFLIES

INSECTS WITH FOUR SCALE-COVERED WINGS

(The measurements given refer to the span of
the outstretched wings)

1 $\begin{cases} \text{Antennae long, club-shaped.} & 2 \\ \text{Antennae not club-shaped. Section II, page 33.} \end{cases}$

2 $\begin{cases} \text{Ground colour of wings white.} & 3 \\ \text{Ground colour of wings other than white.} & 8 \end{cases}$

3 $\begin{cases} \text{Fore-wings with bright orange tips.} & 4 \\ \text{Fore-wings without orange tips.} & 5 \end{cases}$

4. Fore-wings white with large patch of orange and
rusty brown margins to wing-tips. There is a small
brown spot near the outer edge of the orange area.
Hind-wings faintly mottled greenish. Undersides
of hind-wings heavily mottled green. PL. I, 17.

Orange-tip (male), 1½ inches.

Widely distributed in the British Isles and abundant in some areas. On the wing from May to
July. (For female *see* No. 7.)

5 $\begin{cases} \text{All wings conspicuously veined or mottled.} & 6 \\ \text{Wings not conspicuously veined or mottled.} & 7 \end{cases}$

Fore- and hind-wings boldly veined in black or dark brown without other markings.   PL. 17.

Black-veined White, 2½ inches.

A rare British butterfly, occasionally seen in a small part of Kent.   On the wing in June and July.

Veins greyish green on the upper surface, much more green and more clearly defined on the undersides of the wings.   Tips of fore-wings dusky black. Some specimens show one or two blackish spots on the fore-wings and one on each hind-wing.   PL. 17.

Green-veined White, 1½ inches.

6

Widely distributed and generally common.   On the wing in May and again in August in woods and shady lanes.

Wings white or pale cream, heavily marbled with black or dusky brown.   PL. 1.

Marbled White, 2 inches.

Common, though somewhat local, in the southern and midland counties.   Scarce in the north of England.   Absent from Scotland and Ireland. On the wing in open woods, meadows, and fields from late June to August.

Wings white with black patch on angle of fore-wing and a small blackish mark on the front margin of the hind-wing.   PL. 18. **Large White (male), 2½ inches.**

Common in most parts of the British Isles though more abundant in some years than in others.   On the wing from May to September.

Similar to above but each fore-wing marked with two round black spots in the centre and a long, thin black splash on the inner margin.

7

Large White (female), 2½ inches.

8

7 ❭ Fore-wings with dusky brown or black tips and a spot of the same colour on their central areas. The hind-wings with a dark spot near the front margins. PL. 17. **Small White (male)**, 1¾ inches.

Similar to above but with three black spots on each fore-wing, the lower two very close together and partially joined, and an indistinct dark splash along the inner margins.
Small White (female), 1¾ inches.

Common almost everywhere. On the wing from March to September.

Fore-wings with dark brown tips and central spot. Hind-wings faintly mottled greenish. Under-sides of hind-wings heavily mottled green.
Orange-tip (female), 1½ inches.
(For male *see* No. 4.)

Wings creamy white with squarish patch of black at tips of fore-wings.
Wood White (male), 1½ inches.

Similar to above but the patch at the tip of each fore-wing is smaller, greyish, or may be wholly absent. **Wood White (female)**, 1½ inches.

Locally distributed in England and Wales; nowhere common. On the wing from June to August in and near woods.

8 ⎰ Ground colour of wings yellow.   **9**
  ⎱ Ground colour of wings other than yellow.   **12**

9 ⎰ A large butterfly—over 3 inches across outspread wings.   **10**
  ⎱ Wing-span less than 3 inches.   **11**

10. Wings with dentated margins; the hind pair showing well-developed tails. Fore-wings with margins, veins, bases, and a broad band running parallel with hind margin black. Hind-wings with broad black band ornamented with blue spots, black margins, and veins and black-edged red spots at the anal angles. PL. 18.

Swallow-tail, 3–3½ inches.

The largest British butterfly. Local and rare, occurring only in a few fenland districts in south-eastern England. On the wing from June to August.

Wings pale sulphur yellow or pale greenish yellow, with small orange or pale brown spot near the centre of each. PL. 1. **Brimstone**, 2¼ inches.

Common in England and Wales, locally abundant in Ireland. On the wing from March to June and again in August.

Wings rich orange yellow broadly edged with black or blackish brown. Fore-wings with dark central spot; hind-wings with larger, deep orange spot.

Clouded Yellow (male), 2 inches.

Similar to above but with the dark wing margins spotted with yellow.

Clouded Yellow (female), 2 inches.

Locally distributed and erratic in occurrence. In some years abundant, in others scarce. On the wing in May and again in August and September.

Fore-wings pale yellow with black margins, more or less mottled with yellow, and with black central spot. Hind-wings with large orange spot.

11 **Pale Clouded Yellow**, 1¾ inches.

11 〕 Rare and local. Like the Clouded Yellow this pretty butterfly is erratic in its occurrence in this country, most, if not all, the specimens seen being immigrants from the Continent. On the wing in May and June and again in August and September.

12 〈 Ground colour of fore-wings rich red or orange brown marked with darker shades or ornamented with bright colours. **13**

Ground colour other than deep red or orange brown. **24**

13 〈 Fore- and hind-wings of same general ground colour. **14**

Fore- and hind-wings differing in ground colour. **23**

14 〈 Margins of both fore- and hind-wings deeply indented. **15**

Margins of wings not deeply indented. **16**

15 〈 Wings rich velvety red, margined with dark brown. Front margins of fore-wings marked with two black patches separated by a yellow blotch. Each wing shows a large pale-bordered eye spot. PL. 19.
Peacock, 2¼–2½ inches.

A conspicuous and easily recognized butterfly. Widely distributed and common in many areas. On the wing in spring and in August and September.

Fore-wings rich orange brown with front margins edged yellow and boldly barred with black. A black band follows the hind margins and there are a few spots of black on the central portion of each wing. Hind-wings with large dark spot and

15 ⎫ yellow blotch near front margins. Sub-marginal
⎪ band black with small blue crescent markings.
⎪ PL. 20.   **Large Tortoiseshell**, 2¼–2½ inches.

Fairly common in the southern half of England; local
further north and in Wales and Scotland. On the
wing in spring and again from July to September.

Fore-wings orange or reddish brown, broadly
margined in front with yellow broken by three
large, irregular patches of black, the outermost of
which has a white blotch on its outer edge. The
wing margins are bordered by a blackish band
which bears a series of blue crescent-shaped spots.
Central portion of fore-wing marked with one large
and two small black spots. Hind-wings dark
brown at bases bordered with dark brown and
black with small blue spots. PL. 19.
          Small Tortoiseshell, 1¾–2¼ inches.

Generally distributed and common in most parts of
Great Britain. On the wing from early spring to May
and from July to September. This butterfly hiber-
nates at the onset of cold weather and may sometimes be seen flying on warm days in mid winter.

Margins of wings so deeply incised as to appear to
have been torn or nibbled. Ground colour deep
reddish or tawny orange with dark margins. Fore-
wings with three irregular black patches along front
border, three smaller markings of the same kind in
the central area, and a dark brown blotch near the
hind angle. The hind-wings show three or four dark
patches and have dark borders marked with a number
of yellow lunules. PL. 3.   **Comma**, 1¾–2 inches.

Very locally distributed and erratic in occurrence.
Takes its name from a white C-shaped mark on the
⎩ dark underside of the hind-wing.

16 { Fore-wings with conspicuous white-centred brown spot near apex. **17**

{ Fore-wings not as described. **18**

17. Wings orange brown with veins, margins, and transverse lines of dark brown. There is a dark, white-centred spot near the apex of each fore-wing and four similar spots near the margin of each hind-wing. In the male the fore-wing is crossed by a broad brown band extending from the base outwards and upwards to beyond the centre. Bases of hind-wings dark brown. PL. 20.

Wall Butterfly, $1\frac{1}{2}$–$1\frac{3}{4}$ inches.

Widely distributed but rather local in the north of England and Scotland. This butterfly is often seen basking in the sun on hedge-banks, walls, and stones. On the wing from May to August.

18 { Fore-wings marked with white or pale buff. **19**

{ Fore-wings not so marked. **20**

19 { Wings tawny orange. Tips and margins of fore-wings black marked with four white spots and a broken line of white across the wing-tips, continued downwards to the hind angle. Central part of fore-wings with two dark, angular patches. Hind-wings blackish brown at bases with double chain of spots beyond the centre and a series of dark streak-like spots along the hind margins. The undersides of the wings are beautifully patterned in pinkish, gold, brown, black, white, and blue. PL. 19.

Painted Lady, $2\frac{1}{4}$ inches.

An erratic migrant which sometimes appears in considerable numbers in various parts of Great Britain. On the wing in May and June and in August and September.

19) Wings reddish or tawny orange with veins and
transverse lines of black. Variously spotted and
chequered pale buff. The hind-wings with dark
bases, a dark transverse band enclosing pale spots
and a series of buff or yellowish-white lunules on the
margins. PL. 21. **Marsh Fritillary (male)**, 1¼ inches.
(**female**), 1¾ inches.

Locally distributed in damp or marshy districts.
On the wing in May and June.

20 { Butterflies with wing-span of 2 inches or more **21**

Butterflies with wing-span of less than 2 inches. **22**

Wings reddish brown with black veins. On the
fore-wings there are several, usually six, short,
transverse streaks or blotches along the front
margins, an oblique row of irregular streak-like
spots, which sometimes join to form a zigzag, in
the central area, a row of round spots towards the
hind margins, and a sub-marginal line of black
lunules. The hind-wings also have a row of round
black spots and lunules following the line of their
hind borders and a dark transverse band with some
irregular black markings near the wing-bases. The
undersides of the wings are pale yellowish brown
and show two or three silvery spots near the tips
of the fore-wings and a number of larger silvery
white spots, some ringed with cinnamon brown, on
the hind-wings. PL. I.

High Brown Fritillary, 2-2½ inches.

Locally distributed in England and Wales in woodland areas. Most frequent in the southern
counties. On the wing in July and August.

21) Wings reddish brown, sometimes washed dull
green. The darker markings similar to those of the

21 High Brown Fritillary but the undersides of the fore-wings have pale yellowish-green margins. The undersides of the hind-wings yellow towards margins, pale green over basal two-thirds, marked with silvery and chestnut spots. PL. 2.

Dark Green Fritillary, $2\frac{1}{4}$–$2\frac{1}{2}$ inches.

Locally distributed in the British Isles, but common in some parts of England and Wales. On the wing in open country in July and August.

Wings reddish brown with black markings similar to the High Brown Fritillary. Undersides of fore-wings pale yellowish brown with yellow tips, mottled or spotted with green. The undersides of the hind-wings dull green with silver bars—lacking the white and chestnut spots of the last species. PL. 21. **Silver-washed Fritillary,** $2\frac{1}{4}$–$2\frac{1}{2}$ inches.

Fairly common in southern England and Wales in or near woodlands. Local in Ireland, scarce in the north of England and Scotland. On the wing in July and August.

Wings orange brown with dark brown bases, otherwise the dark markings similar to those of the High Brown Fritillary (No. 21). Undersides of fore-wings yellowish brown with yellow wing-tips marked with chestnut brown. Undersides of hind-wings pale buffish brown marked with chestnut and black, with small silver spot near the base, a larger one near the centre, and a row of seven triangular silver spots round the margin. PL. 22.

Pearl-bordered Fritillary, $1\frac{3}{4}$ inches.

Widely distributed in wooded districts in England and Wales; locally common in the south. Scarcer and local in Scotland. On the wing in May and June.

22

22 Similar to the last but somewhat smaller and with the dark markings on the underside of the fore-wings more distinct. PL. 21.

   Small Pearl-bordered Fritillary, 1½ inches.

   Distribution and haunts the same as the Pearl-bordered Fritillary.

   Wings similar to the last except that the spots on the fore-wings merge to form transverse lines or irregular bands, and all the wings are edged with white. Undersides of fore-wings pale golden brown with pale cream tips, spotted and streaked black. Undersides of hind-wings cream dotted with black and with two reddish-brown transverse bands. PL. 2.   **Glanville Fritillary,** 1½ inches.

   A rare British butterfly. Occasionally seen in a few localities in the Isle of Wight. On the wing in June.

   Similar to the last species but on the undersides the tips of the fore-wings and the hind-wings are without the numerous black dots seen in the Glanville Fritillary.   **Heath Fritillary,** 1½ inches.

   Locally distributed in the south of England and west of Ireland. On the wing from May to July about heaths and woods.

23. Fore-wings deep copper brown marked with eight black spots and broadly bordered dark brown. Hind-wings dark, shining brown with broad marginal band of copper red, marked with four black spots near the hind edge. PL. 23. **Small Copper,** 1 inch.

   Widely distributed and common in most parts of the British Isles. On the wing in open country from May to September.

24	Ground colour of wings light tawny brown.	**25**
	Ground colour of wings other than light tawny brown.	**30**

25	Wing-span 1½ inches or more	**26**
	Wing-span less than 1½ inches	**27**

26

Wings pale brownish orange with broad brown margins and a black spot towards the tips of the fore-wings. Hind-wings with brown bases.
Gatekeeper (female), 1½ inches.

Similar to above but with short brown band running obliquely upwards from the base to the centre of each fore-wing.PL.23.**Gatekeeper(male),1½ inches.**

Common in most parts of southern England and Wales. Local further north, in Scotland and south Ireland. On the wing in July and August, often near woods and hedges.

Wings tawny, often with a pale-ringed dark spot near the tips of the fore-wings with another below it. Hind-wings may be clear tawny or show one, two, or three dark brown spots. Underside of fore-wings crossed by white bar and usually showing two black spots near the hind margin. Underside of hind-wing washed greenish brown with white streak or bar and small black spot above the hind margin.
Large Heath, 1¼–1½ inches.

A very variable species in which the male is usually darker than the female. Common in many parts of north England, from Staffordshire upwards, Scotland, and Ireland, frequenting swampy, boggy country. On the wing in June and July.

27 ⎰ Wings showing dark or light markings. 28

⎱ Wings without conspicuous markings. 29

28 ⎨

Wings pale tawny with dull brown margins and a number of yellowish spots near the inner edge of the dark borders. Central area of fore-wing with black, oblique streak.

Large Skipper (male), 1¼ inches.

Similar to above but with dark brown wing margins more distinctly marked with yellow. Fore-wings without the dark oblique central streak.

Large Skipper (female), 1¼ inches.

Common in most parts of England and south Scotland. Local in Ireland. On the wing in June and July.

Similar to the Large Skipper but on the undersides the hind-wings are pale and green-tinged, with eight or nine silvery spots.

Silver-spotted Skipper, 1¼ inches.

Locally distributed in southern England in dry, chalky districts. On the wing in August. Sometimes known as the Pearl Skipper.

Wings tawny orange with dark veins and margins. Fore-wings with dark oblique streak across centres. PL. 23. **Small Skipper (male)**, 1 inch.

Widely distributed in grassy places in England and Wales. Local or rare elsewhere in the British Isles. On the wing in July and August.

(For female *see* No. 29.)

29 ⎰ Wings light tawny with dark edges and small black dot towards the tip of each fore-wing.
PL. 23. **Small Heath**, 1¼ inches.

29 } Widely distributed and common throughout the British Isles. On the wing from May to September.

Wings tawny orange with dark veins and margins.
Small Skipper (female), 1 inch.
(For male *see* No. 28.)

30 {
Ground colour of wings dark brown. **31**

Ground colour of wings other than dark brown. **48**

31 {
Large butterflies—wing-spread over 2 inches. **32**

Smaller butterflies with wing-spread of 2 inches or less. **35**

32 {
Wings conspicuously marked with yellow, white, or red. **33**

Wings not conspicuously marked with yellow, white, or red. **34**

Wings dark chocolate or purple brown broadly banded with pale yellow. On the fore-edge of each fore-wing there are two pale yellow blotches and a row of blue spots follows the inner margin of the yellow wing borders. PL. 22.
Camberwell Beauty, 2¾-3 inches.

Rare and local. Has occurred occasionally in most parts of England and in a few localities in Scotland and Ireland in spring, late summer, and autumn. The broad, pale yellow wing borders are distinctive.

33 }
Wings brownish black with deep purple sheen. Fore-wings with three oblique lines of white spots or splashes. Hind-wings crossed by a wide white

33 transverse band and with black spot, edged orange brown, near the anal angle. PL. 24.

Purple Emperor (male), 2½ inches.

As above but without purple sheen. PL. 24.

Purple Emperor (female), 3 inches.

In both sexes the underside of the wings is reddish brown with pale margins, boldly marked with black and white and a brilliant eye spot on each fore-wing. The Purple Emperor is locally distributed in the south, west, and midland counties of England in or near oak woods, where it flies among the higher branches in July.

Wings velvety black. Fore-wings crossed by broad band of scarlet and with white blotch near the fore edge and a series of white spots of different sizes along the margin from near the wing-tip to the scarlet cross-band. Hind-wings with broad scarlet borders, showing a row of black dots near the hind edge. PL. 3. **Red Admiral,** 2½ inches.

Widely distributed throughout the British Isles and common in many parts. On the wing from June to September

Wings dark brown. Fore-wings with broken band of white running from the front edge to the inner margin. There are two small white marks near the wing-tip and a large spot lower down towards the hind margin. The hind-wing is crossed by a broad white band. Underside of wings pale reddish brown with black spots and white bands. PL. 3. **White Admiral,** 2¼ inches.

Locally distributed in the south of England in woods and shady lanes. On the wing in June and July.

34. Wings dark brown, the outer area banded with pale brown or yellowish buff. On the fore-wings there are two round black spots on the paler bands, and on the hind-wings one black spot towards the anal angle. On the underside of the fore-wing the two black spots stand out prominently on the pale buffish ground colour and the basal half of the wing is reddish brown. The underside of the hind-wing is sooty with greyish variegations.

Grayling, 2¼ inches

Widely distributed and common in most parts of the British Isles. On the wing in July and August. Often seen resting on the ground.

35. ⎰ Butterflies with wing-spread of from 1½ to 2 inches.
    36

    ⎱ Butterflies with wing-spread of less than 1½ inches.
    37

36. ⎰ Wings dark brown. Fore-wings with single white-centred black spot on golden brown patch, which is large in the female, small in the male. PL. 25.
    Meadow Brown, 1½–1¾ inches.

    Common throughout the British Isles. On the wing from June to September.

    Wings sooty brown, each with one or two grey-edged black spots which are much more distinct in the female than in the male. The underside of the wings greyish brown, with three white-edged black spots on the fore- and five similar spots on the hind-wing.
    Ringlet, 1½–1¾ inches.

    Common in woods and shady lanes in most parts of the British Isles in July and August.

36 ⎫ Wings dark brown with large, squarish spots of creamy white. The fore-wing has a black-centred pale spot near the wing-tip and there are three similar spots along the margin of the hind-wing. PL. 20.　　　　　　**Speckled Wood,** $1\frac{1}{2}$–$1\frac{3}{4}$ inches.

Widely distributed in England and Wales, most common in the south, and in Ireland. Local in Scotland. On the wing in shady places from June to September.

Wings dark brown. Fore-wings with patch of deep orange near tip showing three small white-centred dark spots. Hind-wings with band of deep orange marked with three or four dark spots near hind margins. PL. 25.　　**Scotch Argus,** $1\frac{1}{2}$–$1\frac{3}{4}$ inches.

Locally distributed in the north of England and Scotland where it is common in some districts. On the wing near woods from July to September.

37 ⎧ Wings washed purplish blue.　　　　　　　**38**

⎩ Wings not washed purplish blue.　　　　　　**39**

38. Wings blackish brown strongly washed with purple blue on the central areas. Hind-wings with short tails. Underside grey with black and white transverse line and dusky markings along the hind border. On the underside of the hind-wing there is also an orange-edged black dot near the anal angles.　　　　**Purple Hairstreak,** $1\frac{1}{3}$ inches.

Widely distributed in the British Isles except in Ireland, where it is local and rare. On the wing near woods in July and August. In the female the purple blue area is restricted to the fore-wings; the hind-wings being blackish brown.

39 { Underside of wings green.   **40**

    { Underside of wings not green.   **41**

40   Upper surface of wings dull brown. Underside of wings deep green, with transverse line of white spots across hind-wings. In some specimens a few dull white spots also occur on the underside of the fore-wings.   **Green Hairstreak**, 1 inch.

Generally distributed over the British Isles. On the wing, chiefly near woods or about hedgerows, in May and June.

41 { Wings conspicuously marked with cream or yellow.   **42**

    { Wings not so marked.   **43**

{ Fore-wings with yellowish blotches along front edge, a transverse line of confluent spots of the same colour towards the hind margins and a submarginal row of yellow dots. Hind-wings with yellow spot near bases and two rows of similar spots towards the margins, those of the lower series much smaller than the others. PL. 26.

               Chequered Skipper, 1–1¼ inches.

Locally distributed in a few counties in the south and midlands.On the wing in May and June, near woods.

Wings blackish brown with numerous creamy white spots and chequered margins.

             Grizzled Skipper, ¾–1 inch.

42 { Generally distributed in the British Isles in hilly country. On the wing in May and June.

42 Wings brown with yellowish spots along the dark borders. Central area tinged golden brown.
Large Skipper (female), $1\frac{1}{4}$ inches.
(For male *see* No. 28.)

Wings dull golden brown with curved row of yellow spots near the tip of fore-wing and a short yellow streak on the inner edge of the curve.
Lulworth Skipper (female), 1 inch.

A rare and very local species which occurs only in a few parts of Dorset and Devon.

43 Wings marked with tawny, deep orange, or orange brown. **44**

Wings not so marked. **47**

44 Hind-wing with short tail. **45**

Hind-wing without tail. **46**

45. Wings blackish brown. Fore-wings with spots or distinct band of orange towards the tips. Hind-wings with two or three orange marks on the margins at the anal angles. Underside of fore-wings tawny brown with black and white transverse line and small dark streak. Underside of hind-wings with two white transverse lines, the lower of which is broader than the other and extends right across the wing.
Brown Hairstreak, $1\frac{1}{4}$ inches.

A local species confined to a few places in the south and south-west of England, Wales, and Ireland. On the wing in August and September, usually near woods or tall hedgerows. The orange band on the fore-wing is larger and clearer in the female than in the male.

Wings blackish brown with three transverse rows of tawny·blotches or spots across each fore-wing, and a central and marginal row of similar markings on the hind-wing. Underside of wings tawny brown, with white spots and blotches similarly arranged to the pale markings on the upper wing surfaces. PL. 22.

Duke of Burgundy Fritillary, $1–1\frac{1}{4}$ inches.

Locally distributed in southern England; rare or absent elsewhere in Great Britain. On the wing near woods in May and June.

Wings dark or sooty brown. Both fore- and hind-wings with band of orange brown, enclosing a number of small dark spots, towards the margins. PL. 23. **Small Mountain Ringlet,** $1\frac{1}{4}$ inches.

A mountain butterfly found in a few mountainous districts in the lakeland of England and in parts of Scotland and the west of Ireland. On the wing in June and July.

Wings sooty brown powdered with blue at bases. There is a small black, pale-ringed spot on each fore-wing and sometimes a similar mark on each of the hind-wings. The hind-wings have a row of orange-ringed spots along the margins. Wing fringes white spotted with black. Underside of wings pale brown with numerous white-edged black spots and a row of black-centred orange spots near the margins of the hind-wings. PL. 4.

Chalk Hill Blue (female), $1\frac{1}{4}$ inches.
(For male *see* No. 50.)

Very similar to the last species but with the wing-bases more definitely blue and the fore-wings, as well as the hind-wings, usually show some orange spots near the margin. Underside of wings darker

46

46 than in the Chalk Hill Blue with the white-ringed black spots more sharply defined.   PL. 4, 27.

Adonis Blue (female), 1¼ inches.

Locally distributed in the south of England; nowhere abundant.   On the wing in August and September.

(For male *see* No. 50).

Wings sooty brown powdered with blue at bases. There is a band of deep orange on the margin of the hind-wing and a smaller band of darker tawny brown on the margin of the fore-wing, though the latter marking may be obscure and is sometimes absent.   Underside of wings brownish grey with white transverse band and numerous white-ringed black spots.

Silver-studded Blue (female), 1 inch.

(For male *see* No. 51.)

Similar to above but without blue powder at wing-bases.   All wings with white fringes.   On the fore-wing there is a black-centred spot and the orange band is as clear as on the hind-wing.   Underside of wings paler than in the Silver-studded Blue, grey tinged with brown, with a number of white-edged black spots and a band of orange spots along the margin.   PL. 27.   **Brown Argus,** 1 inch.

Widely distributed in the south of England and Wales, often common in chalky districts.   More local further north.   On the wing in June and again in August.

47 Wings blackish brown with or without small, obscure whitish spot near the front edge of the fore-wing.   Hind-wing with short tail.   Underside of wings paler dusky brown with a conspicuous white

47 line on each wing.   The underside of the hind-wing shows a black-edged orange band near the margin. PL. 26.   **White-letter Hairstreak,** 1¼ inches.

The small, pale mark on the fore-wing occurs only in the male.   This butterfly is locally distributed in some English counties from the south coast to Yorkshire.   On the wing in July, usually near trees or hedgerows.

Wings sooty brown powdered blue near bases, with small pale-ringed black spot on each fore-wing and sometimes on the hind-wings.   Hind-wings with orange-ringed black spots near margins.   Wing fringes white spotted with black.   Underside of wings pale brown marked with white-ringed black spots and a row of black-centred orange spots near the margins of the hind-wings.   PL. 26.

Chalk Hill Blue (female), 1¼ inches.
(For male *see* No. 50.)

Wings brown with transverse bars of darker brown enclosing a greyish area, and small white spots round the outer margins of both fore- and hind-wings.   **Dingy Skipper,** 1 inch.

Widely distributed in the British Isles, locally abundant in chalk and limestone districts.   Has a habit of basking in the sun on banks, hillsides, and stones.   On the wing in May and June, sometimes again in August.

Wings sooty brown powdered silvery blue.   Underside of wings greyish white, tinged blue near the bases, with small white-ringed black spots.   PL. 26.
Small Blue (male), ¾ inch.

Similar to above but all upper surface of wings sooty brown, without silvery blue powdering.
Small Blue (female), ¾ inch.

47 〕 Widely distributed but local throughout the greater part of Great Britain. Common on chalk hills in the south of England and locally abundant in limestone districts elsewhere. On the wing in May and June.

48. Ground colour of wings some shade of blue. **49**

49 ⎰ Wings bright or light blue. **50**

⎱ Wings mauvish or purplish blue. **51**

Wings deep, bright blue with black margins and white fringes. Fore-wings with curved row of black spots and a single smaller spot near the centre. Hind-wings with row of small black spots near the dark margins. **Large Blue,** $1\frac{1}{2}$ inches.

A very rare and beautiful butterfly occasionally seen in June and July in a small area of Cornwall. The black wing borders and spots are much more pronounced in the female than in the male.

Wings bright blue with white fringes broken by the tips of the black veins. PL. 4.

Adonis Blue (male), $1\frac{1}{4}$ inches.

50 ⎰

Locally distributed in the south of England; nowhere abundant. On the wing in August and September.

(For female *see* No. 46.)

Wings pale blue with dark borders and black-dotted white fringes. The hind-wings show a row of black spots near the hind margins. PL. 4.

Chalk Hill Blue (male), $1\frac{1}{4}$–$1\frac{1}{2}$ inches.

Common on chalk hills and downs in the southern counties. Local elsewhere in England. On the wing in July and August.

(For female *see* No. 46.)

Wings mauve blue narrowly edged black, with white fringes. **Common Blue (male)**, 1–1¼ inches.

Wings mauve blue thickly powdered with brown. There is a black spot on each fore-wing and a row of orange, black-centred spots on the hind margin of all the wings.

Common Blue (female), 1–1½ inches.

Widely distributed and common in most parts of Great Britain. On the wing from June to September.

Wings mauve blue with thin black edge to the tips of the fore-wings. Wing fringes white. Underside very pale blue or bluish white, marked with small black dots. Pl. 4. **Holly Blue (male)**, 1¼ inches.

Similar to above but tips of fore-wings heavily bordered black and with row of small black spots along the margin of the hind-wings. Pl. 4.

Holly Blue (female), 1¼ inches.

Common in parts of the southern half of England and Wales. Local further north and in Ireland. On the wing in April and May, and again from July to September.

Wings purplish blue with black edges. Underside pale greyish or whitish blue with black spots and a band of orange near the margin of both fore- and hind-wings. Pl. 27.

Silver-studded Blue (male), 1 inch.

Locally distributed in England, Wales, and south Scotland on heaths and commons. On the wing from July to September. (For female *see* No. 46.)

Wings purple blue with black veins and borders. Underside grey with black and white transverse

51 ⎱ line on all wings and a few dusky marks near the
hind borders. The hind-wings also show an
orange-ringed black spot on each anal angle. PL. 27.
Purple Hairstreak (male), 1⅛ inches.

Widely distributed in the British Isles except in
Ireland, where it is local and rare. On the wing
near woods in July and August. In the female the
purple blue area is restricted to the fore-wings, the
hind-wings being blackish brown.

APPENDIX I

Adonis Blue (*Agriades bellargus*)

Black-veined White (*Aporia crataegi*)
Brimstone (*Gonepteryx rhamni*)
Brown Argus (*Aricia medon*)
Brown Hairstreak (*Zephyrus betulae*)

Camberwell Beauty (*Euvanessa antiopa*)
Chalk Hill Blue (*Lysandra corydon*)
Chequered Skipper (*Cyclopides palaemon*)
Clouded Yellow (*Colias edusa*)
Comma (*Polygonia c-album*)
Common Blue (*Polyommatus icarus*)

Dark Green Fritillary (*Argynnis aglaia*)
Dingy Skipper (*Nisoniades tages*)
Duke of Burgundy (*Nemeobius lucina*)

Gatekeeper (*Epinephele tithonus*)
Glanville Fritillary (*Melitaea cinxia*)
Grayling (*Hipparchia semele*)
Green Hairstreak (*Callophrys rubi*)
Green-veined White (*Pieris napi*)
Grizzled Skipper (*Hesperia malvae*)

Heath Fritillary (*Melitæa athalia*)
High Brown Fritillary (*Argynnis adippe*)
Holly Blue (*Celastrina argiolus*)

Large Blue (*Lycæna arion*)
Large Heath (*Coenonympha tiphon*)
Large Skipper (*Augiades sylvanus*)

APPENDIX I

Large Tortoiseshell (*Eugonia polychloros*)
Large White (*Pieris brassicae*)
Lulworth Skipper (*Thymelicus actaeon*)

Marbled White (*Melanargia galatea*)
Marsh Fritillary (*Melitæa aurinia*)
Meadow Brown (*Epinephele jurtina*)

Orange-tip (*Anthocharis cardamines*)

Painted Lady (*Pyrameis cardui*)
Pale Clouded Yellow (*Colias hyale*)
Peacock (*Vanessa io*)
Pearl-bordered Fritillary (*Brenthis euphrosyne*)
Purple Emperor (*Apatura iris*)
Purple Hairstreak (*Zephyrus quercus*)

Red Admiral (*Pyrameis atalanta*)
Ringlet (*Aphantopus hyperanthus*)

Scotch Argus (*Erebia æthiops*)
Silver-spotted Skipper (*Augiades comma*)
Silver-studded Blue (*Plebeius aegon*)
Silver-washed Fritillary (*Dryas paphia*)
Small Blue (*Cupido minimus*)
Small Copper (*Chrysophanus phlaeas*)
Small Heath (*Cœnonympha pamphilus*)
Small Mountain Ringlet (*Erebia epiphron*)
Small Pearl-bordered Fritillary (*Brenthis selene*)
Small Skipper (*Adopœa flava*)
Small Tortoiseshell (*Vanessa urticae*)
Small White (*Pieris rapae*)
Speckled Wood (*Pararge egeria*)
Swallow-tail (*Papilio machaon*)

Wall (*Pararge megæra*)
White Admiral (*Limenitis sibylla*)
White-letter Hairstreak (*Thecla w-album*)
Wood White (*Leucophasia sinapis*)

SECTION II

MOTHS

1 {All wings long and narrow Fore-wings **much** longer than hind-wings.   Body thick and heavy. **2**

{Not as above described.   **10**

2. Very large moths—wing-span 4 inches or more. **6**

3. Large moths—wing-span from 3 to 4 inches. **7**

4. Medium-sized moths—wing-span from 2 to 3 inches. **8**

5. Small moths—wing-span less than 2 inches. **9**

6 {Thorax with conspicuous, pale, skull-like mark. Abdomen banded blackish brown and yellow. Fore-wings dark brown with wavy lines of black and yellowish buff; central areas powdered white. Hind-wings dull yellow or orange buff marked with two broad black bands. PL. 5.

Death's-head, 4½ inches or more.

Occurs from time to time in almost all parts of the British Isles, though irregularly and in small numbers.   The largest of British moths.

Thorax without skull mark. Abdomen banded red, black, and white. Wings greyish; the fore-wings obscurely mottled, the hind-wings showing dark bands. PL. 5.

Convolvulus Hawk, 4½ inches.

33

6 ⎤ Occurs irregularly in many parts of Great Britain, chiefly in England, in June and July.

Abdomen barred black and rose pink. Fore-wings ash grey, sometimes tinted pink at bases, clouded with white or buff and with blackish-brown patch along inner margins. Hind-wings paler in ground colour than fore-wings, with pink bases and two broad black bands. PL. 28.

Privet Hawk, 4 inches or more.

Occurs locally in England and southern Scotland. Most frequent in the south of England. On the wing in June and July.

⎧ Wings and body ash grey. Fore-wings with dark central area marked with white spot. Hind-wings showing large patch of reddish brown at bases. Margins of wings indented. PL. 28.

Poplar Hawk, 3¼ inches.

Common throughout Great Britain except in northern Scotland. The female is paler than the male. On the wing from May to July. Our commonest Hawk moth.

Abdomen barred black or dark brown and white. Wings ash grey. Fore-wing with dark band along inner margin and one or more obscure transverse bands. Near the centre of each fore-wing there are three black dashes. Hind-wings somewhat browner than fore-wings, without markings. PL. 29.

Pine Hawk, 3¼–3½ inches.

A rare British moth, occasionally seen in southern England, particularly in Suffolk. On the wing at dusk about flowers in June and July. The cater-
7 ⎦ pillar feeds on pine needles.

7 Fore-wings with sharply pointed tips; reddish grey or buff, barred and mottled with dark brown. Hind-wings pink fading to greyish buff at the margins, each bearing a large blue eye-spot. PL. 28.
Eyed Hawk, 3¼ inches.

Fairly common in southern England but local or scarce further north and in Scotland and Ireland. On the wing from May to July.

Ground colour of wings yellowish or pinkish brown, often suffused green. Fore-wings scalloped at edges, marked with two patches and an irregular band of olive green on their central areas. Hind-wings with dark oblique band. PL. 29.
Lime Hawk, 2¾–3 inches.

Fairly common in the south of England, scarce in the midlands, absent further north.

8 Fore-wings olive brown suffused rose pink; inner margins white. Hind-wings rose pink with large black area at base. Thorax pink marked olive brown. Abdomen olive brown with pink central line. PL. 5.   **Elephant Hawk**, 2¼–2½ inches.

Fairly common in Great Britain except in the north of England and Scotland, where it is local or scarce. On the wing after dusk in June, usually about night-scented blossoms.

All wings pale tawn, broadly margined rose pink. Hind-wings dusky brown at bases and fringed white. Body deep rose pink variegated yellowish fawn. PL. 5. **Small Elephant Hawk**, nearly 2 inches.

Common in most parts of the British Isles, with the exception of northern Scotland. On the wing in
9 May and June.

9 | Fore-wings dark brownish grey, marked with darker waved lines. Hind-wings orange yellow. Body dark grey with forked tail tuft. PL. 29.
Humming-bird Hawk, 1¾ inches.

Common throughout the British Isles. Flies by day from May to September, when it may be seen hovering over flowers as it sucks their nectar through its long, trunk-like proboscis.

Wings transparent except for dark reddish brown margins, broad on fore-wings, narrow on hind-wings. Body golden tawny. Abdomen banded with black on two segments and orange towards tip. PL. 29
Narrow-bordered Bee Hawk, about 1½ inches.

Flies by day, hovering over flowers, in May and June. Fairly common in most parts of the British Isles.

Similar to above but with broad, dark margins to all wings. Abdomen with broad band of reddish brown. **Broad-bordered Bee Hawk**, 1½–1¾ inches.

Locally common in the south and midlands of England. Rare or absent elsewhere. On the wing in May and June. Flies by day.

10 { All four wings of same general colour; unmarked or but lightly marked or freckled. **11**

Not according to above description. **34**

11 { Ground colour of wings white or pale grey. **12**

Ground colour other than white or pale grey. **26**

12 { All wings without markings. **13**

Wings lightly marked. **18**

13 {
Wings divided into plume-like segments.
Large White Plume Moth, about 1 inch.

Common especially about bindweed, on which the eggs are laid. Often enters houses attracted by lights.

Wings not so divided. **14**
}

14 {
Body mainly or wholly white. **15**

Body not white. **17**
}

15 {
Body all white. PL. 30. **White Satin**, 2 inches.

Common in the south of England, local further north. Rare in Scotland and Ireland. On the wing in July and August.

Body with coloured tail. **16**
}

16 {
Tail golden yellow. PL.30. **Yellow-tail**, $1\frac{1}{4}$–$1\frac{3}{4}$ inches.

Common in the south of England, less so in the north. Rare in Scotland, absent from Ireland. On the wing in June and July.

Tail brown. **Brown-tail (female)**, $1\frac{1}{2}$ inches.

A rare British moth. Occasionally seen near the coast in south-eastern England. On the wing in late July and August. (For male see No. 20.)
}

17. Body smoky brown. Wings pure white thinly margined with brown.

Ghost Moth (male), about 2 inches.

Widely distributed throughout the British Isles, flying in June and July. The flight is peculiar and characteristic, the moths swaying backwards and forwards in the air in companies.

(For female see No. 187.)

18 { Wings lightly spotted or freckled.   **19**

{ Wings marked with wavy lines.   **25**

19 { Abdomen mainly white or white with yellow tail.   **20**

{ Abdomen yellow or gold.   **21**

{ Abdomen greyish.   **24**

20 {
Body white with small black dots on abdomen. Fore- and hind-wings white with few black dots. PL. 30.   **Muslin Moth (female)**, about 1½ inches.

Widely distributed in England, Wales, and Scotland; locally common. On the wing in May and June.   (For male *see* No. 33.)

Abdomen white with yellow extremity. Fore-wings white with one or two dark dots. Hind-wings white, without markings.   **Yellow-tail (male)**, 1¼ inches.   (*See* No. 16.)

21 {
Fore-wings with one or two dark dots, hind-wings unmarked.   **22**

Fore- and hind-wings both showing spots.   **23**

22.   Abdomen yellow or golden brown with small black spots along centre. Female with white tail.   **Water Ermine**, 1½ inches.

Locally distributed near marshes and fens mainly in south-eastern England. Rare in Scotland, absent from Ireland On the wing in June.

23 {
Fore-wings creamy white, lightly but variably spotted with black or dark brown over their whole surface. Hind-wings pure white with very few spots. Thorax white, abdomen yellow. PL. 30   **White Ermine**, 1½–1¾ inches.

23 Common in most parts of Great Britain. On the wing in June and July.

Wings long, rather narrow, creamy or buffish white. Abdomen greyish brown.

Common Swift (female), 1¼ inches.

Widely distributed and common in many parts of Great Britain. On the wing from June to August, over fields, meadows, etc.

(For male *see* No. 187.)

Wings suffused grey, sparsely marked with black dots or short streaks. Hind-wings white. PL. 31.

Miller Moth, 1½ inches.

Widely distributed, but uncommon, from southern England to Sutherland. On the wing from late May to early July near woods and heaths.

24 Wings narrow. Fore-wings finely spotted with black. Hind-wings more sparsely dotted with dark grey. Abdomen grey. PL. 31.

Wood Leopard, 1¾–2½ inches.

Locally distributed in the southern half of England, rare or absent elsewhere in Britain. A strong-flying moth which is on the wing in July and August. The female is considerably larger than the male. Also known as the Leopard Moth.

Wings white; the fore-wings showing three and the hind-wings two grey wavy lines.

White Wave, 1¼ inches.

25 Common throughout the British Isles. On the wing from May to August.

25 ⎤ Wings creamy white dusted with brown. Fore-
wings with three, hind-wings with two transverse
rusty brown lines.   **Common Wave,** 1¼ inches.

Common throughout the British Isles. On the
wing from May to August.

26 ⎰ Ground colour of wings cream or yellow.   **27**

Ground colour of wings other than cream or yellow.
30

27 ⎰ Wings sulphur yellow.   **28**

Wings not sulphur yellow.   **29**

28 ⎱ Hind-wings with short tails. Wings pale sulphur
yellow with three thin bars of olive brown crossing
each fore-wing and one similar bar on each hind-
wing. Wing tails margined in reddish brown with
a spot of the same shade on either side. PL. 31.
     Swallow-tail, 2¼ inches.

Common in most parts of England, Wales, and
Ireland, rarer in Scotland. On the wing in July.

Hind-wings without tails. All wings bright sulphur yellow with irregular markings of reddish
brown along the front edge of the fore-wings.
PL. 31.   **Brimstone Moth,** about 1¼ inches.

Common throughout the British Isles. On the
wing from May to September.

29 ⎰ Wings varying in colour from yellowish buff to
cream. Each fore-wing crossed by oblique row of
dark dots and with a few small spots near the wing
edges. Hind-wings with two or three dots near the
hind margin and usually a small central spot.

29) Abdomen yellowish buff with black dots down the
centre.   **Buff Ermine,** about 1⅝ inches.

Widely distributed and common in most parts of
the British Isles.   On the wing in June and July.

Wings yellowish or greyish buff crossed by two
thin transverse lines of brown.
                        Riband Wave, 1 inch.

Common throughout the British Isles in June and
July.

30 { Ground colour of wings green.   **31**

{ Ground colour of wings other than green.   **32**

Wings bright green, marked with wavy lines and
spots of white.   Thorax green; abdomen pale
yellow.   PL. 6.   **Large Emerald,** 2 inches.

A very handsome moth which is common in most
parts of the British Isles in June and July.

Wings pale bluish green, sometimes almost white;
the fore-wings showing two and the hind-wings one
transverse white lines.   **Light Emerald,** 1¾ inches.

Common in most parts of Great Britain.   On the
wing in July.

Wings dull green fading to grey, with brown-spotted
cream fringes.   Fore-wings with two, hind-wings
with one wavy white lines.
                    Common Emerald, 1 inch.

Common in most parts of the south of England;
local in the midlands, rare further north and in
31) Ireland.   On the wing in June and July.

31 Wings pale bluish green with two white curved lines on each fore-wing and one on each hind-wing.
Small Emerald, 1¼ inches.

Common in the south and east of England but rare elsewhere in the British Isles. On the wing in July and August.

Wings very pale bluish green or greenish white, crossed by two white transverse lines.
Little Emerald, 1 inch.

Widely distributed in England, Wales, and Ireland. Local in Scotland. On the wing from May to July.

Ground colour of wings orange or brown. **33**

Ground colour of wings black.
Chimney Sweeper, 1 inch.

32 Wings and body black or greyish black without markings. Flies by day in sunshine. Locally but widely distributed throughout the British Isles except in north Scotland.

All wings deep orange finely freckled with grey.
Orange Moth (male), 1½ inches.

All wings orange yellow finely speckled with reddish brown. PL. 6. **Orange Moth (female), 1½ inches.**

33 Common in many wooded districts in southern England. Local elsewhere. Absent from Scotland. On the wing in June and July.

All wings dark brown sparsely spotted with black.
Muslin Moth (male), 1¼ inches.
(For female *see* No. 20.)

34 $\left\{\begin{array}{l}\text{All four wings of same ground colour but fore- and} \\ \text{hind-wings differing in colour or distribution of} \\ \text{markings.} \hfill \textbf{35} \\[1em] \text{Ground colour of fore- and hind-wings different.} \quad \textbf{83}\end{array}\right.$

All four wings of same ground colour but fore- and hind-wings differing in colour or distribution of markings. **35**

Ground colour of fore- and hind-wings different. **83**

35 { Ground colour of wings white. **36**

Ground colour of wings other than white. **43**

36 { Wings conspicuously spotted or blotched with black or dark brown. **37**

Wings not conspicuously spotted or blotched. **38**

Wings white, boldly spotted with black round the margins. On the fore-wings a double row of black spots runs in a curved line to the hind margin; the space between the spots being orange. Hind-wings marked with smaller round spots. Abdomen orange spotted with black. Pl. 6. **Magpie,** 1½ inches.

This species is very variable in the distribution of the wing markings. It is common in most parts of Great Britain in July and August.

Wings white, blotched along the margins with dark brown. Some of these markings may join up to form an irregular border. The central areas may be clear, sparsely spotted or crossed by more or less confluent blotches. Pl. 6. **Clouded Border,** 1 inch.

A variable but distinctive moth. Fairly common in the neighbourhood of sallows and willows on which the caterpillar feeds. On the wing from May to late July.

37 { Wings creamy white with mauve-grey centres and with brownish patches near the margins of both fore- and hind-wings. **Clouded Magpie,** 1¼ inches.

37 Another very variable moth. Widely distributed but local in England, Wales, Ireland, and south Scotland. On the wing in May and June.

Wings white bordered with dark brown spots closely set and partially confluent. Fore-wings with several long, blackish spots towards the middle and two streaks of yellow bordered with dark dots near the bases. Hind-wings with two large central spots. Head and thorax yellow, abdomen blackish. **Small Magpie**, 1 inch.

Common in many parts of Great Britain, especially in southern England. On the wing in June and July.

38 Wings white, finely peppered with minute black dots and thin black cross-lines. Some specimens show a few larger black spots near the margins of the fore-wings. PL. 32. **Peppered Moth**, 1½ inches.

Widely distributed and generally fairly common. On the wing in May and June.

Wings not as above. **39**

39 Wings narrow, white, thinly scaled. Fore-wings marked with many blue-black dots; hind-wings more lightly spotted with grey. PL. 31.
Wood Leopard, 1¾–2½ inches.
(*See* No. 24.)

Wings not as above. **40**

40 Fore-wings boldly streaked with dark brown along front and inner margins and with pale brownish edges. Hind-wings white with brownish markings at anal angles. Body brown.
Swallow Prominent, 1¾ inches.

44

40 ⎱ Widely distributed and common in many parts of Great Britain, especially in south and east England. On the wing from May to August.

⎰ Wings not as above. **41**

41. Fore-wings strongly barred or blotched. Hind-wings without bars or blotches. **42**

42 ⎧ Wings creamy or buffish white. Fore-wings with irregular, broad central band of greyish brown. Hind-wings with greyish central dot.
Silver-ground Carpet, 1 inch.

Widely distributed and generally common. On the wing in May and June and again in August and September.

Wings creamy white, brownish at edges. Fore-wings boldly banded with rich purple brown and with triangular patch of the same colour at bases. Hind-wings with small central dot. Pl. 33.
Purple-bar Carpet, 1 inch.

Widely distributed throughout the British Isles. On the wing in June and July, occasionally in August.

43 ⎧ Ground colour of wings grey. **44**

⎩ Ground colour of wings other than grey. **46**

44. Fore-wings showing well-marked central band. **45**

45 ⎰ Wings pale grey, darker at tips. Fore-wings with broad dark grey central band outlined in black on its inner margin. Outer edge of wing marked with black dots. Hind-wings unmarked except for a few marginal dots. Pl. 32. **Poplar Kitten,** 1½ inches.

45 Generally distributed in England wherever poplars are common. Absent from Scotland, rare in Ireland. On the wing from June to September.

Wings ashy (male) or dusky grey (female). Dark central band margined in brownish or slaty grey. In the male the hind-wings are light brownish grey without markings. In the female they are greyer and show faint white marks.

Pale Oak Eggar, $1\frac{1}{4}$ inches.

Fairly common in wooded districts in southern England. Local or rare elsewhere. On the wing in August and September.

Wings pale or whitish grey. Fore-wings with conspicuous purple brown band, which is edged with black, and a triangular mark of the same colour at the wing bases. Hind-wings with dark central dot and several inconspicuous waved lines.

Flame Carpet, 1 inch.

Widely distributed throughout the British Isles and common in many parts. On the wing in May and June and again in August.

Wings greyish white. Fore-wings with outer dark grey borders separated by clear space from dark grey central band. Wing bases same colour as wing borders. Hind-wings bordered with brownish grey and with a few central dots and waved lines. **Common Carpet, 1 inch.**

Widely distributed and generally common. On the wing in May and June and often again in August and September.

46 Ground colour of wings yellow or orange. **47**

Ground colour of wings other than yellow or orange. **53**

47 A large moth with wing-span of two inches or more.

47 Wings yellow to reddish tawny. Each fore-wing shows two silvery white marks and a dark, oblique line. Hind-wings unmarked except for a straight line running across the middle, which is sometimes inconspicuous. PL. 32. **Drinker,** 2–2½ inches.

Widely distributed and fairly common in many parts of Great Britain. On the wing in late June and July. Wing-span less than 2 inches. **48**

48 All wings boldly speckled or heavily marked with dark brown. **49**

Wings not so marked. **50**

49 Wings orange yellow with four rows of irregular purple-brown spots traversing the fore-wings and a variable number of similar spots, arranged in one or two curved rows, on the hind-wings. PL. 32.

Speckled Yellow, ¾ inch.

Common in woodland areas in the south and west of England, flying by day. Elsewhere local, becoming rare in the north. On the wing in late May and June.

Wings yellow heavily blotched with black. Thorax black. Abdomen yellow or orange with broad black line down centre. PL. 33. **Wood Tiger,** 1½ inches.

Widely distributed and fairly common throughout the British Isles. May be seen flying by day in open woods, heaths, moors, etc. On the wing in May and June.

50 Edges of wings deeply indented or scalloped. **51**

Wing edges not indented or scalloped. **52**

51 Wings buffish yellow or tawny. Fore-wings with two curved oblique dark lines. Hind-wings with thinner, less conspicuous single waved line.

September Thorn, 1½ inches.

51 Common in most parts of southern England. Further north it becomes local or scarce. On the wing in August and September.

Similar to above but wings clouded reddish brown on the margins. Between the two dark transverse lines on the fore-wings there is a dark dot.
August Thorn, 1½ inches.

Distribution and season of flight the same as September Thorn.

Similar to September Thorn but thorax bright canary yellow.
Canary-shouldered Thorn, 1½ inches.

Common in most parts of Great Britain about woods and damp places. On the wing in August and September.

Wings dull buffish yellow overlaid by a dusky tint. Fore-wings with two dark oblique lines enclosing an indistinct light-centred spot. Hind wings unmarked. **Dusky Thorn,** 1½ inches.

Fairly common in southern England, local further north. Absent from Scotland. On the wing in August and September.

Wings pale buffish yellow sprinkled with brown. Fore-wings with three dark transverse lines. Hind-wings with pale central band.
Early Thorn, 1½ inches.

Widely distributed in Great Britain and common in many areas. On the wing in March and April and again in July and August.

Wings buff yellow. Fore-wings crossed by two dark lines enclosing light brown area with dark

51 ⎱ central dot. Hind-wings with one line light brown and dark central spot. PL. 33. **Scalloped Oak,** 1½ inches.

Widely distributed throughout Great Britain and generally common. On the wing in July and August.

52 ⎰

A thick-bodied moth. Wings buff yellow. Fore-wings with two cross-lines usually enclosing a brown area. Hind-wings unmarked or with an obscure central line. PL. 33. **Lackey,** 1½ inches.

Common in many parts of the south of England but local and scarcer in the midlands and north. Absent from Scotland and northern Ireland. On the wing in July and August.

A small-bodied moth. Wings yellowish buff. Fore-wings crossed by one conspicuous brown line which has a thinner greyish line on either side. All three lines run through the hind-wings.

Clay Triple Lines, 1 inch.

Common in the south of England and Wales, usually in the neighbourhood of beech woods. Local and scarce in the north. On the wing in May and June and again in August and September.

53 ⎰ Ground colour of wings buff.   **54**

Ground colour of wings other than buff.   **59**

54 ⎰ Wings with indented or scalloped edges.   **55**

Wing edges not scalloped.   **56**

55 ⎰ Wings brownish buff. Fore-wings with three dark transverse lines. Hind-wings with pale central band.   **Early Thorn,** 1½ inches.

(*See* No. 51.)

55 Wings pale buff. Fore-wings tipped purple brown. Basal portions of both fore- and hind-wings deep brown. There is a small white mark on the dark portion of each wing. **Purple Thorn,** $1\frac{1}{2}$ inches.

Fairly generally distributed in the south of England, though nowhere abundant. Local in the midlands and north. Rare in Scotland. On the wing in April and May and again in July and August.

56 All four wings crossed by conspicuous pink, red, or purple line.   **57**

Wings not so marked.   **58**

57. Wings buff dusted with grey, crossed by oblique red or purple line. The fore-wings also have a short ruddy central line and two fine grey transverse lines, one of which is continued on the hindwings. PL. 33.   **Blood-vein,** $1\frac{1}{4}$ inches.

Widely distributed in Great Britain. Common in the south of England, local in the north, rare in Ireland. On the wing from June to September.

Wings creamy buff sprinkled with brown. Both fore- and hind-wings marked with curved transverse bands of dark brown, three on each wing, the middle one on the fore-wings bifurcated.
Common Heath, 1 inch.

Common throughout Great Britain. On the wing from May to July. The male is darker than the female.

58 Wings buff, slightly tinged pink. Fore-wings with two dark wavy lines and a small central dot.

58 Hind-wings with dark wavy line above a brown or clouded band. **Waved Umber,** 1½ inches.

Fairly common in parts of south England and Wales. Rare elsewhere. On the wing in April and May.

59 Ground colour of wings grey. **60**

Ground colour of wings other than grey. **67**

60 Moth large—wing-span 2½ inches or more. **61**

Moth with wing-span of less than 2½ inches. **62**

61 Wings grey tinted with brown and covered with a fine network of dark or blackish brown. The fore-wings show two thick dark lines near the hind margins. PL. 33. **Goat Moth,** 3 inches.

Widely distributed in Great Britain. Owes its name to the pungent odour emitted by its caterpillar, which bores into the wood of trees. On the wing in June and July but most often seen resting on tree trunks.

Wings dark brownish grey, bases and central areas darker than outer portions. Upper part of fore-wing with six dark spots. Hind-wings unmarked except for two pale transverse lines. PL. 34.
Old Lady, 2½ inches.

Fairly common in the south of England and Ireland, less so in northern England and Scotland. On the wing in July and August.

62 Fore-wings with distinct central band. **63**

Fore-wings without distinct central band. **64**

Wings pale grey. Fore-wings crossed by broad transverse band of darker grey edged with black. Edges of wings dotted. Hind-wings without markings except for small dots on margins. PL. 32.
Poplar Kitten, 1½ inches.

Fairly common in all parts of England where poplars grow. Rare in Ireland, absent from Scotland. On the wing in June and July.

Wings brownish or smoky grey with darker bases and transverse central band on fore-wings. Hind-wings without markings except for dark dots round margins.

63

Pale Oak Eggar (female), 1¼ inches.
(*See* No. 45.)

Wings pale grey sprinkled darker grey. On the fore-wings two dark, curved, transverse stripes enclose a central band which varies in depth of colour from dark grey (male) to pale buff-grey (female). Hind-wings almost without markings except for a cloudy blotch or spot near the hind margin. PL. 35. **Pale Tussock (male),** 1½ inches.
(female), 2 inches.

Widely distributed in England and Wales and common in many parts, particularly in the south. Local in Ireland, rare or absent from Scotland.

64

All wings pale grey marked with thin wavy transverse lines. **65**

Wings not as described. **66**

65. Wings pale grey finely dusted with brown. Fore-wings with two dark brown transverse lines and cloudy markings of the same colour near the

65   margins.   The outer dark line is continued on the hind-wing which also has a scalloped marginal line.
Engrailed, 1½ inches.

Common in most parts of Great Britain.   On the wing from March to July.

66 {

Wings grey finely powdered with black.   There is a black spot, often orange-edged, near the bases and three black lines, more or less broken, extend from the front almost to the inner margins. Hind-wings with thin marginal line and a small central spot.   **Dark Tussock (male),** 1½ inches.
                  (female), 2 inches.

Locally distributed in England, most often seen north of the midlands.   More generally distributed in Scotland.   On the wing in June and July.

Wings pale grey tinged greenish or pale brown, powdered brownish grey.   Fore-wings crossed by four irregular blackish lines, the two outer ones often indistinct. Hind wings with one wavy transverse line.
      Pale Brindled Beauty (male), 1¾ inches.

Widely distributed in England, Wales, and southern Scotland.   On the wing from January to March.   The female is wingless.

67   Ground colour of wings brown.   **68**

68 {
Large moth—wing-span over 2 inches.   **69**

Moth with wing-span not exceeding 2 inches.   **72**

69 {
General colour ruddy brown.   **70**

General colour not ruddy brown.   **71**

Wings rich ruddy brown tinged purple. Fore-wings with three waved greyish-black lines running more or less parallel to the dentated margins. Hind-wings with two or three dusky transverse lines, less distinct than on fore-wings. PL. 34.

Lappet Moth, 3 inches.

Widely distributed in England but most often seen in the south. Absent from Scotland and Ireland. On the wing in June and July.

Wings deep mahogany red with broad yellow band running transversely through each wing. White round spot in the centre of fore-wings. PL. 35.

Oak Eggar (male), $2\frac{1}{2}$ inches.

70

Wings and body orange or foxy brown. All wings with broad, pale, yellowish transverse band. Each fore-wing with white central spot.

Oak Eggar (female), 3 inches.

Generally distributed and locally common. On the wing in July and August.

Wings and body reddish brown. Fore-wings crossed by two pale transverse lines.

Fox Moth (male), $2\frac{1}{4}$ inches.

As above but wings paler and tinged grey.

Fox Moth (female), $2\frac{1}{2}$ inches.

Generally distributed throughout the British Isles and common in many localities. On the wing in May and June.

71. Wings dark brown, greyish at bases. Each fore-wing shows a buff transverse line and a number of black and buff spots which follow the line of the wing margin. Hind-wings lighter in colour

71.   towards bases with an indistinct buff line across the centre area. PL. 43. **Lobster Moth,** 2¼–2½ inches.

Widely distributed in England in the neighbourhood of beech woods. Rare in Ireland, absent from Scotland. On the wing in June and July. Its name refers to the peculiar shape of the caterpillar.

72   { General colour of wings reddish brown.   **73**

        { General colour other than reddish brown.   **74**

73   {

Wings reddish brown, darker near bases. Forewings with white spot in centre, a short white line at base, and a narrow, waved, white transverse band. Hind-wings with indistinct, pale, transverse band, otherwise unmarked. PL. 35.
          Small Oak Eggar, 1½–1¾ inches.

Widely distributed in south and east England, local elsewhere. On the wing in February and March.

Wings orange brown. Fore-wings with kidney-shaped white spot. Hind-wings without markings. PL. 35.   **Vapourer (male),** 1¼ inches.

Generally distributed throughout the British Isles, common in many parts. On the wing from August to October. The female is wingless.

74   { All wings boldly spotted or blotched.   **75**

        { Wings not all boldly spotted or blotched.   **76**

75   {

Wings dark brown with black lines and spots. Fore-wings with large white spot near front margin. Hind-wings with broad white central band and small white spot near hind margin.
          Four-spotted Moth, 1 inch.

75 ⎫ Widely, though locally, distributed in south and
   ⎪ south-west England; not generally common. Flies
   ⎪ in sunshine in May and June and again in August.
   ⎪
   ⎪ Wings dark brown broken up by paler lines,
   ⎪ broadly edged with deep chocolate. The hind-
   ⎪ wings with large white or buff spot near the base.
   ⎪ Pl. 35.   **Mother Shipton,** 1 inch.
   ⎪
   ⎪ Widely distributed throughout the British Isles
   ⎪ except in the northern half of Scotland. Locally
   ⎩ common. On the wing in May and June.

76 ⎰ All wings traversed by conspicuous red or purple
   ⎱ line.   **77**

   ⎰ Wings not so marked.   **78**

      ⎧ Wings pale or buff brown. A pinkish, red, or purple
      ⎪ stripe extends from apex of fore-wing to the
      ⎪ inner margin of hind-wing.
      ⎪   **Blood-vein,** 1¼ inches.
      ⎪   (*See* No. 57.)
77 ⎨
      ⎪ Similar to above but wings strongly angulated.
      ⎪ Fore-wings with black central dot.
      ⎪   **Small Blood-vein,** 1 inch.
      ⎪
      ⎪ Generally distributed in England and Wales but
      ⎪ local north of the midlands. Absent from Scot-
      ⎩ land. On the wing in July and August.

78 ⎰ General colour of all wings dark brown without
   ⎱ conspicuous markings.   **79**

   ⎰ Wings not as above described.   **80**

79 ⎰ Fore-wings dark greyish brown with pale nervules.
   ⎱ Hind-wings without markings. Pl. 36.
   ⎱   **Gothic Moth,** 1½ inches.

79) Widely distributed and common in most parts of
the British Isles. On the wing in June and July.

Fore-wings greyish brown marked with two black,
transverse, wavy lines enclosing a ring-like marking
of the same colours, and with pale curved line near
wing margins. Hind-wings unmarked.

Double Dart, $1\frac{3}{4}$ inches.

Common in most parts of the British Isles. On the
wing from June to August.

80 { All four wings showing waved lines. **81**

{ All wings not as described. **82**

Wings pale greyish brown dusted and mottled
darker brown. Fore-wings marked with two dark,
wavy, transverse lines enclosing a dark-mottled
area. Near the wing margin there is a pale or
white wavy line. The hind-wings show one dark
waved line and a pale submarginal line.

Mottled Beauty, $1\frac{1}{2}$ inches.

Common in most parts of the British Isles. On the
wing in June and July.

81 { Wings yellowish brown. Fore-wings with two
dark transverse lines, the outer of which borders a
dark band. Between the lines is a small central
dot. Hind-wings banded with reddish brown and
showing central black wavy line.

Waved Umber, $1\frac{1}{2}$ inches.

Widely distributed in the south and midlands of
England and south Wales. Local in the north,
rare in Scotland and Ireland. On the wing from
April to June.

82. Wings reddish or buffish brown. Fore-wings marked with dark kidney-shaped spot and with an area of darker brown extending from below this spot along the inner margin of the wings. Hind-wings unmarked; often tinged grey.

Red Sword-grass, 2¼ inches.

Locally distributed throughout the British Isles but nowhere common. On the wing in March and April and in September and October.

83 {
Fore-wings darker than hind-wings.   **84**

Fore-wings lighter than hind-wings.   **182**

Wings membranous with dark margins.   **191**
}

84 {
Fore-wings yellow.   **85**

Fore-wings other than yellow.   **92**
}

85 {
Fore-wings without conspicuous markings.   **86**

Fore-wings spotted, barred, or banded.   **87**
}

86. Fore-wings pale buff yellow. Close examination may reveal a small black dot in the middle and two other dots towards the margins. Hind-wings white, sometimes dusted with grey on the hind margins.   **Common Wainscot,** 1¼ inches.

Common in most parts of the British Isles. On the wing in June and July.

87 {
Fore-wings spotted, without other markings.   **88**

Fore-wings not as described.   **89**
}

Fore-wings yellow with pink margins and central spot of grey bordered with red. Hind wings white or cream with dark central spot and broken dusky marginal band. **Clouded Buff (male),** 1½ inches.

Widely distributed in the southern half of England, local further north and in Ireland. On the wing in June and July. (For female *see* No. 93.)

88

Fore-wings yellow with two black spots. Hind-wings paler and without markings. PL. 3.
Four-spotted Footman (female), 2 inches.

Locally distributed in the south of England, scarce elsewhere in Britain and absent from Scotland. On the wing in July and August.

Fore-wings pale yellow or yellowish buff with deeper-tinted margins, marked with a number of small black spots. Hind-wings cream or white without markings. **Dew Moth,** 1 inch.

A local species which occurs chiefly in the southern counties near the coast. On the wing in June and July.

89

Fore-wings crossed by transverse lines but not definitely banded. **90**

Fore-wings showing transverse band or bands. **91**

90

Fore-wings cloudy yellow crossed by three greyish or reddish brown transverse lines and with brown-dotted fringes. Hind-wings paler, without markings except for an indistinct cross-line and brown dots on the fringes.
Spinach Moth, 1¼ inches.

90 Generally distributed in England, often seen in gardens. Local in Wales and Scotland. Absent from Ireland. On the wing in July and August.

Similar to above but ground colour of fore-wings clear straw yellow. Wing fringes brown.
Barred Straw, 1¼ inches.

Widely distributed in the British Isles but most frequent in the southern half of England. On the wing in July and August.

Fore-wings deep yellow crossed by two transverse lines enclosing a central band of purplish brown. Hind-wings pale yellowish cream, without markings. **Barred Yellow,** 1 inch.

Generally distributed and locally common in England and Wales. Local in Scotland and Ireland. On the wing in June and July.

Fore-wings pale yellow with irregular violet-brown band near the base and another near the centre. There is a violet-brown patch near the wing-tip, a brown-bordered central spot, and a row of dark dots following the wing margin. The hind-wings are yellowish white without markings.
Sallow, 1¼–1½ inches.

Widely distributed and common in most parts of the British Isles. On the wing in September.

Fore-wings bright yellow dusted reddish-brown, with transverse band of purplish brown near the centre and another towards the hind margin. The yellow areas show two brown transverse lines and paler yellow spots. Hind-wings buff yellow with grey spot and cloudy band near hind margin. Pl. 36.
91 **Frosted Orange,** 1½ inches.

91 ⎱ Widely distributed throughout England and Wales. Local in Scotland, rare in Ireland. On the wing from August to October.

92 ⎰ Ground colour of fore-wings orange.   **93**

Ground colour of fore-wings buff.   **94**

Ground colour of fore-wings other than orange or buff.   **97**

Fore-wings tawny orange crossed by two dark transverse lines and with central dot. Near the tip there is a round white spot. Hind-wings paler, with indistinct transverse line.

Feathered Thorn, 1¾ inches.

Generally distributed over most of the British Isles; locally common in wooded areas in the southern and midland counties. On the wing in October and November.

Fore-wings deep orange with reddish margins and dark central mark. Hind-wings orange with cloudy black base, central spot and marginal band.

Clouded Buff (female), 1½ inches.
(*See* No. 88.)

Fore-wings yellowish or reddish orange, crossed by two brown transverse lines and with obscure whitish line near the margins. Near the centre is a roughly kidney-shaped mark, which is sometimes ill defined. Hind-wings creamy white without markings.   **Orange Sallow**, 1⅓ inches.

93 ⎰ Generally distributed in England, but local elsewhere in the British Isles. On the wing in August and September.

93 Fore-wings orange, spotted and blotched purplish brown and with a band—often clouded or broken—of the same colour running obliquely across the wing. Hind-wings pale cream or white.

Pink-barred Sallow, 1⅓ inches.

Widely distributed and common in most parts of the British Isles. On the wing in September and October.

94 Fore-wings with central transverse band. **95**

Fore-wings without central transverse band. **96**

Fore-wings buff with two transverse lines enclosing a darker central portion in the middle of which is a blackish dot. Wing margins of similar shade to central band. Hind-wings greyish buff.

Dun-bar, 1¼ inches.

Common in most parts of the British Isles. On the wing in July and August.

Fore-wings buff dusted with reddish and dark brown, with row of black dots on hind margins. There are two conspicuous brown transverse lines and a brown central dot. The hind-wings are buff dusted with brown, with greyish central dot and an obscure transverse line.

Dotted Border (male), 1⅓ inches.

Common throughout the British Isles except in northern Scotland. Flies in March and April. The female is small with very short, vestigial wings.

Fore-wings pale buff dusted reddish brown, with central dot and dark, wavy, transverse lines each bordered by brownish band. Hind-wings pale buff with greyish central spot.

95 **Mottled Umber (male),** 1½ inches.

95 Widely distributed throughout the British Isles and generally common except in Scotland, where it is local in the northern counties. On the wing in October and November. The female is wingless.

96. Fore-wings yellowish or whitish buff varied with rusty brown and showing a few dark dots near the wing edges. Hind-wings white, greyish towards margins. **Light Arches**, 1¾ inches.

Widely distributed and common in most parts of the British Isles except in northern Scotland. On the wing in June and July.

97 { Fore-wings brown. **98**

{ Fore-wings other than brown. **144**

98 { Tips of fore-wings pointed and hooked. **99**

{ Tips of fore-wings not pointed and hooked. **102**

99 { Margin of fore-wing deeply indented or scalloped. **100**

{ Margin of fore-wing not deeply indented or scalloped. **101**

100. Fore-wings pale brown, darker at tips, crossed by two dark transverse lines between which is a small central dot. Hind-wings buff with darker marginal line and central dot.

Scalloped Hook-tip, 1¼ inches.

Widely distributed in the British Isles and common where birch-trees are abundant. On the wing in May and June and in August and September.

Fore-wings brown with two central dots, crossed
by two pale transverse lines. Hind-wings yellowish brown with two pale transverse lines and two
central dots. **Oak Hook-tip (male)**, 1 inch.

Similar to above but hind-wings paler with
markings indistinct.
Oak Hook-tip (female), 1¼ inches.

Widely distributed, though not generally common,
in the southern half of England; local elsewhere.
On the wing in May and June and again in
August.

Fore-wings notched below tips, grey-washed
brown, crossed by two pale transverse lines and
with pale marginal line. Between the two transverse lines there are two pale-bordered dark dots.
Hind wings buff brown with one transverse line.
Beautiful Hook-tip, 1¼ inches.

Widely distributed in the southern half of England.
Local or scarce elsewhere in England and Wales;
absent from Scotland and Ireland. On the wing
from June to August.

Fore-wings pale brown crossed by three wavy
transverse lines, beyond the outermost of which
there is a thick black line or band. On the third
transverse line is an irregular-shaped blotch.
Hind-wings paler, with central dot and four or five
wavy dark lines which often fade out at, or a little
beyond, the middle of the wing. PL. 2.
Pebble Hook-tip, 1¼ inches.

Widely distributed and common in many parts of
England, Wales, and Scotland. On the wing in
May and August.

101

102 {
Head with snout-like projection, caused by the elongation of certain of the mouth parts (palps). **103**

Head without snout-like projection. **104**
}

103 {
Fore-wings with pointed tips, buff brown crossed by two somewhat darker, rather indistinct, transverse lines and with submarginal row of black dots. Hind-wings pale greyish brown. **Snout**, $1\frac{1}{4}$ inches.

Common throughout the British Isles wherever nettles grow. On the wing in June and July.

Fore-wings dark brown on central areas, much paler and greyish on outer portions, with dark brown margins. Wing-tip with triangular brown mark. Hind-wings greyish buff or pale grey.
Beautiful Snout, $1\frac{1}{4}$ inches.

Locally distributed in southern England and in Ireland. On the wing in June and July.
}

104 {
Hind-wings showing bright yellow or orange. **105**

Hind-wings not showing yellow or orange. **110**
}

105 {
Moth with wing-span of 2 inches or more. **106**

Moth with wing-span of less than 2 inches. **107**
}

106 {
Fore-wings dark or greyish brown. Hind-wings bright yellow with conspicuous black band. PL. 36.
Yellow Underwing, $2-2\frac{1}{4}$ inches.

Common in most parts of the British Isles. On the wing from June to August or later.
}

106 Similar to above but fore-wings sometimes buff brown or dark olive brown. Hind-wings with very broad black band covering almost half the wing. PL. 37.

Broad-bordered Yellow Underwing, 2–2¼ inches.

Widely distributed in wooded districts throughout Great Britain. On the wing in June and July.

107 Hind-wings with broad black band near margins.**108**

Hind-wings without broad black band near margins. **109**

Fore-wings dark buffish or reddish brown. Hind-wings deep yellow with conspicuous black band and crescent-shaped black central spot.

Lesser Yellow Underwing, 1½ inches.

Common throughout Great Britain. On the wing in July and August.

Fore-wings reddish brown. Hind-wings yellow with broad black band but without crescent-shaped central spot.

Least Yellow Underwing, 1¼ inches.

Locally distributed in England and Ireland. Absent from Scotland.

Fore-wings greyish brown with darker mottling or transverse bands. Hind-wings orange yellow with blackish bases and very broad black marginal band. PL. 37. **Lesser Broad-bordered Underwing,** 1½ inches.

Widely distributed over most of the British Isles. On the wing in July and August, usually near 108 woods or tall hedgerows.

66

108 Fore-wings dark brown with white central dot. Hind-wings yellow with broad black band.

Beautiful Yellow Underwing, 1 inch.

Widely distributed over the British Isles on heaths and moors. On the wing by day from April to July.

Fore-wings dark brown with black transverse lines and a white blotch near the front edge, sometimes extending across the wing. Hind-wings deep orange with blackish brown bases, a narrow black marginal band, and a dark central crescent-shaped spot, the lower end of which joins the dark basal area. **Orange Underwing,** 1½ inches.

Fairly common in the south and east of England, scarce and local elsewhere. Flies by day in March and April, usually near birch-trees.

109. Fore-wings purplish brown with paler borders and darker cross bands. Hind-wings yellow or orange with dark brown basal areas, sometimes covering half the wings, and thick dark brown transverse line towards the dark hind margins.

Burnet Companion, 1¼ inches.

Generally distributed over the British Isles, locally common, in grassy places. On the wing in June.

110 Hind-wings bright coppery brown. 111

Hind-wings not bright coppery brown. 112

111. Fore-wings brown mottled with dark and blackish brown and buff or white. Hind-wings bright copper brown. PL. 37. **Copper Underwing,** 2 inches.

Locally distributed in the south of England. Rare or absent elsewhere in Great Britain. On the wing from July to September.

112 { Hind-wings showing bright red or rose pink. **113**

Hind-wings not showing red or rose pink. **114**

113 {

Fore-wings deep brown broadly netted with white. Hind-wings bright red boldly marked with large black spots and blotches. PL. 7.

Garden Tiger, $2\frac{1}{2}$–$2\frac{3}{4}$ inches.

Generally distributed and common in many parts of the British Isles. On the wing in July and August.

Fore-wings reddish brown with two small black central dots. Hind-wings rose pink with dusky hind margins and two or more central spots. The pink colour may cover the greater part of the wings or be limited in extent, the rest of the area being pale lilac. Abdomen red marked with black along the centre. PL. 7. **Ruby Tiger**, $1\frac{1}{4}$ inches.

Widely distributed and fairly common in many parts of Great Britain. On the wing from May to July.

114 {

Ground colour of hind-wings some shade of brown. **115**

Ground colour of hind-wings not brown. **126**

115 {

Moth with wing-span of over 2 inches. **116**

Wing-span not over 2 inches. **117**

116 {

Fore-wings conspicuously marked with white and crossed by two thick black transverse lines with white edges. Hind-wings reddish or tawny brown with black central transverse line and a few cloudy brown spots below it. PL. 38.

Kentish Glory (male), $2\frac{1}{4}$ inches.

116 ⟩ A handsome and easily recognized moth. Locally distributed in the southern half of England where birch-trees are plentiful. On the wing in April, flying in sunshine. The female is larger and paler (*see* 135.)

Fore-wings greyish brown with white margins and a white central patch enclosing a large eye-spot. Hind-wings tawny brown with paler margins, dark marginal band, and large central eye-spot. PL. 7.
Emperor Moth (male), 2¼ inches.

Widely, though locally, distributed over the British Isles. On the wing in April and May, flying by day.
(For female *see* No. 147.)

117 ⎨ Fore-wings reddish brown.   **118**

Fore-wings not reddish brown.   **119**

118. Fore-wings ruddy or tawny crossed by a dark zig-zag transverse line or band, sometimes by two other, less distinct, cross lines, and with dark central spot or blotch. The inner margin forms a sharp, dark brown tooth which overlaps the fore-margin of the hind-wing. Hind-wings buffish brown with blackish patch near the anal angle. PL. 41.
Coxcomb Prominent, 1½ inches.

Widely distributed throughout the British Isles. On the wing from May to August.

119 ⎨ Fore-wings showing conspicuous white or whitish spot or patch.   **120**

Fore-wings without conspicuous white spot or patch.   **121**

120 ⎨ Fore-wings deep purplish brown, with two black transverse lines and white central spot which is edged with black and has reddish-brown centre.

120 Hind-wings greyish brown with paler bases and small dark central dot.   PL. 38.   **Dot**, $1\frac{1}{2}$ inches.

Locally distributed in the southern half of England; scarce or rare elsewhere. Absent from Scotland. On the wing from August to late September.

Fore-wings medium to dark brown, often with ruddy tinge, with two indistinct transverse lines and a fine white sub-marginal line. The central spot is pale yellowish brown with white edges and there is a smaller pale spot near the wing-bases. Hind-wings greyish brown with darker margins and small dark central dot.   PL. 38.
                    Bright-line Brown-eye, $1\frac{1}{2}$ inches.

Widely distributed and common in many districts. On the wing in June and July.

Fore-wings mid-brown with ruddy tinge, paler near bases, with dark transverse lines and central shade, throwing into prominence the pale ear-shaped marking. Hind-wings pale greyish brown with ruddy fringes.   PL. 39.
                    Ear Moth, $1\frac{1}{4}$ inches.

Widely distributed and generally common in marshy districts. On the wing both in daylight and after dusk in August and September.

Fore-wings greyish brown crossed by obscure transverse dark lines and with pale cream-coloured submarginal line. Each wing shows two pale markings, the more conspicuous being light grey bordered with white, and has two small white dots near its outer edge. Hind-wings greyish brown with paler bases and small central spot.   PL. 39.
                    Cabbage Moth, $1\frac{3}{4}$ inches.

120 ⎱ Common in most parts of the British Isles. On the wing from May to August. Often found in gardens and allotments, where its caterpillars feed on cabbage plants.

121 ⎰ Fore-wings showing pale markings.   **122**

⎱ Fore-wings without pale markings.   **123**

122 ⎰ Fore-wings brown with slight greenish tinge, crossed by darker transverse lines; wing margins paler than central areas. The outermost of the transverse lines is edged with white and there is a large, pale brown, central spot. Hind-wings pale greyish brown. **Green-brindled Crescent, 1½ inches.**

Widely distributed in the British Isles except in north Scotland. Common in many regions. On the wing in September and October.

Fore-wings greyish brown bordered with pale grey, more or less mottled with darker shades and crossed by widely separated transverse lines of black and reddish brown. In front of the thorax is a pale, black-fringed mark supposed to resemble a pair of spectacles. Hind-wings greyish brown with pale bases.   **Spectacle, 1¼ inches.**

Widely distributed throughout the British Isles and common in many parts. On the wing in June and July.

123 ⎰ Fore-wings showing conspicuous black markings. **124**

Fore-wings without conspicuous black markings. **125**

Fore-wings greyish brown, darker on the outer portions, with pale submarginal line and often with some obscure dark transverse lines. Each wing has two conspicuous black marks, the outer of which is larger and roughly heart shaped; the inner one being flattened and in the form of a short streak. A third small dark mark may be shown but this is often ill defined. Hind-wings greyish brown. PL. 39.

Heart and Dart (female), 1½ inches.

Widely distributed and generally common. On the wing in June and July.

(For male *see* No. 142.)

124

Similar to above but the inner of the two dark marks on the fore-wing is thicker and somewhat club-shaped. **Heart and Club,** 1½ inches.

Locally distributed but fairly abundant in some of the southern counties of England. On the wing in June and July.

Fore-wings greyish or dark brown, sometimes with reddish tint. There are three dark spots along the front edges and below them a characteristic open U-shaped mark—from which this moth takes its name—with a small black streak beneath it. Hind-wings greyish with ruddy brown fringes.

Hebrew Character, 1¼ inches.

Widely distributed and common in most parts of the British Isles. On the wing in March and April.

125

Fore-wings greyish brown mottled with darker and lighter shades, and with two longitudinal black streaks at the wing bases and another near the centre. There are two transverse lines, often very indistinct, and a pale zigzagged submarginal line. Hind-wings pale greyish brown with lighter bases. PL. 39. **Dark Arches,** 2 inches.

125 Widely distributed and common throughout the British Isles. On the wing from June to August.

Fore-wings rusty brown, very variable in shade, mottled pale grey near the margins. The paler forms show darker variegations but there are no definite markings. Hind-wings brown, lighter than the fore-wings but varying in depth of shade. **Clouded-bordered Brindle**, 1½ inches.

Common throughout the British Isles in June and July.

Fore-wings dark reddish brown, sometimes mottled or clouded with yellowish, crossed by fine dark transverse lines and with small, very inconspicuous, pale spots on the front margins. There is a pale submarginal line which, however, may be indistinct. Hind-wings greyish brown, darker in the female. **Brown Rustic (male)**, 1½ inches.
(female), 1¼ inches.

Generally distributed and locally common. On the wing in June and July.

Fore-wings greyish brown, crossed by several darker transverse lines and by dark central band. Hind-wings paler, with two or three fine, darker brown lines. **Winter Moth (male)**, 1 inch.

Widely distributed and common in most parts of the British Isles. The male flies from October to December. The female is much smaller and flightless.

126 Hind-wings some shade of grey. **127**

Hind-wings not grey. **133**

127 {

Fore-wings showing conspicuous whitish streak which extends from the base across the wing to the tip. In ground colour the fore-wings are brownish grey with two dark, oval spots below the streak and with paler margins. Hind-wings ash grey.

The Streak, 1⅜ inches.

Widely distributed and common in most districts where broom grows. On the wing in September and October.

Not according to above description. **128**

Fore-wings olive brown with five large, pinkish, white-bordered spots which show brownish centres. Hind-wings ashy grey. PL. 39.

Peach Blossom, 1⅜ inches.

Widely distributed in wooded areas in England, Wales, and Ireland. More local in Scotland. On the wing from June to August.

Fore-wings light reddish brown each with pale grey patch near the front margin. There is a large, oval, pebble-like mark bounded by dark and light lines near the wing-tip. Hind-wings pale grey with dark central crescent-shaped spot and dark margins. PL. 41. **Pebble Prominent, 1¼ inches.**

Widely distributed in the British Isles where sallows and willows grow. On the wing in May and June and again in August.

128 {

Fore-wings purplish or greyish brown, crossed by two dark transverse lines. Near the centre of the wing there are two yellowish or white marks, one of which resembles the figure 8. Hind-wings pale grey with blackish streak near the anal angle and indistinct central dot. PL. 40.

Figure of Eight, 1⅜ inches.

128 {
Widely distributed in England, most common in the south and east, becoming local further north and in Ireland. Rare in Scotland. On the wing in October and November.

Fore-wings reddish brown with whitish nervules and dark double transverse lines which have white edges. There are two black-edged white central dots and a number of whitish spots or streaks on the wing margins. Hind-wings ashy grey with smoky margins. **True Lover's Knot,** $1-1\frac{1}{4}$ inches.

Common in most parts of the British Isles. On the wing in June and July.

Moths not agreeing with above descriptions. **129**
}

129 {
Fore-wings showing conspicuous light spot or patch. **130**

Fore-wings with pale markings other than spot or patch. **131**

Fore-wings without well-defined pale markings. **132**
}

130 {
Fore-wings reddish to dark brown with darker shadings and dark double transverse lines. Near the centre is a white or pale buff, kidney-shaped spot. Submarginal line pale with dark edge. Hind-wings ashy grey. **Common Rustic,** 1 inch.

Common throughout the British Isles. On the wing in July and August.

Fore-wings light brown crossed by indistinct dark transverse lines. Submarginal line pale marked with dark arrow-head-shaped spots. Central spot
}

130 whitish grey, standing out prominently on a pyramidal black blotch. Hind-wings pale grey with darker central spot. **Heath Rustic,** 1⅓ inches.

Common on heaths and moors in most parts of the British Isles. On the wing in August and September.

Fore-wings brown tinged purple or pink, paler at bases and margins, with dark double transverse lines. Near the centre there is a pale buffish-white spot with dark margins. Hind-wings ashy or pinkish grey. **Small Angle Shades,** 1¼ inches.

Widely distributed throughout the British Isles, locally common. On the wing in June and July.

Fore-wings reddish or greyish brown crossed by transverse lines, which are sometimes indistinct. Submarginal line pale yellowish white or buff. Towards the fore edge of the wings there are two pale spots, the outer one white or pale buff and square in outline with dark edges, the inner one a much smaller dark-centred ring. Hind-wings ashy grey in the female, almost white in the male, with dark margins. **Square-spot Rustic,** 1¼ inches.

Widely distributed and common in most parts of the British Isles. On the wing in August.

Similar to above but the pale square marking on the fore-wings has a dark centre and the wing margins show a line of dark crescent-shaped spots. Hind-wings pale grey with darker margins.
                    Small Square-spot, 1⅓ inches.

Generally distributed and common throughout the British Isles. On the wing in August and September.

131 {

Fore-wings greyish or buffish brown with the nervules edged with paler shades. Centre of wings darker. Each wing has two pale rings with dark centres. Submarginal line pale buff edged on the inner side with black. Hind-wings grey with reddish-brown tinge. **Common Quaker,** 1¼ inches.

Widely distributed and common in most parts of the British Isles. On the wing in March and April.

Fore-wings pale brown washed dull green, crossed by black transverse lines, the outermost of which is edged with white. Central spot large, pale brown with black border. Hind-wings brownish grey. **Green-brindled Crescent,** 1½ inches.
(*See* No. 122.)

132 {

Fore-wings brown washed olive green and variegated with grey and black. Submarginal line whitish, edged dark olive or blackish brown. Hind-wings ash grey with darker margins.
Brindled Green, 1¼ inches.

Widely distributed and common in many parts of England, more local in Scotland, rare in Ireland. On the wing in September.

Fore-wings greyish brown with small central black dot. Hind-wings pale ashy grey, darker towards margins and with dusky central dot.
Mouse Moth, 1¼ inches.

Widely distributed and generally common. On the wing in July and August.

133. Hind-wings cream or white.   **134**

134 {

Large moths—wing-span 2 inches or more.   **135**

Wing-span less than 2 inches.   **136**

135 {
Fore-wings pale brown conspicuously marked with white and crossed by two thick black lines with white edges. Hind-wings pale brownish buff to creamy white. PL. 38.

Kentish Glory (female), 2¾ inches.

Fore-wings purplish brown fading to pale grey near the inner margins. Wing-tips with large oval patch of yellowish buff clouded or spotted with pale brown. Dark, double, transverse lines cross the wings near the bases and border the buff wing-tips. PL. 40 **Buff-tip, 2½ inches.**

Widely distributed throughout the British Isles. On the wing in June and July.

136 {
Fore-wings showing pink. **137**

Fore-wings not showing pink. **138**

137 Fore-wings dark olive brown on the central areas with distinct triangular patch, paler greyish brown at the margins with oblique band of buff crossing the wing beyond the dark central portion. Wing-bases and front edges pink. Hind-wings cream, crossed by three brown transverse lines. PL. 40.

Angle Shades, 1¾ inches.

Widely distributed throughout the British Isles. On the wing in May and June and again in September and October.

138 {
Fore-wings pale reddish brown with darker margins. Crossed by two or three dark transverse lines, of which the most prominent runs down to a dark tooth-like projection on the inner margin. Hind-wings cream washed with grey and with blackish patch at anal angle.

Coxcomb Prominent, 1½ inches.
(*See* No. 118.)

Not agreeing with above description. **139**

139 {
Fore-wings with pale markings. **140**

Fore-wings without pale markings. **141**

Fore-wings dark brown with black streak at base, crossed by two pale transverse lines. Submarginal line pale with dark arrowhead-shaped spots on its inner sides. Near the centre of each fore-wing there are two or three spots, somewhat lighter in colour than the surrounding area, the largest of which may be bordered with white. Hind-wings almost white with brown margins. **Dark Brocade, 1½ inches.**

Generally distributed and common in most parts of the British Isles. On the wing in June and July.

Fore-wings brownish buff clouded dark grey, crossed by two white lines, the inner one running obliquely outwards and downwards from the front wing edge, the outer running transversely from the wing-tips. Wing-bases greyish brown. Front margin of wings almost white and below them two or three pale-ringed spots. Hind-wings buffish or yellowish grey. PL. 40. **Buff Arches, 1½ inches.**

Widely distributed in England and Ireland in wooded areas. Rare elsewhere in the British Isles. On the wing in June and July.

Fore-wings reddish or greyish brown crossed by transverse lines which are sometimes indistinct. Submarginal line pale yellowish white or buff. Towards the fore edge of the wings there are two pale spots, the outer one white or pale buff and square in outline with dark edges, the inner one a much smaller dark-centred ring. Hind-wings white with dark margins.

Square-spot Rustic (male), 1¼ inches.
(*See* No. 130.)

140 }

140 Fore-wings purplish brown with conspicuous stripe of cream or pale buff near the fore edge. Submarginal line pale, wavy, sometimes indistinct. Hind-wings white. PL. 40. **Flame Shoulder,** 1¼ inches.

Common in most parts of the British Isles. On the wing in June and August.

141
Fore-wings with conspicuous dark markings. **142**

Fore-wings without conspicuous dark markings. **143**

142
Fore-wings greyish brown, darker on inner margins, with pale submarginal line and dark transverse lines—the latter sometimes indistinct. There are two conspicuous black marks, the outer one large and roughly heart-shaped, the inner flattened and forming a short streak. A third dark mark may be present but is often obscure. Hind-wings white. PL. 39.　　　　**Heart and Dart (male),** 1½ inches.
(*See* No. 124.)

Fore-wings greyish brown finely speckled with blackish brown. On the central area there are three dark spots and the wings are crossed by dark, zigzag transverse lines. Submarginal line pale brown or buff. Hind-wings white with brown nervules and margins. PL. 41.
Turnip Moth (male), 1¼–1¾ inches.

Generally distributed and common in most parts of the British Isles. On the wing in June and July. The caterpillar of this moth often causes great damage to turnips and similar roots.

143
Fore-wings greyish brown dusted dark brown with a number of small dark spots along the front edge. Submarginal line pale. Central area with two or

143 three small dark spots of which some or all may be very indistinct. Hind-wings white and almost transparent, with brown nervules and margins.

Pale Mottled Willow, 1 inch.

Generally distributed and common in most parts of the British Isles. On the wing from June to August.

Fore-wings buffish brown to very dark brown speckled with darker shades and with three ill-defined dark spots on the central areas, crossed by dark zigzag transverse lines which are often very obscure. Submarginal line pale. Hind-wings white with brown nervules and margins.

Turnip Moth (male), 1¼–1¾ inches.
(*See* No. 142.)

144 {
Ground colour of fore-wings white or grey. **145**

Ground colour of fore-wings other than white or grey. **170**
}

145 {
Moth with wing-span exceeding 2 inches. **146**

Moth with wing-span of 2 inches or less. **149**
}

146 {
Hind-wings showing bright red. **147**

Hind-wings not showing bright red. **148**
}

147 {
Fore-wings ash grey with darker zigzag transverse lines. Hind-wings bright red with broad black central and marginal bands. PL. 42.

Red Underwing, 2¾–3 inches.

Locally distributed in south and east England. On the wing in August and September.
}

147 Fore-wings white boldly blotched with brown. Hind-wings bright orange red with large blue-black spots along the hind margins and near the centre. Abdomen red-banded and spotted black.
Garden Tiger, 2¾ inches.

Generally distributed and common in many parts of the British Isles. On the wing in July and August.

Fore-wings pale purplish grey with white banded margins and a white zigzag transverse line. Near the centre is a white patch bearing a conspicuous eye spot. Hind-wings similar to fore-wings but paler, also with large eye spot. PL. 38.
Emperor Moth (female), 3 inches.
(*See* No. 116.)

Fore-wings purplish grey fading to white towards the inner margins crossed by two transverse lines each edged with chocolate brown, the outer one bordering a large oval yellow or buff blotch near the wingtip. Hind-wings cream. PL. 40. **Buff-tip,** 2½ inches.
(*See* No. 135.)

Fore-wings greyish white, darker in the centre area, crossed by dark transverse lines, one near the wing bases, the other, which is double, beyond the centre of the wing. Hind-wings white with dusky central spot. Some specimens also show a faint cloudy transverse band. PL. 35.
Pale Tussock (female), 2¼ inches.

Locally distributed in England, most frequently seen in the south. On the wing in May and June.
(For male *see* No. 162.)

148 Fore-wings greyish white with yellow and black nervules and a variable number of dark spots and dusky markings, chiefly near the fore and inner margins and towards the bases. Hind-wings

148 white (male) or ashy grey (female) with dark nervules. Thorax greyish white marked with small black spots. Abdomen banded dusky grey and white. PL. 41. **Puss Moth, 2½–3 inches.**

Generally distributed throughout the British Isles and fairly common in most parts. On the wing in May and June. The caterpillar feeds on willow and poplar.

149 Ground colour of fore-wings white. **150**

Ground colour of fore-wings grey. **151**

Fore-wings white boldly marked with four or five black zigzag transverse lines, those near the centre often running together, and black blotches along the front edges. Wing margins spotted with black. Thorax black and white. Abdomen rosy red banded with black. Hind-wings pale grey, darker towards the spotted margins. PL. 42.

**Black Arches (male), 1½ inches
(female) 2 inches.**

Locally distributed in England and Wales as far north as Yorkshire but most frequently seen in the south On the wing in July and August.

Fore-wings white dusted grey, with short, black streak at base and a number of small black spots scattered sparsely over the wings, the central series sometimes forming a broken transverse line. Hind-wings white. PL. 31. **Miller Moth, 1½ inches.**

Locally distributed in England, southern Scotland, and southern Ireland. On the wing in July and August.

150 Fore-wings white freckled with black and with two blackish, wavy transverse lines deeply bordered

150 〕 with dark brown. Hind-wings greyish white with
     two brown transverse lines. PL. 42.

                              Oak Beauty, 1¾–2 inches.

     Widely distributed but local in England and Wales.
     On the wing in March and April.

151 〔 Hind-wings pale yellow.   **152**

     〔 Hind-wings not pale yellow.   **153**

     〔 Fore-wings lead grey with yellow stripe along front
       margin, tapering to a point near wing-tip. Hind-wings
       pale yellow. PL. 42. **Common Footman,** 1¼ inches.

       Generally distributed in England and Wales but
       local in the north and in Scotland and Ireland.
       On the wing in July.

152 〔 Similar to above but the yellow stripe along the
       front edge of the fore-wings is of equal width
       throughout its length—not tapering to a point
       near the wing-tips.   Hind-wings pale yellow dusted
       with grey.   **Scarce Footman,** 1¼ inches.

       Locally distributed in the southern half of England
       and in Ireland.   Rare elsewhere in the British Isles.

153 〔 A small moth with snout-like projection in front of
       head.   **154**

     〔 Not according with above description.   **155**

154. Fore-wings whitish grey with large central area of
      deep brown and brown triangular patch near wing-
      tips.   Hind-wings pale grey.

                      Beautiful Snout (female), 1¼ inches.

      Locally distributed in the southern half of England
      and in Ireland.   On the wing in June and July.

155 {
Fore-wings showing dark central band. **156**

Fore-wings without dark central band. **157**
}

156 {

Fore-wings grey with broad dark grey central band bordered with black. Wing-tips clouded dark grey. Wing bases and wing margins showing small black spots. Hind-wings white with dark dots on margins. PL. 32. **Poplar Kitten,** $1\frac{1}{2}$–$1\frac{3}{4}$ inches.

Widely distributed in England and Wales where poplars grow, locally common. Scarce in Ireland, absent from Scotland. On the wing from June to September.

Similar to above but smaller and with the outer border of the central band strongly indented.
Sallow Kitten, $1\frac{1}{4}$–$1\frac{1}{2}$ inches.

Widely distributed throughout the British Isles. On the wing in June and July.

Fore-wings grey, varying in shade from ashy to dusky, with darker central band bounded by two dark brown transverse lines. Wing margins dotted dark grey. Hind-wings pale ash grey with small dots on margins.
Pale Oak Eggar (female), $1\frac{1}{4}$ inches.
(*See* No. 45.)
}

157 {
All wings showing many dark zigzag lines. **158**

All wings not showing many dark zigzag lines.
159
}

158. Wings yellowish grey. Fore-wings covered with wavy dark brown lines. Submarginal line pale; wing borders brown. Hind-wings paler than fore-wings, with dark brown wavy lines below the

158. central area, which shows a dark dot.   Submarginal line pale, wing borders brown.

Scallop Shell, $1\frac{1}{4}$ inches.

Widely distributed in the southern and midland counties of England.   Local elsewhere in the British Isles.

159 {
Ground colour of hind-wings white. **160**

Ground colour of hind-wings not white. **163**
}

160 {
Fore-wings long and narrow. **161**

Fore-wings not long and narrow. **162**
}

161. Fore-wings pale grey with black line running outwards from the bases and fine blackish nervules. Each wing shows a creamy white blotch near the middle and two minute black dots.   Hind-wings white with brown nervules and hind margins.
PL. 43. **Shark (male), 2 inches.**

Widely distributed over most of the British Isles. Common in some parts of southern England.   On the wing in June and July.

(For female *see* No. 164.)

Fore-wings pale grey freckled with darker shades especially towards the centre, crossed by two dark transverse lines.   Wing margin dotted dusky grey or black.   Hind-wings white, sometimes tinged pale grey, with dusky central spot and incomplete band below the middle.   PL. 35.

Pale Tussock (male), $1\frac{3}{4}$ inches.
(*See* No. 148.)

Fore-wings pale grey variegated with somewhat darker mottling, crossed by two dark transverse lines and with short longitudinal line extending from the base.   Hind-wings pure white.   PL. 43.

162 {
Sycamore Moth, $1\frac{3}{4}$ inches.

162 ⟩ Fairly common in the south and east of England. Local in Ireland, absent from other parts of the British Isles.   On the wing in June and July.

Similar to above but fore-wings dark grey˙ with white or pale grey dark-centred spot.   Body dark grey.   Hind-wings white with dusky nervules and hind margins.   **Poplar Grey,** 1½ inches.

Widely distributed over most of the British Isles and common in many parts of southern England. On the wing from June to August.

Fore-wings pale to medium grey, crossed by **two** thin, pale transverse lines which have dark edges. A well-defined black streak extends from the wing base to the inner transverse line and two others are shown towards the outer part of the wing, crossing the outer transverse line.   On the front edge of the wing there is a fourth dark streak, slanting downwards and outwards.   Hind-wings white. PL. 43.
Grey Dagger, 1½ inches.

Widely distributed and common in many parts of the British Isles.   On the wing in June and July.

Very similar to the last species but somewhat smaller and usually rather darker in colour.
Dark Dagger, 1¼–1½ inches.

Widely distributed in England and Wales but rare or absent elsewhere.   The Grey and Dark Dagger moths are almost indistinguishable but the caterpillars are quite different.   The larva of the Grey Dagger is black with a high, pointed hump on the fourth segment of the body and a broad, clear yellow stripe along the back.   That of the Dark Dagger is also black but the hump is much smaller and the back line is orange and white.   There is also an orange and black stripe along each side.

163 {
  Fore-wings long and narrow.   **164**

  Fore-wings not long and narrow.   **165**
}

164 {
Fore-wings brownish or ashy grey, obscurely marked with darker grey and with a short pale streak at the wing base and black nervules. Hind-wings brownish grey with paler bases.
           Chamomile Shark, $1\frac{3}{4}$ inches.

Widely distributed in England, Wales, and south Scotland. Local in Ireland. On the wing from April to June.

Fore-wings pale grey with thin black nervules, a black streak at the base, and some similar but smaller markings on the outer portions. There is a creamy white central blotch with two minute black dots. Hind-wings pale brownish grey with paler bases. PL. 43.   **Shark (female),** $1\frac{3}{4}$ inches.
                       (*See* No. 161.)
}

165 {
  Fore-wings greenish grey.   **166**

  Fore-wings not greenish grey.   **167**
}

166 {
Fore-wings greenish grey with pale, almost white, front margins, crossed by black transverse lines. Central spot greenish white with sometimes a second smaller marking of the same colour. Sub-marginal line dark. Wing margins pale, dotted with greenish grey. Hind-wings pale grey with dusky margins.   **Yellow-horned Moth,** $1\frac{1}{2}$ inches.

Generally distributed in England, Wales, and Scotland where birch-trees grow. Rare in Ireland. On the wing in March and April.
}

166 Fore-wings greenish or olive grey, mottled with reddish or greyish brown, crossed by five dark, waved, transverse, narrow bands of varying width. These bands may extend across the whole wing or be broken below the middle line and conspicuous only near the front wing margin. There is a pale spot or patch near the margin of each fore-wing. Hind-wings pale ashy grey with dusky margins. **July High-flyer,** 1 inch.

Common in most parts of the British Isles about hedgerows, woods, and heaths. On the wing in July and August.

167 Fore-wings showing white or pale-coloured markings. **168**

Fore-wings without white or pale-coloured markings. **169**

Fore-wings grey, washed purple, crossed by two dark transverse lines, the inner of which forms an open zigzag while the outer slopes obliquely inwards. Central spot white with two small central dots, the marking having the form of the figure 8. On the outer side of this spot there is another white blotch or irregular shape. Hind-wings pale grey with dark patch at anal angle. PL. 40. **Figure of Eight,** 1⅓ inches. (*See* No. 128.)

168 Fore-wings grey, sometimes tinged pinkish, browner and darker near centre, crossed by two brown transverse lines and with black, longitudinal streak extending from near the base to the first transverse line. Submarginal line pale. The front edge of the wing shows two pale markings; the outer one crescent shaped. Hind-wings grey. **Early Grey,** 1¼ inches.

168 Widely distributed throughout the British Isles; common in southern England. On the wing in March and April.

Fore-wings brownish grey mottled and clouded darker grey, crossed by two double black transverse lines, the outer pair with two white spots near the inner edge. Near the front margin of the wing there are two nearly round black-edged, pale grey blotches.Sub-marginal line broken,white.Hind-wings pale brownish grey. PL. 43. **Knot-grass,** 1½ inches.

Widely distributed over most of the British Isles; common in England and Wales. On the wing from June to August.

Fore-wings brownish grey, usually light in shade, darkest near front edges, crossed by two brown transverse lines which have pale borders. Central spot dark brown. Hind-wings pale brownish grey with dark central spot and pale grey transverse line, which may be broken or indistinct.
March Moth (male), 1¼ inches.

Common in most parts of the British Isles in March and April. The female is small and wingless.

Fore-wings brown grey with black central spot and two closely apposed or confluent black spots below it. Hind-wings pale brownish grey with darker margins. **Mouse Moth,** 1½ inches.

Widely distributed and generally common. On the wing in July and August.

Fore-wings grey sprinkled with black, crossed by two black transverse lines, the outer one double.
169 Both these lines and a dark streak at the wing-base
90

169 are dusted with orange. Hind-wings pale grey with dusky central spot and margins.

> **Dark Tussock (male), 1½ inches**
> **(female) 2 inches.**

Locally distributed in England, Wales, and Scotland, chiefly in the midlands and north. On the wing in June and July.

Fore-wings brownish or leaden grey with black central spot which may be edged with pale grey. Submarginal line buff grey edged reddish brown on the inner side. The two transverse lines are double but may be absent. Hind-wings brownish grey, only slightly paler than fore-wings.

> **Red-line Quaker, 1¼–1½ inches.**

Widely distributed throughout the British Isles; common in many parts of southern England. On the wing in September and October.

Fore-wings brownish grey, usually light in shade but very variable, darker near front edges, crossed by two brown transverse lines with pale borders. Central spot dark brown. Hind-wings pale brownish grey with dark central spot and pale grey transverse line, sometimes broken or obscure.

> **March Moth (male), 1½ inches.**
> *(See* No. 168.)

170
Ground colour of fore-wings green.	**171**
Ground colour of fore-wings not green.	**180**

171
Hind-wings showing red.	**172**
Hind-wings not showing red.	**173**

Fore-wings dark bluish green boldly spotted with white and cream. Hind-wings scarlet with large black central spot and a broken band of black near the hind margins. Abdomen scarlet with black streak down the centre. PL. 8. **Scarlet Tiger,** 2 inches.

This striking, handsome moth is locally distributed in the south of England and South Wales. On the wing in June, usually in damp places.

172

Fore-wings dark bluish green with five large crimson spots, two or more of which may be joined. Hind-wings crimson with black margins. PL. 8.
Five-spot Burnet, 1¼ inches.

Locally distributed in England and Wales, common in parts of southern England. Flies by day from June to August.

Similar to above but with six crimson spots on the fore-wings. **Six-spot Burnet,** 1¼ inches.

173

Fore-wings crossed by conspicuous white lines or streaks. **174**

Fore-wings not crossed by white lines or streaks. **175**

Fore-wings bright green crossed by three silvery white lines or streaks, the outermost broader than the other two. Wing margins fringed reddish. Hind-wings white (female) or pale yellow (male).
Green Silver Lines, 1¼ inches.

Widely distributed in England, Wales, and Ireland, more local in Scotland. On the wing in June and July.

174

Fore-wings bright green, crossed by two straight parallel lines of silvery white. Hind-wings white.
Scarce Silver Lines, 1½ inches.

174 { Locally distributed in the south and midland counties of England. Rare in Ireland, absent elsewhere in the British Isles. On the wing in July.

175 { Hind-wings white. **176**

Hind-wings not white. **177**

176 {

Fore-wings green with white front edges. Hind-wings and abdomen white.
Cream-bordered Green Pea, ¾ inch.

Locally distributed in damp districts in southern and eastern England. On the wing in May and June.

Fore-wings pale green with darker central band and basal patch. Submarginal line pale, wavy. Hind-wings greyish white with black central dot and dark transverse lines.
Autumn Green Carpet, 1 inch.

Widely distributed throughout the British Isles, common in many places. On the wing from June to September.

177 { Fore-wings with dark transverse central band. **178**

Fore-wings without dark central band. **179**

178 {

Fore-wings yellowish green with dark brown transverse central band edged with black and white lines, joining two small dark triangular patches near the front wing edges. Wing-tips show dark marking. Hind-wings pale grey crossed by darker lines near the hind margins.
Green Carpet, 1 inch.

Widely distributed throughout the British Isles, common in many parts. On the wing from June to August.

178 Fore-wings greyish green with pinkish suffusion, central band and basal patch darker greyish or blackish green. Hind-wings dark greyish brown with black central dot and two or three dark transverse lines. **Red-green Carpet,** 1 inch.

Widely distributed over the whole of the British Isles. On the wing in September and October.

Fore-wings pale green with darker central band and basal patch. Submarginal line pale, wavy. Hind-wings pale grey with dark central dot and transverse lines. **Autumn Green Carpet,** 1 inch.
(See No. 176.)

Fore-wings bronzy green. Hind-wings dark grey. PL. 8. **Forester,** 1 inch.

Widely distributed in England, local elsewhere in the British Isles. On the wing in June in meadows and fields.

Similar to above but smaller.
Cistus Forester, ¾ inch.

Locally distributed in England and Wales; nowhere common.

Fore-wings darkish or olive green, variegated with brown and grey and powdered with darker brown and brighter green. There is a pale oblique patch near the centre, and a small pale spot below it. The submarginal line is pale brownish grey with darker edges. Hind-wings pale brownish grey with darker margins. **Brindled Green,** 1¼ inches.

179 Widely distributed in England and Wales, generally common. Local in southern Scotland, rare in Ireland. On the wing in September.

179 Fore-wings dark or olive green clouded with brown, crossed by two black zigzag transverse lines with white edges. The central area shows two pale-edged dark patches with a pale buff or white blotch adjoining the outer one. Submarginal line pale with series of wedge-shaped spots on its inner side. Hind-wings brownish grey with pale fringes.
Green Arches, $1\frac{3}{4}$ inches.

Widely distributed in the southern half of England and in Ireland. Local elsewhere in the British Isles. On the wing near woods in June.

180 Ground colour of fore-wings black. **181**

Ground colour of fore-wings not black. **182**

181 Fore-wings black, boldly spotted cream or yellow. Hind-wings yellow with several black spots and a short broken black marginal band. Abdomen yellow with red tail, marked with dark spots. PL. 37. **Cream-spot Tiger, $2-2\frac{1}{2}$ inches.**

Widely distributed in southern England, local in the midlands, scarce or absent elsewhere. On the wing in June.

Fore-wings greyish black with scarlet stripe running from the wing-base to near the tip and two scarlet spots towards the side margin. Hind-wings scarlet with black margins. PL. 7.
Cinnabar, $1\frac{1}{2}$ inches.

Widely distributed throughout the British Isles, locally common. On the wing in June.

182 Ground colour of fore-wings orange. **183**

Ground colour of fore-wings other than orange. **184**

183.　Fore-wings deep orange, with reddish borders, nervules, and central spot. Hind-wings orange with broad black basal area, central spot, and marginal band.　**Clouded Buff (female),** 1½ inches.
(*See* No. 88.)

184 { Fore-wings grey.　**185**

{ Fore-wings other than grey.　**186**

185 {

Fore-wings silvery grey, tinged greenish and flushed pink near the front edges; the central area clouded brownish grey. Each wing crossed by pale wavy transverse lines and showing three silvery grey, dark-edged spots. Submarginal line white, shaded dark brown on inner side. Hind-wings dusky grey with darker nervules and pale fringes.　**Silvery Arches,** 1¾ inches.

Locally distributed in England and south Scotland. On the wing in June and July near birch-trees.

Fore-wings pale grey, clouded brownish grey on the central area which bears two pale buff black-bordered spots and with a short streak, bifurcated at the end, at each wing base. The front edge is dotted with black and shows a black oblique mark. Hind-wings dull grey.
　　　Grey Shoulder-knot, 1½ inches.

Generally distributed in England and Wales, local elsewhere in the British Isles. On the wing in April and September.

186 { All wings long and narrow.　**187**

{ All wings not long and narrow.　**188**

187 {

Fore-wings yellowish brown with orange brown markings in the form of oblique streaks. Hind-wings dusky grey. **Ghost Moth (female)**, 2½ inches. PL. 30. (For male *see* No. 17.)

Fore-wings yellowish brown streaked with white and with small white spots near the margins. Hind-wings brownish grey.
Common Swift (male), 1¼ inches.

Generally distributed and common in most parts of the British Isles. On the wing in June.

Fore-wings ruddy brown varied with darker shades, with white streak or band extending from base along the inner margin and another pale line running obliquely upwards towards the wing-tip. Hind-wings dull grey, tinged reddish brown near the hind margins. **Beautiful Swift**, 1¼–1½ inches.

Widely distributed throughout the British Isles. On the wing in June and July.

Fore-wings golden brown with three oblique white streaks, sometimes more or less broken into spots, edged with black. Hind-wings dusky grey.
Golden Swift (male), 1¼ inches.

Fore-wings pale brownish grey, barred with darker brown. Hind-wings ashy grey.
Golden Swift (female), 1¼ inches.

Common in most parts of the British Isles where bracken grows. On the wing in June.

188 {

Ground colour of fore-wings some shade of brown. **189**

Ground colour of fore-wings creamy white. **190**

Fore-wings violet brown with broad patch of metallic yellow extending from near the base to the margin but divided by a transverse band of brown. Hind-wings greyish brown. PL. 8.

Burnished Brass, $1\frac{1}{2}$ inches.

Widely distributed and common in most parts of the British Isles. On the wing from June to August.

Fore-wings greyish or purple brown, with broad patch of reddish orange extending over the central area, and two light grey transverse lines. Wing margins deeply indented. Hind-wings greyish brown. PL. 8. **Herald**, $1\frac{3}{4}$ inches.

189

Widely distributed in England, Wales, and Ireland, Absent from Scotland. On the wing in spring and again in August and September.

Fore-wings brownish buff or yellowish brown with fine reddish-brown longitudinal lines and pale nervules. Hind-wings brownish grey.

Smoky Wainscot, $1\frac{1}{4}$ inches.

Generally distributed throughout the British Isles and common in most areas. On the wing in July and August.

190. Fore-wings creamy white or pale yellow, with yellow margins and two small dark dots, one near the front edge of the wing, the other near the inner margin. Hind-wings smoky buff to grey with pale yellow fringes. **Four-dotted Footman**, 1 inch.

Generally distributed in England; most frequently seen in the south. Local in Scotland, absent from Ireland. On the wing in June on heaths. The female has yellow fore-wings, those of the male being creamy white. The markings are the same in both sexes.

191 {
Moths with wing-spread exceeding 1 inch.　192

Moths with wing-spread not exceeding 1 inch.　193
}

Body thick and hairy. Fore-wings twice as long as hind-wings. Wing borders reddish brown. Body tawny or greenish yellow with a band of reddish brown covering two segments of the abdomen. End of abdomen tufted. PL. 44.
Broad-bordered Bee Hawk, 1½–1¾ inches.

Locally common in the south and midlands of England; rare or absent further north On the wing in May and June, flying by day.

Similar to above but the borders of the hind-wings very narrow. Body tawny or greenish yellow with a black band covering two of the segments of the abdomen, followed by a band of orange.
Narrow-bordered Bee Hawk, 1½ inches.

192 {
Widely distributed in most parts of the British Isles, locally abundant. On the wing in May and June, flying by day.

Body not hairy. Wings with narrow brown margins. Head and sides of thorax yellow. Abdomen yellow, banded with dark brown. PL. 44.
Hornet Clearwing, 1½ inches.

Locally distributed in England and south Scotland, flying by day in May and June. Often seen resting on the trunks of poplar-trees.

Similar to above but with black head and thorax with yellow collar between.
Lunar Hornet Clearwing, 1½ inches.

Widely distributed over the British Isles except in north Scotland. On the wing in June and July.

Fore-wings crossed by black transverse bar and with bronzy margins. Head and body black, the abdomen narrowly banded with yellow and bearing a black tail tuft. PL. 44. **Currant Clearwing,** ⅔ inch.

Widely, though locally, distributed in the British Isles up to northern Scotland. Common in parts of southern England, rarer further north. Flies in sunshine about currant bushes, on the pith of which the caterpillar feeds, in June and July.

Similar to above but larger and with the cross bar on the fore-wings orange. Thorax black with yellow stripe on each side. Tail tuft black in the male, yellow in the female. Legs yellow with black ring. **Yellow-legged Clearwing,** 1 inch.

193 ⎰ Locally distributed in England as far north as Yorkshire. On the wing in June near oak-trees.

Body bluish black with belt of red or reddish orange across abdomen. Fore-wings reddish orange towards bases. PL. 44.
Large Red-belted Clearwing, 1 inch.

Fairly widely, though locally, distributed in England; usually seen near birch woods. Rarer in Scotland and Ireland. On the wing in June and July.

Similar to above but smaller.
Red-belted Clearwing, ¾ inch.

Locally distributed in England; most frequent in the south. Often seen in orchards and gardens in June and July, where the caterpillar feeds beneath the bark of apple and other fruit trees.

APPENDIX II

ENGLISH AND SCIENTIFIC NAMES OF MOTHS MENTIONED IN
SECTION II

Angle Shades (*Phlogophora meticulosa*)
August Thorn (*Ennomos quercinaria*)
Autumn Green Carpet (*Cidaria miata*)

Barred Straw (*Cidaria pyraliata*)
Barred Yellow (*Cidaria fulvata*)
Beautiful Hook-tip (*Lespeyria flexula*)
Beautiful Snout (*Bomolocha fontis*)
Beautiful Swift (*Hepialus fusconebulosa*)
Beautiful Yellow Underwing (*Anarta myrtilli*)
Black Arches (*Lymantria monacha*)
Blood-vein (*Timandra amata*)
Bright-line Brown-eye (*Mamestra oleracea*)
Brimstone Moth (*Opisthograptis luteolata*)
Brindled Green (*Eumichtis protea*)
Broad-bordered Bee Hawk (*Hemaris fuciformis*)
Broad-bordered Yellow Underwing (*Triphaena fimbria*)
Brown Rustic (*Rusina tenebrosa*)
Brown-tail (*Euproctis chrysorrhoea*)
Buff Arches (*Habrosyne derasa*)
Buff Ermine (*Spilosoma lubricipeda*)
Buff-tip (*Phalera bucephala*)
Burnet Companion (*Euclidia glyphica*)
Burnished Brass (*Plusia chrysitis*)

Cabbage Moth (*Barathra brassicae*)
Canary-shouldered Thorn (*Ennomos alniaria*)
Chamomile Shark (*Cucullia chamomillae*)
Chimney Sweeper (*Odezia atrata*)
Cinnabar (*Tyria jacobaeae*)
Cistus Forester (*Ino geryon*)

APPENDIX II

Clay Triple Lines (*Ephyra linearia*)
Clouded-bordered Brindle (*Xylophasia rurea*)
Clouded Buff (*Diacrisia sanio*)
Clouded Magpie (*Abraxas sylvata*)
Common Carpet (*Xanthorhoë sociata*)
Common Emerald (*Hemithea strigata*)
Common Footman (*Lithosia lurideola*)
Common Heath (*Ematurga atomaria*)
Common Quaker (*Taeniocampa stabilis*)
Common Rustic (*Apamea secalis*)
Common Swift (*Hepialus lupulina*)
Common Wainscot (*Leucania pallens*)
Common Wave (*Cabera exanthemata*)
Convolvulus Hawk (*Herse convolvuli*)
Copper Underwing (*Amphipyra pyramidea*)
Coxcomb Prominent (*Lophopteryx camelina*)
Cream-bordered Green Pea (*Earias chlorana*)
Cream-spot Tiger (*Arctia villica*)
Currant Clearwing (*Sesia tipuliformis*)

Dark Arches (*Xylophasia monoglypha*)
Dark Brocade (*Eumichtis adusta*)
Dark Dagger (*Acronycta tridens*)
Dark Tussock (*Dasychira fascelina*)
Death's-head (*Acherontia atropos*)
Dew Moth (*Endrosa irrorella*)
Dot (*Mamestra persicariae*)
Dotted Border (*Hybernia marginaria*)
Double Dart (*Noctua augur*)
Drinker (*Odonestis potatoria*)
Dun-bar (*Calymnia trapezina*)
Dusky Thorn (*Emnomos fuscantaria*)

Early Grey (*Xylocampa areola*)
Early Thorn (*Selenia bilunaria*)
Ear Moth (*Hydraecia nictitans*)
Elephant Hawk (*Chaerocampa elpenor*)
Emperor Moth (*Saturnia pavonia*)
Engrailed Moth (*Tephrosia bistortata*)
Eyed Hawk (*Smerinthus ocellatus*)

APPENDIX II

Feathered Thorn (*Himera pennaria*)
Figure of Eight (*Diloba caeruleocephala*)
Five-spot Burnet (*Zygaena trifolii*)
Flame Carpet (*Coremia designata*)
Flame Shoulder (*Noctua plecta*)
Forester (*Ino statices*)
Four-dotted Footman (*Cybosia mesomella*)
Four-spotted (*Acontia luctuosa*)
Four-spotted Footman (*Oeonestis quadra*)
Fox Moth (*Macrothylacia rubi*)
Frosted Orange (*Ochria ochracea*)

Garden Tiger (*Arctia caia*)
Ghost Moth (*Hepialus humuli*)
Goat Moth (*Cossus cossus*)
Golden Swift (*Hepialus hecta*)
Gothic Moth (*Naenia typica*)
Green Arches (*Eurois prasina*)
Green-brindled Crescent (*Miselia oxyacanthae*)
Green Carpet (*Amoebe viridaria*)
Green Silver-lines (*Hylophila prasinana*)
Grey Dagger (*Acronycta psi*)
Grey Shoulder-knot (*Graptolitha ornithopus*)

Heart and Club (*Agrotis corticea*)
Heart and Dart (*Agrotis exclamationis*)
Heath Rustic (*Agrotis agathina*)
Hebrew Character (*Taeniocampa gothica*)
Herald (*Scoliopteryx libatrix*)
Hornet Clearwing (*Trochilium apiformis*)
Humming-bird Hawk (*Macroglossa stellatarum*)

July High-flyer (*Hydriomena furcata*)

Kentish Glory (*Endromis versicolor*)
Knot-grass (*Acronycta rumicis*)

Lackey (*Malacosoma neustria*)
Lappet (*Gastropacha quercifolia*)
Large Emerald (*Geometra papilionaria*)
Large Red-belted Clearwing (*Sesia culiciformis*)

Large White Plume Moth (*Aciptilia pentadactyla*)
Least Yellow Underwing (*Triphaena interjecta*)
Lesser Broad-bordered Yellow Underwing (*Triphaena ianthina*)
Lesser Yellow Underwing (*Triphaena comes*)
Light Arches (*Xylophasia lithoxylea*)
Light Emerald (*Metrocampa margaritaria*)
Lime Hawk (*Dilina tiliae*)
Little Emerald (*Iodis lactearia*)
Lobster (*Stauropus fagi*)
Lunar Clearwing (*Trochilium crabroniformis*)

Magpie (*Abraxas grossulariata*)
March Moth (*Anisopteryx aescularia*)
Miller Moth (*Acronycta leporina*)
Mother Shipton (*Euclidia mi*)
Mottled Beauty (*Boarmia repandata*)
Mottled Umber (*Hybernia defoliaria*)
Mouse Moth (*Amphipyra tragopogonis*)
Muslin Moth (*Diaphora mendica*)

Narrow-bordered Bee Hawk (*Hemaris tityus*)

Oak Beauty (*Pacys strataria*)
Oak Eggar (*Lasiocampa quercus*)
Oak Hook-tip (*Drepana binaria*)
Old Lady (*Mania maura*)
Orange Moth (*Angerona prunaria*)
Orange Sallow (*Cirrhia citrago*)
Orange Underwing (*Brephos parthenias*)

Pale Brindled Beauty (*Phigalia pedaria*)
Pale Mottled Willow (*Caradrina quadripunctata*)
Pale Oak Eggar (*Trichiura crataegi*)
Pale Tussock (*Dasychira pudibunda*)
Peach Blossom (*Thyatira batis*)
Pebble Hook-tip (*Drepana falcataria*)
Pebble Prominent (*Notodonta ziczac*)
Peppered Moth (*Pachys betularia*)
Pine Hawk (*Hyloicus pinastri*)
Pink-barred Sallow (*Xanthia lutea*)

APPENDIX II

Poplar Grey (*Acronycta megacephala*)
Poplar Hawk (*Smerinthus populi*)
Poplar Kitten (*Cerura bifida*)
Privet Hawk (*Sphinx ligustri*)
Purple-bar Carpet (*Mesoleuca ocellata*)
Purple Thorn (*Selenia tetralunaria*)
Puss Moth (*Dicranura vinula*)

Red-belted Clearwing (*Sesia myopaeformis*)
Red-green Carpet (*Cidaria siterata*)
Red-line Quaker (*Amathes lota*)
Red Sword-grass (*Calocampa vetusta*)
Red Underwing (*Catocala nupta*)
Riband Wave (*Acidalia aversata*)
Ruby Tiger (*Phragmatobia fuliginosa*)

Sallow (*Xanthia fulvago*)
Sallow Kitten (*Cerura furcula*)
Scalloped Hook-tip (*Drepana lacertinaria*)
Scalloped Oak (*Crocallis elinguaria*)
Scallop Shell (*Eucosmia undulata*)
Scarce Footman (*Lithosia complana*)
Scarce Green Silver Lines (*Hylophila bicolorana*)
Scarlet Tiger (*Callimorpha dominula*)
September Thorn (*Ennomos erosaria*)
Shark (*Cucullia umbratica*)
Silver-ground Carpet (*Xanthorhoë montanata*)
Silvery Arches (*Aplecta tincta*)
Six-spot Burnet (*Zygaena filipendulae*)
Small Angle Shades (*Euplexia lucipara*)
Small Blood-vein (*Acidalia imitaria*)
Small Elephant Hawk (*Metopsilus porcellus*)
Small Magpie (*Eurrhypara urticata*)
Small Oak Eggar (*Eriogaster lanestris*)
Small Square-spot (*Noctua rubi*)
Smoky Wainscot (*Leucania impura*)
Snout (*Hypena proboscidalis*)
Speckled Yellow (*Venilia maculata*)
Spectacle (*Abrostola tripartita*)
Spinach Moth (*Lygris associata*)
Square-spot Rustic (*Noctua xanthographa*)

Streak (*Chesias spartiata*)
Swallow Prominent (*Pheosia tremula*)
Swallow-tail (*Ourapteryx sambucaria*)
Sycamore Moth (*Acronycta aceris*)

True Lover's Knot (*Agrotis strigula*)
Turnip Moth (*Agrotis segetum*)

Vapourer (*Orgyia antiqua*)

Water Ermine (*Spilosoma urticae*)
Waved Umber (*Hemerophila abruptaria*)
White Ermine (*Spilosoma menthastri*)
White Satin (*Stilpnotia salicis*)
White Wave (*Cabera pusaria*)
Winter Moth (*Cheimatobia brumata*)
Wood Leopard (*Zeuzera pyrina*)
Wood Tiger (*Parasemia plantaginis*)

Yellow-horned Moth (*Polyploca flavicornis*)
Yellow-legged Clearwing (*Sesia vespiformis*)
Yellow-tail (*Porthesia similis*)
Yellow Underwing (*Triphaena pronuba*)

BEETLES

UNLIKE butterflies and moths, beetles have never been popular subjects, either for collecting or study, with the amateur naturalist or nature lover. The two main reasons for this are, perhaps, that comparatively few beetles exhibit conspicuous or attractive colours and the majority pass the greater part of their lives hidden beneath herbage, fallen leaves, dung, or stones, so that they are not so generally noticed as are the larger and more flamboyant of the Lepidoptera. Yet the species of beetles which may be found in the British Isles are far more numerous than any other type of insect. The world population of named and classified beetles exceeds a quarter of a million and some 3,700 species inhabit the British Isles. Many of these are rare or confined to a few small localities; others are so minute that they are not likely to be noticed by any one but the specialist who sets out in search of them. There remains, however, a great number of forms which are widely distributed in these islands and sufficiently common to be met with in the course of walks or rambles either inland or by the seashore. A still larger number may be discovered by sweeping a net through thick herbage or by shaking the foliage of trees and bushes over a white sheet. So diverse are these insects in their habits that there is hardly any situation which will not yield its quota of representatives, whether search be made in a town park, the grassy verge of a suburban road, fields, meadows, woods, hillsides, mountains, or seashore. Ditches, ponds, and streams also have their beetle population, for many species have become adapted to an aquatic exist-ence. Even our homes, store-houses, and gardens may furnish a select collection of beetles which live in close association with man, his food, and works.

Except for certain aberrant forms, beetles are easily distinguished from insects of other orders. Their most characteristic feature is the possession of hard, horny, often shell-like, wing-cases or elytra, which represent modified fore-wings. These lie flat on the back when the insect is at rest; their inner margins meeting in a straight line. The hind-wings are membranous and lie folded beneath the elytra, so that except when the beetle spreads its wings they are completely hidden. In

BEETLE
1. Antennae. 2. Head.
3. Thorax. 4. Scutellum.
5. Elytra.

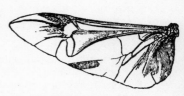

Hind-wing of beetle.

beetles which possess the power of flight the hind-wings are considerably longer than the elytra. This is a necessary provision to enable the body to be airborne, for the horny fore-wings take no part in sustaining and propelling the body in the air. During flight the elytra are held stationary at an acute angle to the body while the membranous hind-wings vibrate rapidly. A number of beetles have lost the ability to fly; the hind-wings being either very small or wholly wanting. In such species the elytra may be soldered together along their inner margins, so that they cannot be raised above the body. Familiar examples of such earth-bound types are furnished by the Cellar Beetle (*Blaps lethifera*), several of the Ground-beetles, and Weevils. The head is hard, with two compound eyes, antennae, and mouth parts adapted for biting, the jaws or mandibles being well developed, hard, and sharp. In some forms, like the Stag Beetle

(*Lucanus cervus*), the upper jaws are enormous, projecting far in front of the head like antlers. The antennae are very varied in shape. They may be very short and thick, bristle-like, long and thread-like, toothed, pectinated, clubbed, or flattened. The thorax is hard and horny with the three divisions all well developed. Of these the prothorax is particularly large and broad. Its upper portion, called the pronotum,

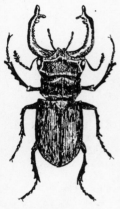

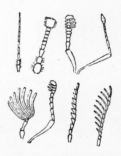

Some types of beetles' antennae.

Male stag beetle.

extends backwards from the junction of the head to the base of the elytra, so that when a beetle is viewed from above only this part of the thorax is seen in front of the elytra. To save confusion in the minds of non-technical readers, in the descriptions which follow the pronotum is referred to as the thorax, but it should be understood that, in fact, the greater part of a beetle's thorax is not seen from above. To see that part in its entirety the insect must be turned on its back, when the middle and hind portions with their legs and wing appendages will be clearly revealed.

In most beetles the elytra completely cover the hind parts of the thorax and abdomen, but there are a good many species in which the wing-cases are very short; either forming a small cape at the base of the hind-body, as in the Devil's Coach-horse (*Staphylinus olens*), or leaving the hind segments of the abdomen exposed, as in the

EXAMPLES OF BEETLE LARVAE
1. Cockchafer.   2. Weevil.   3. Dytiscus.

Burying Beetle (*Necrophorus*). In the female Glow-worm (*Lampyris noctiluca*) both elytra and hind-wings are absent. Inset between the bases of the elytra, behind the pronotum, there is a small triangular plate,

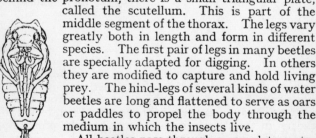

Pupa of Dytiscus.

called the scutellum. This is part of the middle segment of the thorax. The legs vary greatly both in length and form in different species. The first pair of legs in many beetles are specially adapted for digging. In others they are modified to capture and hold living prey. The hind-legs of several kinds of water beetles are long and flattened to serve as oars or paddles to propel the body through the medium in which the insects live.

All beetles pass through a complete metamorphosis in the course of their life history. The eggs are laid near the source of food needed by the grubs, on plants, in the decaying wood of trees, beneath bark, in carrion or dung, underground, or in water. The larva may be active, provided with long legs and powerful jaws to fit it for the pursuit and capture of insects and other prey; caterpillar-like, with short legs and fat, cylindrical, often curved, body, or a legless maggot. The duration of larval life varies, from a few weeks to several years. The pupa is quiescent, with its developing legs and wings covered by hard skin or sheaths. It may lie naked, be enveloped in the larval skin, or be enclosed in a cocoon of some kind, on a plant, under the bark of a tree, on or beneath the ground, or at the bottom of a pond or stream in which the larval stage has been passed. When the perfect beetle emerges from the pupal skin it is at first soft and almost colourless, but exposure to the air soon causes the cuticle to harden and darken, or to assume the metallic shades typical of the species to which it belongs.

SECTION III
BEETLES

(The measurements given refer to the length of the head and body)

1 {
　Very large beetles, over 1½ inches long, with distinct waist between thorax and elytra.   **2**

　Not as above described.   **3**
}

2 {
　Head very broad with mandibles developed into antler-like processes which project an inch or more in front of the head. Head and thorax dark brown, elytra reddish brown.   PL. 9.
　　　　　Stag Beetle (male), 2½–2¾ inches.
　　　　　　　　　　　(*Lucanus cervus.*)

　Similar to above but without antler-like mandibles. Head narrower than thorax.
　　　　　Stag Beetle (female), 1¾ inches.

　Not uncommon in parts of the south of England in woodland districts. The larva burrows in dead tree stumps.
}

3 {
　Antennae short, terminating in a club formed of a number of flat, plate-like joints.   **4**

　Antennae not as described.   **17**
}

4 {
　Elytra red.   **5**

　Elytra not red.   **6**
}

5.   Elytra red. Head black. Thorax black with red on sides. Antennae red with yellowish club. PL. 9.
　　　　　Dung Aphodius, ¼ inch.
　　　　　　　　　(*Aphodius fimetarius.*)

　Common in fields among dung.

6 ⎧ Elytra yellow.   7
  ⎩ Elytra not yellow.   8

7 ⎧ A broad, flattish, rotund beetle. Head and thorax
      dull green or bronze with rough surface. Elytra
      brownish yellow. The male has a long, curved
      horn at the back of the head. PL. 9.
                          Cow Onthophagus, ½ inch.
                              (*Onthophagus vacca.*)

      Fairly common in the southern half of England,
      particularly in sandy localities near the coast.

      Head and thorax black, elytra brownish yellow,
      sometimes with darker spot. Legs red. PL. 9.
                          Erratic Aphodius, ⅓ inch.
                              (*Aphodius erraticus.*)

      Not uncommon among dung in fields and meadows.

      Head and thorax clothed in long yellowish hair.
      Elytra dull yellow with three black bands. Elytra
      shorter than abdomen. PL. 9. **Bee Chafer,** ½ inch.
                              (*Trichius fasciatus.*)

      Scarce and locally distributed in Great Britain.
      Usually seen on flowers in fields. Found chiefly in
      Scotland.

8 ⎧ Elytra brown.   9
  ⎩ Elytra not brown.   12

9 ⎧ Large beetles—1 inch or more long.   10
  ⎩ Beetles less than 1 inch long.   11

Antennae ending in fan composed of seven (male) or six (female) joints. Head and thorax blackish, elytra yellowish or reddish brown with three raised longitudinal ridges.

End of abdomen pointed, protruding beyond the elytra. There is a row of wedge-shaped white marks along the sides of the abdomen beneath the elytra. PL. 9.

10

Cockchafer, 1¼ inches.
(*Melolontha melolontha.*)

Generally common, often abundant, on or about trees. Frequently flies by night, when it may enter rooms attracted by the lights.

Head, thorax, and elytra black. Head as broad as thorax. There is a distinct waist between the thorax and elytra. The abdomen is completely covered by the wing cases. **Little Stag,** 1 inch. PL. 9. (*Dorcus parallelopipedus.*)

Locally distributed in wooded areas. The larva lives in decaying ash, beech, and other trees.

Club of antennae trilobed. Head, thorax, and elytra brown, clothed with yellowish or grey hair. Elytra with three blackish longitudinal stripes. End of abdomen projects beyond the wing-cases. PL. 45. **Summer Chafer,** ¾ inch. (*Amphimallus solstitialis.*)

11

Resembles the common Cockchafer but is smaller and narrower. Locally distributed but sometimes occurs in large numbers, flying at and after dusk in early summer.

11   Similar in general appearance to the Summer Chafer but smaller. Head, thorax, and legs greenish black. Elytra reddish brown.

> **June Chafer,** ⅖ inch.
> (*Phyllopertha horticola.*)

Generally common in fields and gardens in June and July.

Head and thorax metallic green. Elytra, which are shorter than the abdomen, greenish bronze. Tip of abdomen and legs blue black.

> **Bronze Anomala,** ⅜ inch.
> (*Anomala aenea.*)

Locally distributed in sandy districts, chiefly near the coast.

Head and thorax black, elytra yellowish brown finely freckled with black. A short, stout, almost globose beetle with thorax as broad as the elytra, which completely cover the abdomen. In the male the head has a sharp, erect horn. In the female the thorax is ridged.

> **One-horned Onthophagus,** ⅖ inch.
> (*Onthophagus nuchicornis.*)

Common on and beneath dung, in pellets of which the eggs are laid.

12   Elytra green.   **13**

Elytra black.   **14**

13   Whole body shining metallic green with golden sheen. Base of thorax as wide as elytra, narrowing towards the rather small head. Elytra with a few thin transverse streaks of white. Pl. 45.

> **Rose Chafer,** ⅞ inch.
> (*Cetonia aurata.*)

13 A beautiful, easily recognized beetle which takes its name from its liking for rose blossoms. Widely distributed but nowhere common. The larva feeds in dead trees.

Whole body golden green. Smaller and narrower than the Rose Chafer, less square in general outline and lacking the white streaks on the elytra. **PL. 45.**
Beautiful Gnorimus, ¾ inch.
(*Gnorimus nobilis.*)

Rare in Britain. Occurs in favoured districts on flowers in early summer. The larva feeds in dead wood.

Head and thorax metallic green. Elytra greenish bronze, shorter than abdomen. Tip of abdomen and legs blue black. **Bronze Anomala,** ⅜ inch.
(*Anomala aenea.*)
(*See* No. 11.)

14 Large, broad, heavily built beetles, ¾ inch or more long. **15**

Beetles less than ¾ inch long. **16**

Beetle black. Fore part of thorax with three horn-like, forward-pointing protuberances. Thorax as wide as elytra at base but narrowing towards the head. **PL. 45.**
Three-horned Dor Beetle (male), ¾ inch.
(*Geotrupes typhaeus.*)

As above but the horns on the fore part of thorax two in number and shorter. The thorax shows a transverse ridge.
15 **Three-horned Dor Beetle (female),** ¾ inch.

15 ⎫ Generally distributed on heaths and commons in
　　⎪ May.　Feeds on rabbit dung, in pellets of which its
　　⎪ eggs are laid.

　　⎪ Beetle blue black with finely grooved elytra.
　　⎪ Underside of body violet blue.　Upper surface very
　　⎪ convex.　PL. 45.　　　**Lousy Watchman**, 1 inch.
　　⎪ 　　　　　　　　　　(*Geotrupes stercorarius*.)

　　⎪ Sometimes known as the Dumbledore.　Common
　　⎪ in most parts of Great Britain.　Frequently seen
　　⎪ in blundering flight or lying on its back unable to
　　⎪ regain its normal position because of the convexity
　　⎪ of its back.　The underside of the body is usually
　　⎪ covered with mites (*Gamasus coleoptratorum*), hence
　　⎪ this beetle's popular name.　Feeds in horse and
　　⎪ cattle dung.　The mites feed on the fragments of
　　⎪ dung which adhere to their host's body.

　　⎪ Very similar to the last species but the under sur-
　　⎪ face has a green instead of a violet sheen.　PL. 45.
　　⎪ 　　　　　　　　　**Greenish Dor Beetle**, 1 inch.
　　⎪ 　　　　　　　　　　(*Geotrupes mutator*.)

　　⎪ Widely distributed and common.

　　⎪ Similar to the Lousy Watchman but smaller.
　　⎪ Elytra black with greenish sheen.　Underside blue
　　⎪ black.　PL. 46.　　　**Wood Dor Beetle**, ¾ inch.
　　⎪ 　　　　　　　　　　(*Geotrupes sylvaticus*.)

　　⎪ Common in wooded districts in cattle dung.

　　⎪ Elytra nearly hemispherical, about as long as the
　　⎪ head and thorax and almost as broad as long.
　　⎪ Upper and under sides black with blue sheen.　Wing-
　　⎪ cases almost smooth. PL. 45. **Spring Dor Beetle**, ¾ inch.
　　⎪ 　　　　　　　　　　(*Geotrupes vernalis*.)

　　⎭ Rather local in distribution.　Occurs in early
　　　 spring in horse and cattle dung.

15) Beetle shiny black. Thorax wider than elytra, with
parallel sides and pronounced lobe-like projections
on the fore margins. Head shovel-shaped with
slightly curved horn which is long in the male, short
in the female. PL. 46. *Copris lunaris*, 1 inch.

Locally distributed, chiefly on sandy soils among
cattle dung.

Beetle shining black. Thorax as wide as elytra,
separated from hind body by distinct waist. Body
very convex, giving the insect a cylindrical appearance. Front border of thorax scooped out,
leaving three projecting tubercles, one on each
corner and one in the middle. Head with horn, long
and curved in the male, short and straight in the
female. PL. 46. **Cylindrical Sinodendron,** ½ inch.
(*Sinodendron cylindricum*.)

Fairly common in the south of England but scarce
further north. Found in woods, particularly beech
woods, where the larva lives in decaying tree trunks.

16 Beetle black, rather long and very convex, with
hind border of thorax, tip of abdomen, and legs
reddish yellow. Elytra about twice as long as head
and thorax. PL. 46. **Red-legged Aphodius,** ⅖ inch.
(*Aphodius rufipes*.)

Fairly common in many parts of Britain on or
about dung. Sometimes enters rooms in the
evening attracted by lights.

Similar to last species but wholly black, more heavily
built and rather larger. PL. 46. **Black Aphodius**
(*Aphodius fossor*), ½ inch.

Common in fields and meadows on and beneath
cattle dung.

17 { Long, slender-bodied beetles with elytra very much shorter than abdomen, so that the wing-cases appear to form a small cape over the back. **18**

{ Not as above described. **32**

18 { Elytra wholly red. **19**

{ Elytra other than red. **20**

Elytra and legs red. Other parts dull black. Abdomen with yellow lateral spots. PL. 10.
Staphylinus caesareus, ⅝ inch.

Locally distributed and scarce. Occurs in favoured districts on road and field paths.

Elytra, legs, and antennae red. End of abdomen with small patches of yellow hair. Other parts black. **Red-winged Staphylinus**, ½ inch.
(*Staphylinus erythropterus.*)

19 { Locally and uncommon in the north of England in woods.

Similar to above but smaller and with the oval head considerably longer than broad.
Red-winged Othius, ⅜ inch.
(*Othius fulvipennis.*)

Another woodland beetle, locally distributed.

Elytra bright red, legs reddish yellow. Other parts shining black. **Yellow-legged Philonthus**, ¼ inch.
(*Philonthus flavipes.*)

Rare in the south, more frequent in North Wales. Usually found under stones by streams and rivers.

20 { Elytra metallic green.   21

Elytra other than metallic green.   22

21 {
Elytra metallic bronze green, head blackish bronze, thorax dark blue. Head as large as thorax. Abdomen black.   **Brazen Philonthus,** ½ inch.
(*Philonthus aeneus.*)

Fairly common under stones and among dung, decaying vegetable matter, and fungi.

22 { Elytra brown.   23

Elytra other than brown.   24

23. Insect dull chestnut brown except for the head, which is blackish. Elytra very short. Thorax small and oval, with deep indentation down the centre. Legs pale brown.
    Channelled Astilbus, ¼ inch.
(*Astilbus canaliculatus.*)

Fairly common on pastures in the southern half of England, particularly in downland country.

24. Elytra black with or without markings.   25

25 { Beetle marked with red.   26

Beetle not marked with red.   27

26 {
Antennae, thorax, and basal half of abdomen dark red. Head, elytra, and hind half of abdomen black. Legs yellowish red.
    Shore Paederus, ¼ inch.
(*Paederus littoralis.*)

Locally distributed near the seashore and on chalk hills. Found under stones.

26 Similar to above, but whereas in the Shore Paederus the thorax is rounded, being as broad as long, in the present species that part is oval—longer than broad. **Bank Paederus,** ¼ inch.
(*Paederus riparius.*)

Local near streams and rivers.

27
Beetle marked with yellow or orange. **28**

Beetle not so marked. **29**

Body black with golden hairs on head, thorax, and last three segments of the abdomen. Elytra with broad grey band of fine hairs. Head as broad as thorax with strong, prominent jaws. PL. 46.
Hairy Emus, nearly 1 inch.
(*Emus hirtus.*)

A local and scarce beetle found near or under horse and cattle dung.

28
Eyes very large and prominent, antennae projecting between them. Beetle black with head, thorax, and elytra coarsely punctured, so that the surface is rough. Elytra showing yellow or orange spot near the inner margin of each wing-case.
Two-spotted Stenus, ¼ inch.
(*Stenus biguttatus.*)

Locally common by stream sides and on sandy shores.

Similar to above but with the yellow spots on the elytra at the centre of the wing-cases.
Stenus bipunctatus, ¼ inch.

Locally common in damp places by ponds and stream sides.

29 {
Beetle 1 inch or more long.   **30**

Beetle less than 1 inch long.   **31**
}

Whole beetle dull black, abdomen long. Head, thorax, and elytra of equal width. Jaws strong and prominent. PL. 46. **Devil's Coach-horse,** 1¼ inches. (*Staphylinus olens.*)

Common on paths, in gardens, under stones, and elsewhere. Has the habit of curling the hind part of the abdomen upwards when disturbed and emits an offensive odour from small yellow glands near the 'tail.' Easily identified by its dull black colour and large size.

Similar to above but smaller and with much more slender body. Last joint of antennae and legs reddish.   **Dark Rove Beetle,** about 1 inch. (*Staphylinus morio.*)

Common in fields, etc., under stones.

Beetle black with blue sheen. Abdomen long, tapering, and rather thick. Elytra leathery, covering about half the abdomen. Head broader than thorax. PL. 46.

Oil Beetle (female), 1¼ inches. (*Meloë proscarabaeus.*)

A slow-moving, wingless beetle. Generally distributed and common on heaths, paths, pastures, and by grassy roadsides in spring. The larva is found in the nests of bees where it feeds on the eggs and honey stores of its hosts. The male is less thick in body and has longer elytra.

30

30 Similar to the last species but with brighter blue or violet sheen. **Violet Oil Beetle**, 1¼ inches.
(*Meloë violaceus.*)

More local than the Common Oil Beetle but not uncommon in parts of southern England.

Beetle resembling the Devil's Coach-horse (*see* No. 30) in general appearance, but smaller and with head and thorax shining black. Elytra clothed with short, pale grey hairs, margined and fringed rusty brown. Segments of abdomen banded with greyish hairs. Pl. 10. *Creophilus maxillosus*, ¾ inch.

Widely distributed and fairly common. A carrion feeder which is often found in the decaying carcasses of small animals.

31 Beetle bright, shining black with greenish or bronze sheen. Head small and narrow with distinct neck between it and the broader thorax. Elytra bronze black. **Polished Paederus**, ⅜ inch.
(*Paederus politus.*)

Fairly common and widely distributed. Found under stones, among dead leaves, moss, etc.

Beetle black with coppery bronze sheen, brightest on the head and thorax and dull on the elytra. Antennae and legs pitch black.
Handsome Philonthus, ½ inch.
(*Philonthus decorus.*)

Locally common on heaths and moors under stones and moss.

32 Robustly built beetles with elytra shorter than abdomen but covering more than half its length. **33**

Not as above described. **36**

33 { Elytra orange brown and black.   **34**

     { Elytra wholly black.   **35**

34 {

Head and thorax black, the latter bordered with yellow hairs. Elytra orange or reddish brown bordered with black on front and hind margins and with broad central black belt. Abdomen black with fine yellow hairs on the terminal segments. Last pair of legs strongly bowed. Antennae black with orange bases. PL. 10. **Common Burying Beetle,** 1 inch. (*Necrophorus vespillo.*)

Widely distributed and common on or under the dead bodies of mice and other small animals. The Burying Beetles excavate the ground beneath such corpses so that they are buried under the soil. Here the eggs are laid, the larvae feeding on the decaying flesh.

Similar to above but smaller and with the last pair of legs not bowed. Club of antennae orange. PL. 10.   **Searcher Burying Beetle,** ¾ inch. (*Necrophorus investigator.*)

Similar to the Common Burying Beetle but smaller. Last pair of legs not bowed. Antennae wholly black. The yellow hairs on the tip of the abdomen are scanty or may be absent. Central black band on elytra broken in the middle. PL. 10.   **Undertaker Beetle,** ½ inch. (*Necrophorus mortuorum.*)

Both these beetles are widely distributed and fairly common on and near carrion. In habits they closely resemble the Common Burying Beetle.

35 {

Beetle all black except for the orange red clubs of the antennae. Head large and broad, thorax broader than long, widest at the front. Abdomen long. Elytra with parallel sides. Pl. 10.

Black Burying Beetle, 1⅓ inches.
(*Necrophorus humator.*)

Widely distributed and generally common on or near carrion in summer.

Beetle black except for the club-shaped tips of the antennae, which are dull red. Head small. Thorax almost semicircular. Abdomen long. Elytra broader behind than at bases, with three raised longitudinal ridges. Pl. 10. **Shore Sexton**, ¾–1 inch.
(*Necrodes littoralis.*)

Widely distributed on sandy seashores under stones or among dead fish, etc.

Body blue black, soft. Elytra thin and leathery, nearly as long as the abdomen. Head broader than thorax with well-defined neck. Antennae long and slender. **Oil Beetle (male)**, 1 inch.
(*See* No. 30.)

Similar to above but with brighter blue or violet sheen. **Violet Oil Beetle (male)**, 1 inch.
(*See* No. 30.)

36 {

Long-bodied, slender beetles with antennae as long as abdomen. Elytra black with yellow markings or yellowish brown marked with black. **37**

Not as above described. **40**

37 {
  Elytra black marked with yellow.   **38**

  Elytra yellowish brown marked with black.   **39**
}

38 {
  Beetle black with narrow band of yellow on front border of thorax and two curved and one straight transverse marks of the same colour on the elytra. PL. 10.   **Wasp Beetle,** ½ inch. (*Clytus arietis.*)

  An active, long-legged beetle which is fairly common in many parts of Great Britain. May be seen flying in sunshine or walking over flowers and on dead tree trunks in early summer. The larva lives in rotten wood.
}

39 {
  Head and thorax black. Elytra brownish yellow banded with black, narrower behind than at bases. Legs long and slender. PL. 47.   **Four-banded Strangalia,** ⅘ inch. (*Strangalia quadrifasciata.*)

  Common on elder and other blossoms in summer.

  Similar to above but smaller. The elytra narrow sharply from base to apex and are yellowish brown with five black spots and two black bands on each wing-case. PL. 47.   *Strangalia armata,* ¾ inch.

  Smaller than the last species. Elytra yellowish brown with black tips and a black line on the inner margins of the wing-cases, giving the impression of a central, longitudinal stripe. PL. 47.   **Black-tailed Strangalia,** ½ inch. (*Strangalia melanura.*)

  Both these beetles are fairly common on umbelliferous and composite flowers in summer.
}

39 Fore margins of elytra sloping sharply inwards from the broad shoulders; dingy yellow, thinly covered with fine grey hairs and showing eight black spots. PL. 47. **Eight-spotted Pachyta,** ½ inch. (*Pachyta octomaculata.*)

Locally, though widely, distributed. Found in summer on umbelliferous flowers and dead tree trunks.

40 Long-bodied, slender beetles, with antennae as long as, or longer than, head, thorax, and abdomen. **41**

Beetles not as above described. **44**

41 Beetles ¾ inch or more long. **42**

Beetles considerably less than ¾ inch long. **43**

42 Beetle metallic green with coppery sheen. Head narrower than thorax. Antennae about twice the length of elytra. PL. 47. **Musk Beetle,** 1 inch. (*Aromia moschata.*)

Widely distributed and locally common. Found on or about willows, in the decaying trunks of which the larva feeds. This beetle emits a pleasant, musk-like odour, from which it derives its name.

Head and thorax blackish, elytra pale reddish brown. Thorax with small, pointed tubercles on the sides. Antennae about the same length as the body. Elytra much broader at bases than thorax, narrowing towards their apex. PL. 47.

Toxotus meridionalis, 1 inch.

A widely distributed and fairly common beetle found on flowers.

42 ⎱ Beetle brown. Antennae four or five times the length of head and body. Head narrower than thorax, which is sharply angled at the sides. Elytra narrowing somewhat towards their apex. PL. 47. **Timberman (male),** ¾ inch.
(Acanthocinus aedilis.)

As above but antennae only twice as long as head and body. **Timberman (female),** ¾ inch.

A rather scarce British beetle which occurs locally in pine woods in Scotland.

Head and thorax black. Elytra light greyish brown clouded with black, with reddish-brown margins. Each wing-case crossed by two oblique bars of dull yellow. The thorax has a sharp spine on each side. Antennae about the same length as body. PL. 48. **Two-banded Rhagium,** ¾ inch.
(Rhagium bifasciatum.)

Fairly common near pine-trees, on the decaying wood of which the larva feeds.

Similar to above but elytra yellowish brown stippled with black and crossed by two transverse (not oblique) bars of yellow with two black spots between them. The spine on the side of the thorax is shorter than in the last species. PL. 48.
Searcher Rhagium, ¾ inch.
(Rhagium inquisitor.)

Fairly common beneath the bark of beech, oak, pine, and other trees.

⎧ Head, thorax, and elytra black. Antennae and bases of legs red. Antennae about the same length as head and body. Sides of elytra parallel.
Red-horned Grammoptera, ⅓ inch.
43 ⎩ *(Grammoptera ruficornis.)*

43 Widely distributed and common on hawthorns, in the wood of which the larva feeds.

Similar to above but light brown in colour.
Brown Grammoptera, ⅓ inch.
(*Grammoptera tabacicolor.*)

Another fairly common British beetle found on trees and bushes.

Head and thorax brownish grey with elytra, of similar colour, crossed by two indistinct yellow bands. Antennae black and red, about twice the length of the head and body.
Clouded Leiopus, ¼ inch.
(*Leiopus nebulosus.*)

Widely distributed in the British Isles on dead tree trunks and boughs.

44 Slender, soft-bodied beetles with thin elytra. Head prominent. Sides of elytra parallel. **45**

Beetles not as above described. **50**

45 Elytra yellow, orange, or yellowish red. **46**

Elytra other than orange or yellowish red. **47**

46 Head and thorax yellowish red. Elytra yellowish red with black tip. Legs and antennae black.
PL. 48. **Soldier Beetle,** ½ inch.
(*Rhagonycha fulva.*)

Very common from July to September on umbelliferous and composite flowers in fields and by grassy roadsides.

46 ⎫ Head yellow, as large as thorax, with black pro-
tuberant eyes. Thorax yellow with black spot on
each side near front margin. Elytra dull greyish
yellow tipped with black, covered with fine hairs.
Legs dark or blackish brown. PL. 48.

Black-tailed Nacerdes, $\frac{2}{5}$ inch.
(*Nacerdes melanura.*)

Widely distributed and locally common on old
wooden posts and timber of various kinds. Most
often seen by the seashore but also occurs in timber
yards and other places inland.

47 ⎰ Elytra bright red.   **48**

⎱ Elytra green or black.   **49**

Thorax and elytra bright red. Head, antennae,
and legs black. Elytra bright red, broader behind
than at bases. PL. 48.   **Cardinal Beetle,** $\frac{3}{4}$ inch.
(*Pyrochroa coccinea.*)

Widely distributed and not uncommon in many
parts of Great Britain. This beetle flies in sunshine and may be found on flowers and on old tree
stumps. The larva feeds under the bark of
decaying trees.

Similar to above but head bright red like the
thorax and elytra. Antennae very strongly
serrated. PL. 48.   **Comb-horned Cardinal,** $\frac{1}{2}$ inch.
(*Pyrochroa serraticornis.*)

More generally common than the last species, on
flowers and dead wood.

48 ⎰ Head and thorax black with green sheen. Elytra
crimson with green bases and a line of green running

130

48 down the inner margins of the wing-cases for about half their length. PL. 48. **Shining Malachius**, ⅓ inch.
(*Malachius aeneus.*)

Widely distributed and fairly common on flowers.

Head and thorax shining metallic green. Elytra metallic green with bright red tips. PL. 49.
Two-spotted Malachius, ¼ inch.
(*Malachius bipustulatus.*)

A brilliant little flower-haunting beetle, widely distributed and locally common.

Head, thorax, and elytra bright golden green or bronze green. PL. 49. **Blister Beetle**, ¾ inch.
(*Lytta vesicatoria.*)

This beetle emits a peculiar mousy odour. Cantharides is obtained from the body of these insects. Locally distributed in the south and east of England, nowhere common. Found on the foliage of trees and bushes. Also known as the Spanish Fly.

Thorax yellowish red or pale orange, with black centre. Abdomen yellow. Elytra greyish black.
Sailor Beetle, ½ inch.
(*Telephorus nigricans.*)

49

Common and abundant in summer on flowers in fields and waste places, often in company with Soldier Beetles (No. 46).

All parts shining metallic green except the tips of the elytra, which are bright red. PL. 49.
Two-spotted Malachius, ¼ inch.
(*Malachius bipustulatus.*)

A brilliant little flower-haunting beetle, widely distributed and locally common.

50 { Head produced into a snout or long thin beak (rostrum). Antennae, which are often bent or elbowed, with thickened ends.   **51**

Not according to above description.   **66**

51 { Rostrum or snout long and very thin.   **52**

Rostrum short.   **59**

52 { Elytra metallic blue or green.   **53**

Elytra other than blue or green.   **54**

53 { Beetle shining dark blue with fine white down on head and thorax and along sides of elytra. Antennae elbowed. PL. 49. **Downy Rhynchites,** $\frac{2}{8}$ inch. (*Rhynchites pubescens.*)

Widely distributed and not uncommon on oak-trees.

Beetle shining blue or green without down on fore body and elytra.   *Rhynchites betulae*, $\frac{2}{8}$ inch.

A widely distributed beetle which is common on apple- and pear-trees.

53 Head and thorax black. Elytra blue. Rostrum curved and pointed. PL. 49. *Apion pomonae*, ¼ inch.

Generally common on flowering shrubs and fruit trees.

54 { Elytra grey. **55**

{ Elytra other than grey. **56**

General appearance brownish or buffish grey; the beetle being black but covered with grey scales. Rostrum very long, slender, and curved. Elytra broad at bases, narrowing to a point at the apex, so that this part of the body is roughly heart-shaped. Antennae strongly elbowed. PL. 49.
Nut Weevil, ⅖ inch.
(*Balaninus nucum.*)

Common on hazel bushes. The larva is the white 'maggot' so often found in hazel nuts.

55 Head and thorax grey, clothed in fine down. Elytra grey with three raised, longitudinal bands which are spotted with white. Each wing-case also shows a central black spot. Antennae strongly elbowed. Rostrum very slender.
Figwort Cionus, ⅕ inch.
(*Cionus scrophulariae.*)

Widely distributed and common on figwort.

Similar to last species but grey with yellow down on the margins of the elytra.
Mullein Cionus, ⅕ inch
(*Cionus verbasci.*)

Generally common on mullein.

56 ⎰ Elytra red.   57

   ⎱ Elytra brown.   58

57.   Beetle uniform brick red with long, slightly curved
      rostrum.   **Uniform Rhynchites,** $\frac{1}{4}$ inch or less.
                                        (*Rhynchites aequatus.*)

      Common on hawthorn in the southern half of
      England.

58.   Beetle dark brown with narrow transverse border
      of yellow on the elytra. There are also some small
      yellow spots on both the thorax and wing-cases.
      Rostrum tapering and slightly curved. Antennae
      strongly elbowed.   PL. 49.   **Pine Pissodes,** $\frac{2}{5}$ inch.
                                        (*Pissodes pini.*)

      Locally distributed in the north of England and
      Scotland on fir- and pine-trees.

59 ⎰ Elytra grey.   60

   ⎱ Elytra other than grey.   61

      Head and thorax dark brown. Elytra brown
      overlaid with grey scales and showing distinct
      striations. Rostrum rather thick; shorter than
      thorax. Antennae elbowed. PL. 49.
                           Obscure Barynotus, $\frac{1}{2}$ inch.
                                        (*Barynotus obscurus.*)

      Widely distributed and generally common under
      stones.

      Head, thorax, and legs black. Elytra covered
      with pinkish grey scales and marked with five
      black longitudinal lines. Rostrum short and
      thick. Antennae elbowed.
                           Schönherr's Barynotus, $\frac{2}{5}$ inch.
                                        (*Barynotus schonherri.*)

60

60 A local and rather uncommon beetle which may be found under stones in favoured districts.

A small, brown-grey, rotund beetle with brownish-black antennae and legs. Elytra with a shining streak of dark brown on the inner margins of the wing-cases. Rostrum short and thick. Antennae elbowed, rather long. Eyes prominent. PL. 49.
Nut Strophosomus, $\frac{1}{4}$ inch.
(*Strophosomus coryli.*)

Very common on hazel bushes but also occurs on many other shrubby plants. Generally distributed in Great Britain.

Beetle almost globose, brownish grey with thick rostrum, prominent eyes, and short elbowed antennae. All parts covered with greyish scales, rather lighter on the head and the margins of the thorax. Elytra showing pale striations on a darker ground.
Shore Philopedon, $\frac{1}{4}$ inch.
(*Philopedon plagiatus.*)

Locally distributed but often common on sandy slopes near the coast.

61
Elytra black.   62

Elytra other than black.   63

A very convex, shining black beetle with thorax almost as broad as long. Abdomen pear-shaped. Rostrum short and thick, broadest in front. Antennae elbowed. Elytra finely granulated. PL. 49.   **Black Otiorrhynchus,** $\frac{3}{5}$ inch.
(*Otiorrhynchus unicolor.*)

62 Common on sandy hillsides and wooded slopes.

62 — Beetle black with roughened surface. Elytra marked with a number of thin, opaque, greyish bands and lines. Head small, partly hidden in the almost globular thorax. Rostrum stout, slightly curved. PL. 49.   **Pine Weevil,** $\frac{3}{5}$ inch. (*Hylobius abietis.*)

Often abundant in pine forests. The larva feeds under the bark of both growing and felled trees.

63 ⎰ Elytra metallic green.   **64**

⎱ Elytra red.   **65**

64 — Beetle shining green. Rostrum very short and stout. Antennae elbowed. Elytra twice as long as broad. Hind part of thigh with prominent teeth. PL. 11.   **Spurred Phyllobius,** $\frac{2}{5}$ inch. (*Phyllobius calcaratus.*)

Common in hedges and woods, particularly on oaks.

Similar to above but without teeth on thighs.
Nettle Phyllobius, $\frac{2}{5}$ inch. (*Phyllobius urticae.*)

Occurs in abundance on nettles.

Smaller than the last two species but of similar shape. Without teeth on thighs. Paler in colour; being brilliant silvery green.   **Silvery Phyllobius,** $\frac{1}{4}$ inch. (*Phyllobius argentatus.*)

Very common on flowering shrubs and trees.

Metallic green with reddish-purple scales scattered over the elytra and arranged in streaks.
Pear Phyllobius, $\frac{1}{4}$ inch. (*Phyllobius pyri.*)

Another very common little beetle which occurs on hawthorn and other trees and shrubs.

65. Head, antennae, and feet black. Other parts brick red. Thorax very narrow. Head small and long, joining the thorax by a long, thin neck. Elytra square in front, rounded behind. Rostrum short and thick. **Pl. 11.** **Nut Apoderus,** $\frac{2}{3}$ inch. (*Apoderus coryli*.)

Common on hazel bushes, in the rolled-up fragments of the leaves of which the larvae feed.

66 ⎰ Water beetles, i.e. beetles which habitually swim and live in water. **67**

⎱ Beetles which do not habitually live in water. **78**

67 ⎰ Last pair of legs long, flattened, and fringed with hairs to serve as oars or paddles. **68**

⎱ Last pair of legs not as described. **77**

68 ⎰ Antennae long and thin. **69**

⎱ Antennae short, with clubbed ends. **74**

69 ⎰ Beetle $\frac{3}{4}$ inch or more long. **70**

⎱ Beetle less than $\frac{3}{4}$ inch long. **71**

70 Body and head forming a long oval. Colour black or blackish brown with thorax and elytra bordered dull yellow. In the male the wing-cases are smooth and the first pair of legs show a conspicuous swelling of yellowish brown on the first tarsal joints. In

70) the female the elytra are ridged and the first pair of
legs are without the swollen foot parts. Underside of
body yellowish. PL. 11. **Margined Dytiscus**, 1¼ inches.
(*Dytiscus marginalis*.)

The largest of our carnivorous water beetles.
Common in ponds, ditches, and slow-running
streams. Frequently flies from one piece of water
to another in the evening.

Similar to above but smaller. The underside of the
body black. PL. 11. **Black-bellied Dytiscus**, 1 inch.
(*Dytiscus punctulatus*.)

Widely distributed in ponds and streams.

Body shorter and flatter than in Dytiscus; colour
greyish brown. Thorax margined brownish yellow
with band of the same colour across the middle.
Underside of body black, spotted on the sides of the
abdomen with yellow. Elytra of female show four
broad, hairy furrows. Other sexual differences as
in Dytiscus. PL. 11. **Grooved Acilius**, ¾ inch.
(*Acilius sulcatus*.)

Common in ditches, ponds, and streams.

Head and body forming narrow oval. Thorax
yellowish brown with darker stripe in the middle.
Elytra dark brown. Underside of body blackish
brown. Legs reddish brown.
Striped Colymbetes, ¾ inch.
(*Colymbetes striatus*.)

Common in ditches, ponds, and streams. May
often be seen in flight over or near water.

71 {

Head and body about ½ inch long. **72**

Head and body considerably less than ½ inch long. **73**

Outline of head and body ovate and convex. Upper surface black with dull bronze sheen. Each wing-case with small streak or spot of dull brownish yellow below the centre. Underside of body blackish brown. Antennae and legs reddish brown.　　　　　**Black Ilybius,** $\frac{1}{2}$ inch.
(Ilybius ater.)

Locally common in still water.

Similar to above but larger and narrower, and without pale streak or spot on elytra. Antennae and legs dark brown.　　　**Dark Ilybius,** $\frac{2}{3}$ inch.
(Ilybius obscurus.)

Common in streams and rivers. Less frequent in small ponds.

72

Head and body ovate; black, with two small red spots on the head. Elytra with a number of transverse scratches. Antennae red; legs blackish red.
Pl 11　　　　　**Two-spotted Agabus,** $\frac{2}{5}$ inch.
(Agabus bipustulatus.)

Generally common in ponds and ditches, etc.

Head and body ovate; dark brown. Elytra smooth, without scratches, and with two inconspicuous spots on each wing-case, the larger below the centre, the other at the tip. Antennae and legs reddish brown.　　*Agabus biguttatus,* $\frac{2}{5}$ inch.

Locally distributed, usually found in running, rather than still, water.

Body ovate, smooth, and convex. Ground colour yellow, densely but finely stippled with very dark brown, except on the margins of the thorax and elytra. Underside of body black.
　　　　　　　　Pond Agabus, $\frac{1}{2}$ inch.
(Agabus paludosus.)

Locally common in ponds and streams.

73 {

Head and body forming a long oval with pointed apex. Colour blackish brown with broad border of yellowish brown to the thorax and elytra.　PL. 11
Dusky Ilybius, $\frac{1}{3}$ inch
(*Ilybius fuliginosus.*)

Locally common in ponds and streams.

Similar to above but with the yellowish-brown border to the elytra narrowing behind.
Perforated Ilybius, $\frac{1}{3}$ inch.
(*Ilybius fenestralis.*)

Common in ponds and ditches in many parts of Great Britain.

Beetle ovate and very convex.　Colour dull reddish brown with the margins of the thorax and a large patch on the elytra black.　Underside of thorax and tip of abdomen black, otherwise dull red.
Slow Pelobius, $\frac{1}{3}$ inch.
(*Pelobius tardus.*)

Common on the muddy bottoms of ponds and slow-running streams.　This is a very thick-bodied, inactive insect which is sometimes called the Squeaker from the slight squeaky sound it produces by rubbing the last segment of the abdomen in a groove on the underside of the elytra.

74 {

A very large beetle measuring $1\frac{3}{4}$ inches in length.　75

A much smaller beetle.　76

75.　Body and head oval, smooth.　Colour glossy black. Antennae reddish.　In the male the last but one of the tarsal joints on the first pair of legs dilated into a triangular plate.　PL. 50.
Great or Black Water Beetle, $1\frac{3}{4}$ inches.
(*Hydrous piceus.*)

75. This large, slow-moving water beetle is herbivorous. It is locally distributed in ponds and slow-moving streams in the south of England.

Similar to the Great Water Beetle (No. 75) but much smaller. PL. 50. **Lesser Black Water Beetle,** ¾ inch. (*Hydrobius caraboides.*)

Common in ponds and ditches in many parts of England.

Head and body glossy brownish black. Elytra minutely punctured and scratched. Legs reddish brown. PL. 50. **Red-legged Water Beetle,** ⅓ inch. (*Hydrobius fuscipes.*)

76. Common in standing water and slow streams in many parts of England.

Beetle oblong with almost rectangular thorax which is broader than long. Colour yellowish brown with metallic sheen on head and thorax, and a few dark spots on the elytra. Legs dull yellow. PL. 50. **Aquatic Helophorus,** ¼ inch. (*Helophorus aquaticus.*)

Widely distributed and common on weeds in and on the margins of ponds and streams.

First pair of legs long, remainder very short and flattened. Body ovate and convex, black with olive or bronze sheen. Inturned edges of elytra red. PL. 50. **Whirligig Beetle,** ¼ inch. (*Gyrinus natator.*)

77. Common in ponds, ditches, and slow-moving streams, where it may be seen whirling about rapidly on the surface but diving quickly when disturbed. The first pair of legs is used to hold

77 ⎱ the tiny insects on which this small beetle feeds;
the short, flattened hind pairs being used for
swimming.

⎰ Not in accordance with above description.   **78**

78 ⎰ Long-legged, robustly built beetles,
with head, thorax, and abdomen
clearly separated. Abdomen considerably longer than the head and
thorax together.   **79**

⎱ Not as above described.   **105**

Head as broad as thorax. Front edge of
elytra with square shoulders. Sides of
elytra parallel. End of body square or
bluntly rounded.   **80**

79 ⎰ Head narrower than thorax. Front
edge of elytra without shoulders. Hind
body oval.   **89**

80 ⎰ Elytra green.   **81**

⎱ Elytra other than green.   **82**

Beetle green with iridescent gold sheen
on head and thorax. Elytra with five
dull yellow spots. Legs iridescent red.
PL. 51.

81 ⎰   **Tiger Beetle,** ½ inch.
(*Cicindela campestris.*)

142

81 ⎱ A very active beetle which may be seen flying in
sunshine in early summer in fields, woods, etc.
The larva lives in a hole in the ground. Both
beetle and grub feed on other insects.

See also Hybrid Tiger Beetle (No. 83).

82 ⎰ Elytra dark or blackish brown with yellow markings. **83**

Elytra other than above. **84**

83 Elytra very dark brown, each wing-case marked
with three curved lines of bright yellow. PL. 51.
Wood Tiger Beetle, ¾ inch.
(*Cicindela sylvatica.*)

Locally distributed on sandy heaths and woods in
southern England.

Similar to above but smaller. The pale yellow
or buff markings on the elytra are broader than in
the Wood Tiger Beetle. This species is very
variable in ground colour. The elytra are sometimes dark or brownish green. PL. 51.
Hybrid Tiger Beetle, ⅖ inch.
(*Cicindela hybrida.*)

Locally distributed in sandy, coastal districts in
southern England.

84 ⎰ Elytra black **85**

Elytra other than black **86**

85 Beetle black and smooth. Legs black, stout, with
spiny bristles. Head as large as thorax.
Big-headed Broscus, ¾ inch.
(*Broscus cephalotes.*)

85 — Locally distributed, but often common in favoured districts, on sandy seashores, where it hides under stones or tunnels in the sand.

Beetle black with pale yellow antennae and legs. Thorax longer than broad, rounded at sides and narrowing behind. Elytra with shallow, longitudinal lines. **Pale-legged Anchomenus**, ⅜ inch.
(*Anchomenus albipes.*)

Common in damp places; hiding under stones, fallen leaves, moss, etc.

Head, thorax, antennae, and legs red. Elytra dull black. Head and thorax of almost the same size; much narrower than the elytra. **PL. 51.**
Bombardier Beetle, ⅓ inch.
(*Brachinus crepitans.*)

Locally distributed on chalk downs and by river sides in the south of England. Usually found under stones. Owes its name to its ability to eject from the abdomen a fluid which on contact with air volatizes with a slight report.

86 {
Elytra light brown or orange.   **87**

Elytra blue.   **88**
}

Head and thorax bluish green, elytra dull orange with large blue spot. Legs reddish yellow. Thorax longer than broad, much narrower than elytra. **Back-marked Anchomenus**, ¼ inch.
(*Anchomenus dorsalis.*)

Common in fields, meadows, by roadsides, and in ditches. Found under stones or leaves and in
87 — rotting wood.

87 ⟩ Head and thorax bronze green. Elytra pale yellowish brown with a bronze spot in the centre of the fore margin and a dark brown band across the middle. Antennae and legs yellow.

Pale-winged Bembidium, ¼ inch.
(*Bembidium pallidipenne.*)

Common in many coastal districts on wet sand and in damp sandy places inland.

88. Head, thorax, and elytra pale or greenish blue, covered with fine hairs. Underside and legs darker blue. PL. 51. **Blue Corynetes,** ¼ inch.
(*Corynetes caeruleus.*)

Not uncommonly found in old houses and in rotting timber.

89 ⎰ Beetle 1 inch or more in length.　　　　**90**

　　⎱ Beetle less than 1 inch in length.　　　　**92**

90 ⎰ Elytra much wider than thorax with rather square-cut ends. Colour varying from dark coppery brown to greenish bronze. Elytra delicately pitted or lined. PL. 51. **Beautiful Searcher,** 1 inch.
(*Calosoma inquisitor.*)

Uncommon and local. Found on trees, usually in oak woods, where it feeds on defoliating caterpillars.

Not as above described.　　　　**91**

91 ⎰ Head long. Elytra forming a long oval; dull blue-black edged brighter purple blue or violet. PL. 51.
Violet Ground Beetle, 1–1¼ inches.
(*Carabus violaceus.*)

Common in gardens, fields, and woods, under stones, moss, etc.

91 } Stouter than the last species. Thorax black with purplish sheen; elytra coppery or bronze with greenish sheen, showing three rows of punctures on each wing-case. **Woodland Ground Beetle,** $1-1\frac{1}{4}$ inches. (*Carabus sylvestris.*)

Another very common beetle; found not only in woods but also in fields, gardens, and by grassy paths.

Head and thorax dark or blackish brown. Elytra coppery, sometimes with slight greenish sheen. Legs and antennae black. The wing-cases have several rows of small granules and slightly raised ridges. PL. 51. **Field Ground Beetle,** 1 inch (barely). (*Carabus arvensis.*)

May be identified by its smaller size and by the details of its sculptured elytra. Despite its name this beetle is found in woods and on hillsides, as well as in fields, on sandy soils. Fairly common in suitable areas but less generally so than the two previous species.

92 {
Beetle about $\frac{3}{4}$ inch long.   93

Beetle $\frac{1}{2}$ inch or less in length.   94

Thorax and sides of elytra coppery red, remainder of elytra shining green with three longitudinal ridges. PL. 52. **Shining Ground Beetle,** $\frac{3}{4}$ inch. (*Carabus nitens.*)

A very striking-looking beetle. Locally distributed on moors and mosses.

Head small and long, with large eyes. Thorax much narrower than elytra, contracted at base. Elytra oval and very convex. Colour black with rough surface. PL. 52. **Beaked Cychrus,** $\frac{3}{4}$ inch.
93 } (*Cychrus rostratus.*)

93 Takes its name from the long, narrow head, which has the appearance of a beak. Widely distributed but local in damp situations. Most often found in hilly areas.

Beetle uniform dull black. Thorax wider than long; fitting closely to the base of the elytra. Wing-cases flattened, oval; narrowing behind to form a point at the apex. PL. 52. **Cellar Beetle,** $\frac{3}{4}$ inch.
(*Blaps lethifera.*)

A slow-moving beetle. Common in cellars and other dark, damp places. Emits an unpleasant odour.

94 Elytra iridescent bronze, copper, or purple. **95**

Elytra not iridescent. **96**

Head and thorax shining metallic green. Elytra coppery with golden sheen. Thorax rounded, considerably broader than head. Antennae and legs black. Wing-cases with five or six punctures or pits. PL. 52. **Six-pitted Anchomenus,** $\frac{3}{8}$ inch.
(*Anchomenus sexpunctatus.*)

Locally distributed in damp spots on heaths and moors.

Thorax as broad as elytra. Sides of wing-cases almost parallel. Elytra bronze green with coppery or purple sheen, strongly striated. Antennae and legs red. PL. 52. **Bronze Harpalus,** $\frac{2}{5}$ inch.
(*Harpalus aeneus.*)

Common in fields, by grassy roadsides, etc.

95 Beetle shining coppery purple, sometimes with greenish sheen. Thorax rounded. Sides of elytra

95 | almost parallel. Antennae black, short. Legs dull red with black thighs. **Coppery Pogonus,** ¼ inch.
(*Pogonus chalceus.*)

Widely distributed and locally common on sea-shores.

96 | Elytra yellowish red or brownish yellow. **97**

Elytra other than yellowish red or brownish yellow. **98**

97 | Head black, thorax red, elytra reddish yellow with black patch in the middle of each wing-case. Antennae and legs red.
Two-spotted Badister, ¼ inch.
(*Badister bipustulatus.*)

Locally common on chalk hills and downs in southern England. Found under stones.

Thorax broader than long. Sides of elytra almost parallel. Colour brownish yellow.
Pale Nebria, ½ inch.
(*Nebria livida.*)

Locally distributed on cliffs near the sea on the east coast of England.

98 | Elytra black marked with red. **99**

Elytra black without red markings. **100**

99. | Head and thorax black. Elytra black with two bright red spots on each wing-case. PL. 52.
Four-spotted Ips, ¼ inch.
(*Ips quadripunctata.*)

Common on pine-trees. The larva lives beneath the bark.

148

100 ⎰ Elytra black; thorax reddish yellow.   **101**

    ⎱ Both elytra and thorax black.   **102**

101.   Head and elytra dull black. Thorax, antennae, and legs reddish yellow.

> **Black-headed Calathus,** $\frac{1}{4}$ inch.
> (*Calathus melanocephalus.*)

Widely distributed and common in fields and on hillsides.

102 ⎰ Legs red or yellow.   **103**

    ⎱ Legs black.   **104**

Thorax as broad as elytra, sides of wing-cases almost parallel. Head, thorax, and elytra dull black. Antennae and legs red.

> **Red-horned Harpalus,** $\frac{1}{2}$ inch.
> (*Harpalus ruficornis.*)

Common in fields, gardens, etc. Found under stones and in mould.

Similar to above but smaller. Thorax narrowly edged red.   **Broad Harpalus,** $\frac{2}{5}$ inch.

> (*Harpalus latus.*)

Locally common in sandy districts.

Thorax nearly as broad as elytra and of uniform width. Colour dull black. Elytra oval, grooved. Antennae and legs yellow.

> **Yellow-legged Calathus,** $\frac{2}{5}$ inch.
> (*Calathus flavipes.*)

103 Generally distributed in fields and on downs and hillsides.

149

103 ⎱ Thorax narrower behind than in front, making this
part bluntly heart-shaped. Elytra oval, shining
black, grooved. Legs brownish red.

Busy Pterostichus, ¼ inch.
(*Pterostichus diligens.*)

Widely distributed in damp places in fields, by
ditch sides, etc. Generally common.

104 ⎰

Beetle shining black. Thorax longer than broad,
narrower behind than in front, and bluntly heart-
shaped. Elytra oblong, grooved. Legs and antennae black. **Bog Pterostichus,** ⅝ inch.
(*Pterostichus madidus.*)

Widely distributed and common on damp fields,
by ditches, etc., under stones.

Thorax broader than long—little longer than head.
Legs slender. Beetle black with brownish black
antennae and legs. Elytra striated. Pl. 52.
Short-collared Nebria, ½ inch.
(*Nebria brevicollis.*)

The name refers to the very short thorax characteristic of this species. The beetle is common in fields
and other grassy places throughout Great Britain.

105 ⎰

Thorax and base of elytra of similar
width, not distinct but merging, giving
the beetle a smooth oval outline. Elytra
at least twice as long as broad. **106**

As above, but elytra not twice as long as broad. **120**

106 ⎰

Elytra metallic green. **107**

Elytra other than metallic green. **110**

107 {
Elytra more than twice as long as broad. Beetle long and narrow. **108**

Elytra not more than twice as long as broad. Beetle not long and narrow. **109**

Thorax longer than broad with hind angles produced into sharp-pointed processes which overlap the bases of the elytra. Body long and narrow. Antennae long, toothed on the inside. Thorax and tips of elytra bronze green, sometimes with purple reflections, remainder of elytra yellowish brown. PL. 52. **Copper Corymbites,** $\frac{1}{2}$ inch.
(*Corymbites cupreus.*)

Locally distributed on grassy slopes and hillsides. Usually found under stones.

Similar to above but broader. Head, thorax, and elytra shining metallic green or bronze. Legs darker green or reddish. Thorax with central furrow. PL. 52. **Bronze Corymbites,** $\frac{3}{5}$ inch.
(*Corymbites aeneus.*)

Locally distributed in hilly districts on grass and low herbage or under stones.

Similar in shape to the Copper Corymbites but shining greenish yellow. Antennae black. In the male the teeth on the long antennae are very long, giving these organs the appearance of slender combs. PL. 53. **Comb-horned Corymbites,** $\frac{1}{2}$ inch.
(*Corymbites pectinicornis.*)

A local beetle. Less common than the last two species but found in similar haunts.

108 {
Beetle long and very narrow. Elytra very much longer than broad, tapering somewhat to their blunt extremity. Colour dark green with golden

108   or purplish sheen.   In the male the antennae are dilated.   **Broad-horned Agrilus,** ¼ inch.
(*Agrilus laticornis.*)

Locally distributed in the south of England on trees and bushes.

Beetle golden green with reddish sheen.   Head and body oval.   Elytra about twice as long as broad, extremity bluntly rounded.   Head bent downwards, almost hidden by thorax.   Antennae long. Legs black.   **Cat's-ear Beetle,** ¼ inch.
(*Cryptocephalus hypochaeridis.*)

Common on cat's ear (*Hypochaeris*) and other composite flowers in summer.

Similar to above but paler, golden green.
     Golden Cryptocephalus, ¼ inch.
(*Cryptocephalus aureolus.*)

Another common, brilliant little beetle found on composite flowers in summer.

Beetle golden green with dark blue stripe at the inner margins of the elytra.   Body very convex. Head not turned beneath thorax. Elytra about twice as long as broad.   Pl. 53.   **Golden Apple Beetle,** ¼ inch.
(*Chrysomela fastuosa.*)

Generally common on nettles and other wayside plants.

Thorax golden green, elytra coppery green; otherwise similar to the last species.
     St. John's Wort Beetle, ¼ inch.
(*Chrysomela hyperici.*)

Common on St. John's wort and other low-growing
109   plants.

109 〕 Head and elytra shining golden green or bluish green. Thorax orange. Legs long, basal halves reddish yellow, distal halves and antennae black. Wing-cases twice as long as broad, wider behind than at bases. *Sermyla halensis*, ¼ inch.

Common on field flowers, especially on yellow bed-straw.

Elytra shining bluish green. Thorax, bases of antennae and legs, and tip of abdomen red. PL. 53. **Knot-grass Beetle**, ¼ inch. (*Gastrophysa polygoni.*)

Widely distributed and generally common on knot-grass (*Polygonum*).

110 〔 Elytra red or yellow.   **111**

Elytra other than red or yellow.   **112**

Body a blunt oval; convex. Elytra about twice as long as wide. Head and thorax black. Elytra shining orange yellow with two round black spots on each wing-case—one in front near the side margins, the other more central, a little below the middle. Legs black. This beetle resembles a large, oblong ladybird. PL. 53. **Four-spotted Clythra**, ⅔ inch. (*Clythra quadripunctata.*)

Locally distributed on birch near nests of the wood ant, in which the eggs are dropped and the larvae feed.

Similar to above but thorax dull yellow with a large black central patch. Elytra dull yellow with two round black spots on each. PL. 53. **Four-spotted Silpha**, ½ inch. (*Silpha quadripunctata.*)

111 〕 Locally distributed in woods especially on oak-trees.

111 ⎤ Body very convex. Elytra about twice as long as broad. Head almost hidden in the broad thorax. Head and thorax golden green, elytra coppery red, highly polished. **Polished Apple Beetle**, ⅓ inch.
(*Chrysomela polita.*)

Widely distributed and generally common on flowers in summer.

Beetle very convex, oval. Elytra less than twice as long as broad. Head, thorax, and elytra reddish yellow with a dark brown spot on each wing-case. **Carrion Phaleria**, ¼ inch.
(*Phaleria cadaverina.*)

Generally fairly common on seashores, where it may be found under the dead bodies of the sea creatures on which it feeds.

112 ⎰ Elytra some shade of brown. **113**

⎱ Elytra black. **114**

Beetle long and narrow with elytra many times longer than wide. Colour brown, lined with darker brown or black. Antennae long, slightly toothed. PL. 53. **Lined Click Beetle**, ⅖ inch.
(*Agriotes lineatus.*)

Generally common on plants of various kinds. The larva is known as the wire-worm and is very destructive to the roots of grass, corn, and other crops. There are several other closely related species differing little in general appearance.

Beetle long and narrow, covered with fine grey down. Head and thorax blackish brown; elytra rather lighter in colour with reddish-brown borders. Tip of abdomen reddish. PL.53. **Red Click Beetle**, ½ inch.
113 ⎦ (*Athous haemorrhoidalis.*)

113 Widely distributed and common on hazel bushes and other low shrubs and herbage. The click beetles get their name from their trick, when turned on their backs, of springing into the air with a slight clicking sound.

Head small, rather sunk beneath the thorax, which is broad at the base and almost semicircular in outline. Elytra rather more than twice as long as broad, with parallel sides and bluntly rounded extremity. Head and thorax black. Elytra black with broad band of dull yellowish brown bearing six black spots on the basal half. Antennae and legs black. Pl. 53. **Bacon Beetle**, $\frac{1}{3}$ inch. (*Dermestes lardarius.*)

Locally distributed. Often found in larders and provision shops. Besides bacon this beetle damages hides, leather, etc.

Head hidden beneath broad, rounded thorax which is pale greyish brown with darker border. Elytra greyish brown, darker than thorax, about three times as long as broad. Antennae short and flattened. Pl. 53. **Glow-worm** (male), $\frac{1}{2}$ inch. (*Lampyris noctiluca.*)

The female has neither elytra nor wings. Both sexes have small, light-giving spots on the hind abdominal segments, but those of the male are smaller and their light much less bright than in the female. This well-known beetle is widely distributed and common in damp, grassy places. The male insect often flies into lighted rooms after dusk. The larva, which resembles the wingless female, feeds on small snails and slugs.

114 Elytra black with markings of some other colour. 115

Elytra wholly black. 116

115 {

Elytra about twice as long as broad. Beetle shining black with one, often indistinct, deep red spot on each wing-case near its base and a yellow streak near its tip.   **Scarab Sphaeridium**, $\frac{1}{4}$ inch.
(*Sphaeridium scarabaeoides*.)

Common in fresh dung.

Similar to above but with deep red spot at shoulders and another of lighter shade near the tip of each wing-case.   Thorax and elytra thinly edged yellow. PL. 53.   **Two-spotted Sphaeridium**, $\frac{1}{4}$ inch.
(*Sphaeridium bipustulatum*.)

As above but with two spots near the tip of each wing-case.   **Four-spotted Sphaeridium**, $\frac{1}{4}$ inch.
(*Sphaeridium quadrimaculatum*.)

Both these small beetles are fairly common in many localities on fresh dung.

116 {

Thorax red.   **117**

Thorax black.   **118**

117.   Beetle thick-set, oval, and flat-bodied, with rather pointed extremity.   Thorax red with fine yellow down.   Elytra black; each wing-case with three raised longitudinal lines.   PL. 54.
Red-and-black Carrion Beetle, $\frac{5}{8}$ inch.
(*Silpha thoracica*.)

Fairly common on small dead animals and fungi.

118 {

Beetle long and narrow   **119**

Beetle short and broad.   **120**

119 {

Head almost as wide as the very convex thorax. Elytra many times longer than broad with rounded extremities. Whole beetle shining black with fine grey down. Wing-cases slightly lined and finely punctured. **Black or Hairy Athous,** ½ inch.
(*Athous hirtus.*)

Widely distributed and common on tall-growing herbage and bushes.

Beetle oval, flat. Head narrower than thorax. Thorax wider than long. Elytra rather more than twice as long as wide, grooved, sides almost parallel, extremely bluntly rounded. Colour deep black or brownish black. PL. 54. **Meal Beetle,** ½ inch.
(*Tenebrio molitor.*)

Common in stores of grain and flour. The larva is the meal-worm.

120 {

Beetle flat-bodied, thick-set. Head small, thorax dome-shaped with very broad base. Elytra barely twice as long as broad, with three raised longitudinal lines. Head, body, and legs shining black. PL. 54. **Black Carrion Beetle,** ½ inch.
(*Silpha atrata.*)

Common on and in carrion and animal refuse. The larva is destructive to the foliage of beet and mangold.

As above but rather larger. Upper surface covered with fine grey down. **Beet Carrion Beetle,** ⅔ inch.
(*Silpha opaca.*)

Another common species, the larva of which is sometimes a pest on beet and similar crops. The adult beetle is a carrion feeder.

Beetle not as above described. 121

121 ⎰ Elytra yellow, orange, or red.   **122**

    ⎱ Elytra other than yellow, orange, or red.   **125**

122 ⎰ Markings on elytra black.   **123**

    ⎱ Markings on elytra paler than ground colour.   **124**

Body hemispherical. Thorax black with white on side margins. Elytra red with two or more black spots on each wing-case. PL. 55.

        Two-spotted Ladybird, ¼ inch or less.
        (*Coccinella bipunctata.*)

Very common almost everywhere. The number of spots on the elytra is very variable. The several species of ladybirds and their larvae feed on aphides (green-fly). These beetles exude a bitter, yellowish fluid from the leg joints which makes them distasteful to birds and lizards.

123

As above but elytra orange red with seven black spots. PL. 55.   **Seven-spotted Ladybird**, ¼ inch.
        (*Coccinella septempunctata.*)

Widely distributed and generally common.

Thorax with white on front as well as on side margins. Elytra orange or yellow with from five to seven black spots. **Variegated Ladybird**, ¼ inch.
        (*Adonia variegata.*)

Widely distributed and generally common.

Thorax black marked with yellow. Elytra red with about eight yellow-ringed black spots.
        Eyed Ladybird, over ¼ inch.
        (*Anatis ocellata.*)

Locally distributed. Often fairly abundant where it occurs.

124 {

Thorax and elytra yellow. Thorax with five, elytra with twenty-two, black spots.

Twenty-two-spotted Ladybird, less than ¼ inch.
(*Thea vigintiduopunctata.*)

Widely distributed but less common than the two- or seven-spotted forms.

Thorax and elytra pale reddish brown. Thorax with light margins; elytra with sixteen pale spots. PL. 55. **Sixteen-spotted Ladybird**, ¼ inch.
(*Micraspis sexdecimguttata.*)

Another widely distributed form that is less generally common than several of the black-spotted ladybirds.

125 {

Elytra black.   126

Elytra other than black.   127

126 {

Beetle dull blue-black, very convex with elytra only a little longer than broad. Head tucked beneath the broad, rounded thorax. Feet dilated, brown on the undersides. PL. 54. **Bloody-nosed Beetle**, ¾ inch.
(*Timarcha tenebricosa.*)

A slow-moving, heavy beetle which takes its name from its habit of ejecting a red fluid from its mouth when alarmed. Common in spring and summer on paths and in fields and woods, on bushes.

Similar to above but much smaller. PL. 54.
Lesser Timarcha.
(*Timarcha coriaria.*)

Common on heaths, commons, etc.

126 Body hemispherical. Elytra black with two or more red spots on each wing case.

> **Two-spotted Ladybird** (dark variety), $\frac{1}{4}$ inch or less.
> (*Coccinella bipunctata.*)

This dark variety of the common Two-spotted Ladybird is very often met with in company with the more usual form. (*See* No. 123.)

127 Elytra green. 128

Elytra brown. 129

128 Body hemispherical, depressed. Head hidden beneath thorax. Elytra much broader than abdomen, with raised side margins which almost hide the legs. Head, thorax, and elytra green, legs yellowish brown. PL. 55.

> **Mint Tortoise Beetle,** $\frac{1}{3}$ inch.
> (*Cassida equestris.*)

Common on several kinds of wild mint.

Beetle very thick-set, almost spherical. Colour brown, upper surface covered with fine golden hair. Elytra lined and with dark velvety spots. PL. 54.

> **Pill Beetle,** $\frac{2}{5}$ inch.
> (*Byrrhus pilula.*)

Common in spring on pastures, roads, and sunny banks. When alarmed this beetle withdraws its legs and head under the body, assuming a form in which it is almost indistinguishable from a dung
129 pellet of a rabbit.

129 Head hidden beneath thorax. Beetle globular, shining brown, covered with fine golden hair. Antennae and legs rather long. PL. 55.

Shining Niptus, less than $\frac{1}{4}$ inch.
(Niptus hololeucus.)

Not uncommon in cupboards and store-rooms, where it feeds on sugar, flour, and other dry provisions. Looks more like a small spider than a beetle. Originally a native of the Near East, whence it was introduced into Europe in merchandise.

BUGS, PLANT-LICE, AND
THEIR ALLIES

THE insects included in this section constitute the order Hemiptera. They vary very widely in shape and general appearance. In some the body and fore-wings are hard, in others soft. Some are fully winged in both sexes; in others one or both sexes may be wingless. But despite this diversity all have one feature in common. The mouth parts, instead of being adapted for biting as in beetles, or taking the form of a long, coiled proboscis, as in butterflies and moths, are fashioned into a sharp, beak-like structure which, when not in use, is folded backwards under the head against the underside of the thorax. These insects feed on plant or animal juices, to obtain which they pierce the skin of the food supply with two pairs of minute but sharp stylets and suck the fluid through the hollow beak. The order is divided into two sub-orders. Of these the first is the Heteroptera, or bugs, the second the Homoptera, which includes, besides the plant-lice proper, those curious little insects popularly known as frog-hoppers, white-flies, and scale-insects or mealy bugs.

The bugs are characterized by the possession of fore-wings which are leathery for the greater part of their length but become membranous towards their tips. They may be likened to the elytra of beetles but, because of their lack of uniformity in consistency, are sometimes termed hemelytra, that is hemi-, or half, elytra. The hind-wings are membranous and, except during flight, are hidden, or partly hidden, by the leathery wing-cases. The head is roughly triangular in shape, with compound eyes and antennae. The thorax, as in beetles, shows a well-developed pronotum, which is the portion seen when the insect is looked at from above. In many species of bugs the scutellum, which in beetles is small and usually inconspicuous, is very large, forming in some cases a shield-like structure extending to the tip of the abdomen. The legs are usually adapted for walking but, as in beetles, the front pair may be modified to capture prey, and the hind-legs be lengthened and flattened to serve as oars or paddles in aquatic species. Several bugs are without hind-wings and in a few, including some of the

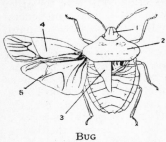

Bug

1. Head. 2. Thorax. 3. Scutellum.
   4. Fore-wing. 5. Hind-wing.

water-bugs, there are neither fore- nor hind-wings. Metamorphosis in all members of the Hemiptera is incomplete. Though the young may exhibit some differences in structure from the adult, these are never so strongly marked as those which differentiate the larva from the pupa, or the pupa from the perfect insect, in butterflies, moths, or beetles. The chief distinction between the nymph and the adult condition often consists in the absence of wings in the early stages.

The great majority of British bugs feed on plant juices and may be found on vegetation of various kinds on land or in water. A few have adopted a carnivorous diet, Perhaps the most generally known of these, at least by name, is the Bed-bug (*Cimex lectularius*) which in less hygienic days was almost universally familiar as an unwelcome domestic guest throughout these islands. Other carnivorous species live in ditches, ponds, and streams, preying on insects and any other creatures they are able to overpower. The Water Scorpion and Water Boatman are examples of aquatic bugs of this kind.

The only other type of insect with which a bug is likely to be confused is a beetle. To the beginner in the study of insects the two may at first appear to have several features in common, but there are two points of structure which at once distinguish the one from the other. All beetles have mouth parts of the biting type. No member of that order has a sucking proboscis like that of a bug. It is true that in some of the weevils the long rostrum may seem to bear a resemblance to the piercing beak of a bug, but the mouth parts of these beetles, situated at the end of the rostrum, are adapted for biting and are typical of the order to which the insects

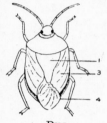

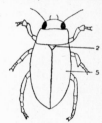

BUG

1. Large scutellum.
3. Leathery part of elytra.
4. Membranous area of elytra.

BEETLE

2. Small scutellum
5. Horny elytra.

belong. Again, whereas the elytra of beetles meet in a straight line along their inner margins, in bugs the fore-wings, when folded, overlap one another for part of their length and, although these hemelytra are often opaque and hard, they are never horny and shell-like as are the elytra of beetles.

The insects which form the second sub-order of the Hemiptera, the Homoptera, differ so much from one another that it is difficult to give a general summary of their characteristics. All have piercing and sucking mouth parts essentially similar to those of the Heteroptera. The winged forms differ from the bugs in that the fore-wings, which may be opaque and leathery, as in the frog-hoppers, or clear and membranous, as in the aphides, are of the same texture or consistency throughout their length. A brief account of the characteristics of the various types included in the sub-order is given in the descriptive parts of the text devoted to each.

SECTION IV

BUGS, FROG-HOPPERS, PLANT-LICE, WHITE-FLIES, SCALE INSECTS

Wings usually overlapping over the abdomen. Fore-wings leathery with membranous area at tips.

Sub-section A, page 166.

Wings, when present, usually sloping over the sides of the abdomen. Fore-wings either leathery or membranous but of the same consistency throughout their length.

Sub-section B, page 179.

SUB-SECTION A

BUGS

(The measurements given refer to the length of head and body)

1 { Insects found in water.   **2**

     Insects not found in water.   **11**

2 { Head very long and narrow. Body long and thin. **3**

     Not as above described.   **4**

3.   Head very attenuated, about half the length of the narrow abdomen. Antennae and legs very long and slender. Colour dark grey or greyish black. PL. 56.   **Water Gnat, ½ inch.**
(*Hydrometra stagnorum*.)

166

3. This curious insect, although very common, is not usually seen unless a careful search is made for it, on account of the extreme thinness of its wingless body. The Water Gnat walks slowly on the surface of ponds, ditches, and streams, feeding on small, floating insects.

4 $\begin{cases} \text{Head small, body very long and narrow.} & \textbf{5} \\ \text{Body not very long and narrow.} & \textbf{8} \end{cases}$

5 $\begin{cases} \text{Abdomen with long, tail-like appendage.} & \textbf{6} \\ \text{Abdomen without long, tail-like appendage.} & \textbf{7} \end{cases}$

6. Head small, eyes prominent. Body very narrow and long. Abdomen bearing a long, thin, caudal appendage. Legs very long, the first pair modified for the purpose of holding prey. General colour brown; the abdomen beneath the wings red. Head and body, 1½ inches; caudal appendage, 1 inch. PL. 56. **Water Stick-insect.**
(*Renatra linearis.*)

The long, thin 'tail' is composed of two portions which interlock by a series of fine teeth. This organ is a breathing siphon by means of which air is drawn into the body, the insect rising at intervals from the bottom of the pool in which it lives to protrude the tip of its respiratory apparatus through the surface. The Water Stick-insect is carnivorous, seizing small insects and other aquatic creatures in its modified fore-legs and sucking their juices through its short proboscis. The eggs are attached to the leaves of water plants. The young are very similar in shape to the adult insect except that they are paler in colour.

Head small, body narrow and tapering somewhat towards the extremity. Legs long and slender. Colour dark grey marked with dull yellow on the sides of the body. PL. 12. **Pond Skater,** about ½ inch.
(*Gerris lacustris.*)

A common insect in pools and streams, where it may be seen moving quickly over the water surface in search of the small insects on which it feeds. The first pair of legs is used to hold the prey, the second and third for rowing and steering the body. All parts of the Pond Skater are covered with fine downy pile which prevents the insect from becoming waterlogged when it dives beneath the surface to escape danger.

Similar to above but with yellowish-red patch on the thorax.
Red-marked Pond Skater, about ½ inch.
(*Gerris thoracica.*)

Similar to the Common Pond Skater but with broader body. **Broad Pond Skater,** about ½ inch.
(*Gerris gibbifera.*)

Considerably larger than the Pond Skater mentioned above, with very long legs. Wingless.
Great Pond Skater, ¾ inch.
(*Gerris naias.*)

All the above species are widely distributed and common in suitable situations.

Body shorter and broader than in the Pond Skaters. Hind-legs with thighs much broader than in the first two pairs. Colour dark brown, with two stripes of orange along the back. Usually wingless, but if wings are present they are membranous. PL. 56. **Water Cricket,** ½ inch.
(*Velia currens.*)

7

7 ⎱ Common in ponds, streams, and rivers, often in large companies. This is a very active insect, which may be seen running and skipping over the surface of water or diving rapidly when alarmed.

8 ⎰ Abdomen bearing tail-like appendage. **9**

⎱ Abdomen without tail-like appendage. **10**

9. Head small, partly hidden beneath the thorax. Body oval and flattened. Fore-legs modified to form pincer-like weapons for seizing and holding prey; the thigh being broad and grooved to receive the thinner, curved shank which closes on it like the blade of a pocket-knife. The tip of the abdomen bears two slender, bristle-like appendages, about half an inch long, which form the breathing siphon. Colour brown. Head and body, 1 inch; appendages, $\frac{1}{2}$ inch. PL. 58 **Water Scorpion.**
(*Nepa cinerea.*)

A rather slow-moving insect which stalks, or lies in wait for, its prey at the bottoms of ponds and streams. It is very voracious, feeding on small fish, worms, insects, etc. May occasionally be seen taking short flights from one piece of water to another. The young resembles the adult except that the breathing siphon is short.

⎧ Body broad, oval, and flattened. Fore-legs with broad thighs and thin shanks, so hinged as to close together to hold captured insects, etc. Hind pair of legs flattened and fringed to serve as oars or paddles. Colour greenish brown. PL. 56.
Lesser Water Scorpion, $\frac{1}{2}$ inch.
10 ⎭ (*Naucoris cimicoides.*)

10 Similar in general appearance to the Water Scorpion (No. 9) but without its tail-like siphon. Locally distributed in pools and streams; not generally common.

Head almost as broad as thorax. Body convex and keeled above, flattened below. Third pair of legs much longer than others, flattened, with broad fringes of hairs. General colour dull yellow with black scutellum. PL. 12. **Water Boatman,** ⅝ inch.
(*Notonecta glauca.*)

This insect always swims on its back, moving itself along with its long, oar-like hind-legs, which when at rest are held at right angles to the body. It is generally common in ponds and streams. When diving the body is encircled by a silvery air bubble due to the hairy covering. The Water Boatman is carnivorous, feeding on any creatures it is able to overpower. May often be seen in flight over water.

Similar to the above but with the upper surface spotted with blackish brown.
Spotted Water Boatman, ⅝ inch.
(*Notonecta maculata.*)

Widely distributed and locally common in ponds and streams.

Head almost as broad as thorax, body flat above—not concave and keeled as in the Water Boatman. First pair of legs much shorter than the middle pair. Hind-legs much longer than the others, flattened and fringed with hairs. Colour dark greenish or blackish brown. Legs dull yellow. PL. 56.
Lesser Water Boatman, ½ inch.
(*Corixa geoffroyi.*)

10 〉 Unlike the Water Boatman this insect swims back upwards, using its long hind-legs as oars. Though very common in many ponds and streams it is less active than the last two species and not so often seen at the surface.

Similar to the Lesser Water Boatman but about half its size. **Small Water Boatman,** ¼ inch.
(*Corixa nigrolineata.*)

Widely distributed and generally common in ponds and streams.

11 〈 Scutellum very large; at least half as long as abdomen. **12**

Scutellum not as described. **19**

12 〈 Insect with red or yellow markings. **13**

Insect without red or yellow markings. **14**

Insect bronze brown finely punctured with black. Scutellum with orange red, roughly triangular, mark at tip. Antennae and legs red. Fore part of thorax very broad with slightly hooked projecting borders. Margins of abdomen spotted yellow and black. PL. 12.
Red-legged Bug, ⅔ inch.
(*Tropicornis rufipes.*)

Widely distributed. Common in fields, hedgerows, and gardens.

Similar to above but smaller and paler in colour. The red spot on the tip of the scutellum is smaller, and the projecting corners of the fore part of the thorax are sharply pointed. PL. 57.
Two-pointed Picromerus, ½ inch.

13 〉 (*Picromerus bidens.*)

13 ⎫ More locally distributed than the Red-legged Bug but usually fairly common on dry heaths and among heather.

Insect pale shining brown, finely punctured. Scutellum triangular, prolonged behind into a narrow extension, which is yellow. Body rather long, tapering. Abdomen barred with crimson— noticeable only when the wings are raised. PL. 57.
Bloody Acanthosma, ½ inch.
(*Acanthosma haemorrhoidale.*)

A fairly common insect. The crimson-barred abdomen from which it takes its name makes it conspicuous and easy to identify in flight.

Body oval and broad. General colour red with black spots or patches on thorax and elytra.
Ornate Strachia, ¼ inch.
(*Strachia ornata.*)

Often common on cruciferous plants, both wild and cultivated.

Body oval, rather broad. Black with brassy green sheen. Elytra marked with yellowish red or cream.
Strachia oleacea, ¼ inch.

Common on hedgerow plants and in fields in many parts of the British Isles.

14 ⎰ Insect black and white.   **15**

⎱ Insect other than black and white.   **16**

15 {
Body almost as broad as long. Colour glossy black marked with splashes of white on thorax and elytra. **Two-coloured Schirus,** ¼ inch.
(*Sehirus bicolor.*)

A common little insect which may be swept from nettles and other low-growing herbage in most parts of Great Britain.
}

16 {
Insect green. **17**

Insect other than green. **18**
}

17 {
Head, scutellum, and elytra bright olive green punctured with black. End of elytra transparent.
Juniper Bug, ¼ inch.
(*Pentatoma juniperinum.*)

A local and scarce insect, occurring chiefly, as its name implies, on juniper on chalky hills.

Brighter green than the last species with the triangular scutellum ending in a narrow extremity. Body tapering. **Three-striped Acanthosma,** ⅜ inch.
(*Acanthosma tristriatum.*)

More widely distributed than the Juniper Bug but, like it, usually found on juniper bushes.
}

18 {
Scutellum reaching to tip of abdomen, almost covering the elytra. Colour pale greyish brown, finely punctured with black. There are two clear spots at the base of the scutellum and a pale line down its centre. PL. 57. **Hottentot Bug,** ⅖ inch.
(*Eurygaster maurus.*)

This bug bears a strong resemblance to the Tortoise Beetle (page 160), the pale line on the scutellum
}

18 looking like the line of junction of the two wing-cases. It is widely distributed and may often be found on umbelliferous and other flowers and in corn-fields.

Insect bronze brown with paler legs; the harder parts all punctured with black. Scutellum triangular with narrow extension at the rear. Body tapering. *Acanthosma interstinctum*, ½ inch.

Common in suitable localities on or near birch-trees.

Insect greyish brown, reddish on head and fore part of thorax. Edges of abdomen reddish brown spotted with black.

Grey Elasmostethus, ⅖ inch.
(*Elasmostethus griseus*.)

Locally common on birch-trees.

Scutellum covering whole inner margins of elytra. Body oval. The front of the thorax near the head has two small knob-like projections. Colour greyish brown. PL. 57. *Podops inunctus*, ¼ inch.

Widely distributed and common in some localities on plants of various kinds.

19 Insect large—¾ inch long. **20**

Insect small—considerably less than ¾ inch long **21**

20 Body long and oval. Legs and antennae long. Head small with distinct neck and short, curved rostrum. Colour dark brown. PL. 57.

Fly Bug, ¾ inch.
(*Reduvius personatus*.)

20 An uncommon British insect, rarer now than formerly. Carnivorous, feeding on other insects, including the Bed-bug, in quest of which it sometimes enters buildings. Will also suck human blood.

21 Insect marked with black and red.   **22**

Insect not so marked.   **23**

Body soft, oval, and rather narrow. Antennae with four joints, of which the first, or basal one, is much thicker than the others. Elytra large, completely covering the abdomen. Colour black with a red spot on the tip of the hind portion of the elytra. Other red markings are sometimes shown, this species being very variable.

Red-and-black Capsus, ⅖ inch.
(*Capsus capillaris.*)

Common on nettles. A pretty, fragile little insect.

Body long and rather narrow. Elytra very short, covering but a third of the abdomen. General colour shining blue-black with bright red elytra and legs. **Red-winged Prostemma**, ½ inch.
(*Prostemma guttula.*)

This striking-looking bug is carnivorous, feeding on small insects which are seized by its modified forelegs. A scarce species occasionally found among low herbage.

Body rather slender and soft. Antennae long. Head, thorax, and elytra red, banded and spotted with black. Membranous portion of fore-wings blackish with clear white spots. Pl. 12.
Lygaeus equestris, ⅖ inch.

22 A local and rare insect, found among moss and low herbage.

22 Head broad, triangular; eyes prominent. General colour red with black spot on sides of head. The fore and hind borders of the thorax, the base of the scutellum, and the elytra also show black markings. Legs and antennae black.

Henbane Bug, $\frac{1}{3}$ inch.
(*Rhopalus hyoscyami.*)

Locally distributed in the southern half of England; often found on henbane.

Body almost elliptical. Head distinct from thorax; antennae long. Elytra without membranous hind portions. Hind-wings usually absent. Head and antennae black, thorax black bordered with red, scutellum black, elytra red with one large and one small black spot on each wing-case; abdomen black edged with red. PL. 57.

Red or Fire Bug, $\frac{1}{3}$ inch.
(*Pyrrhocoris apterus.*)

A local and generally scarce British insect, though it has from time to time occurred in large numbers in a few favoured localities. Feeds on plant juices. Usually found near trees.

23 { Colour black and yellow. **24**

Colour other than black and yellow. **25**

24. Body oval. Head, antennae, and legs yellow. Thorax yellow with black hind margins. Scutellum orange. Elytra black with three yellow dots near the hind margin.

Three-spotted Phytocoris, $\frac{1}{4}$ inch or less.
(*Phytocoris tripustulatus.*)

Common in most parts of Great Britain on nettles and hedgerow plants.

25 {

General colour brown.   **26**

General colour other than brown.   **27**

Body oblong, flat, with margins of the abdomen projecting beyond the elytra on each side. Colour of upper parts dull brown. Abdomen beneath the wings red. Antennae four-jointed with the second and third joints red. PL. 57.

Margined Syromastes, ½ inch.
(*Syromastes marginalis*.)

Not uncommon near brambles and other shrubby herbage. May also be found on box-trees.

Body short, oval, and flat. Colour reddish brown. The insect bears a strong superficial resemblance to the Bed-bug, for which it is often mistaken. In the present species, however, the elytra are fully developed.   **Reddish Platygaster**, ⅓ inch.

Common among herbage in many parts of Great Britain.

Body very flat and broad. Fore-part of head projecting between the short antennae. Abdomen broader than wings. General colour brown with white on margin of thorax and elytra. Antennae tipped with white hairs. PL. 57.

Flat Aradus, ¼ inch.
(*Aradus depressus*.)

This may be taken as an example of a number of bugs remarkable for their greatly flattened bodies. All live under the bark and in small crevices of dead trees, etc. Their depressed form is an adaptation to this mode of life. The Flat Aradus, like several other related species, is very common in most parts of Great Britain.

26 }

26 Elytra vestigial, or wholly absent. Antennae thick, four-jointed. Legs short and thick. Colour rusty brown with red eyes. **Sea Bug**, about $\frac{1}{4}$ inch.
(*Aepophilus bonnairei.*)

A curious insect which lives under submerged stones on the coasts of south England and Ireland. It feeds on small marine worms.

27 General colour black or grey.   **28**

General colour green.   **29**

Body rather narrow and soft. Head, thorax, and scutellum black with bronzy sheen. Elytra grey.
Nettle Heterogaster, $\frac{1}{3}$ inch.
(*Heterogaster urticae.*)

Generally distributed and common on nettles.

28 Body narrowly oval, rather soft and fragile. Colour black. Legs may be either black or dusky red. **Black Capsus**, $\frac{1}{4}$ inch.
(*Capsus ater.*)

Widely distributed and common on low-growing plants. May be taken as a type of a large tribe all the species of which are small and closely resemble one another.

29. Body oval, narrow, soft, and fragile. Antennae with four joints, of which the first is much thicker than the rest. Elytra completely covering the abdomen. Legs long. Antennae very long, equalling the total length of head and body. Colour pale green.   **Long-horned Green Bug**, $\frac{1}{2}$ inch.
(*Megaloceraea longicornis.*)

Frequents grassy places, where it may be seen flying in sunshine or running actively over the leaves of plants.

SUB-SECTION B

FROG-HOPPERS, PLANT-LICE, AND THEIR ALLIES

1 { Thorax hard and horny or leathery.   **2**

  { Thorax not hard or leathery.   **9**

2 { Fore part of thorax produced behind into long, angular spine.   **3**

  { Fore part of thorax not so produced.   **4**

Fore part of thorax produced behind into long, angular hood with central spine reaching almost to the hind extremity of the body. Fore margin of thorax with pair of sharp-pointed horns. Colour brownish black with lighter brown wings. Head and thorax covered with fine golden down. Pl. 58.
Horned Tree-hopper, $\frac{1}{3}$ inch.
(*Centrotus cornutus.*)

This curious little insect is one of the only two British representatives of the Membracids or Tree-hoppers, a family represented in some tropical countries by a large number of forms, many of which assume remarkable shapes by reason of the great development of the hood-like extension of the thorax. The hind pair of legs is longer than the others. The Horned Tree-hopper may be found on both trees and low herbage. The immature form, or nymph, is without the hood which characterizes the adult condition.

Similar to above but smaller and without the horns on the sides of the fore margin of the thorax.
Greenweed Centrotus, barely $\frac{1}{4}$ inch.
(*Centrotus genistae.*)

Locally distributed. Most often found on dyer's greenweed (*Genista tinctoria*).

4 {
General colour greyish brown with darker mottlings.   **5**

General colour other than above.   **6**
}

5 {

Head broad, short, and rounded. Elytra opaque. Antennae short, placed between and slightly in front of the eyes. Hind-legs long, adapted for leaping. Colour yellowish grey mottled with dark and blackish brown. PL. 58.
Common Frog-hopper, ¼ inch.
(*Philaenus spumarius.*)

This is the very common little insect the nymph of which produces the curious white patches of froth seen on plants in summer and familiarly known as cuckoo-spit. The foam-like substance is formed by the soft-bodied, yellow nymph from the surplus fluid sucked from the plants on which it lives, which is whipped to a froth by a peculiar, rapid movement of the tip of the abdomen. Within this protective envelope the young Frog-hopper remains until it assumes the form of the adult. The mature Frog-hopper may be found on a variety of plants, rarely quitting its leaf until disturbed, then leaping away with great agility.

Similar to the Common Frog-hopper but the frothy exudation of the nymph is found only on grasses.
Livid Frog-hopper, ¼ inch.
(*Philaenus lividus.*)

Like the Common Frog-hopper but much larger. Found mainly on sallow and alders.
Alder Frog-hopper, ½ inch.
(*Aphrophora alni.*)
}

6 {
Colour greyish green or black and green.   **7**

Colour black and red.   **8**
}

Colour greyish green. Head broad and flattened. Sides of fore part of thorax raised to form a pair of ear-like projections. Body broad and flat.
Eared Leaf-hopper, $\frac{5}{8}$ inch.
(*Ledra aurita.*)

7 Occurs on oak-trees. This is the largest of British leaf-hoppers, the great majority of which are very small insects. Several species are common on a great variety of plants, leaping, like fleas, when disturbed.

General colour black with streaks of green.
Green-and-black Leaf-hopper, $\frac{1}{4}$ inch.
(*Evacanthus interruptus.*)

A bright, very active little insect which may be found on the leaves of herbage and shrubby plants.

8. Colour black with conspicuous patches of cinnabar red. PL. 12. **Black-and-red Frog-hopper,** $\frac{1}{3}$ inch.
(*Cereopis vulnerator.*)

A very strikingly coloured frog-hopper which may be found locally on sallows and willows. As in other frog-hoppers, the nymph lives in a covering of froth, but is unique in feeding on the roots of grasses beneath the soil.

9 Both fore- and hind-wings, if present, clear, membranous. **10**

Wings covered with fine white powdery wax. **13**

10 A jumping insect. **11**

Not a jumping insect. **12**

11. Small, very active insects. Wings clear and membranous; held in a high, roof-like position when at rest. Antennae long, delicate, many-jointed.
Jumping Plant-lice.

A great many species of these tiny insects occur in Britain, varying much in colour. All feed on the juices of plants and may be found on leaves. Among the most common forms are the greenish-yellow Apple-sucker (*Psylla mali*), the dark red Pear-sucker (*Psylla pyri*), and the bright green Hawthorn-sucker (*Psylla peregrina*). Several insects of this kind are destructive orchard pests. Like the Aphides, the Jumping Plant-lice produce honey-dew on the leaves of the trees on which they feed. Some species also exude a wax-like substance.

12 {
Insect either winged or wingless. If wings are present both fore and hind pairs are fully developed. The wingless forms are long-legged and active.
13

If wings are present the fore pair only is developed. Wingless forms are inactive with the legs very short or aberrant.
14
}

13. Aphides or Green-fly, among the most familiar of agricultural and horticultural pests. They differ from the Jumping Plant-lice in their longer legs, more delicate wings, and in their inability to jump. The fifth abdominal segment usually bears a pair of tubular projections. From eggs laid in late summer or autumn wingless females emerge in the spring and, without mating, give birth to insects similar to themselves. Throughout the summer this viviparous reproduction continues, from time to time a number of winged females being produced in broods consisting mainly of the apterous type.

13. The winged females migrate to areas removed from the place of their birth to establish new centres of distribution. At the end of the summer males are produced, together with non-parthenogenetic females. These mate together and the females lay eggs which remain through the winter to produce a further generation of wingless females the following spring. Despite the name of Green-fly

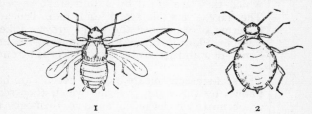

PLANT-LICE (Aphides)
1. Winged female.   2. Wingless female.

commonly bestowed on them, Aphides are by no means always green. The Bean-aphis is black, the Cabbage-aphis greyish green with black spots; other forms are reddish, grey, or brown. Though so often seen on the leaves and stems of plants, several aphides carry out their destructive work underground, feeding on roots. The honey-dew secreted by these insects is a favourite food with certain kinds of ants, which protect their benefactors and distribute them on suitable plants near the ant colony or keep them in the nest itself.

14 Small insects with wings thickly covered with fine waxy powder, causing them to look like tiny moths. All are small—about $\frac{1}{8}$ inch across the outspread wings. PL. 58.   **White-flies.**
(Family Aleurodidae.)

14 Species of this family occur on both garden and greenhouse crops, one of the best known being the Cabbage Snow-fly. Others are found on tomatoes, cucumbers, strawberries, currants, brambles, and many more wild and cultivated plants. In some species the wings are pure white, in others they show a variable number of minute dark dots. Eggs are laid on the food plant, to the leaves of which they are glued by a thin stalk or pedicle. The larvae are flattened and hide beneath a covering of wax until the wings grow. Like the Jumping Plant-lice and Aphides, these insects exude honey-dew and are visited and protected by ants.

The scale-insects, mealy bugs, or coccids are better known by the waxy covering which they secrete and beneath which they hide and lay their eggs, than by their appearance. All are small. The males are winged but the hind pair is vestigial. The females are wingless and remain motionless on the food plant. After pairing the female secretes a waxy substance which, with the cast skins, forms a scale beneath which she feeds. Several species of scale-insects are injurious to orchard trees. Among the best known of these are the Mussel-scale (*Mytilaspis pomorum*) of the apple and the Oyster-scale found on several kinds of fruit trees. Certain non-British coccids yield valuable commercial commodities. These include the cochineal insect which yields the cochineal dye, the lac insect from which shellac is manufactured, and several species from which wax is obtained.

EARWIGS

THE earwigs form the small order Dermaptera, which includes about nine hundred known species, though only five are found in the British Isles. The head is broad, with strong biting jaws, compound eyes, and rather long, many-jointed antennae. The fore-wings are modified into short, leathery wing-cases, beneath which the large,

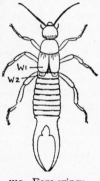

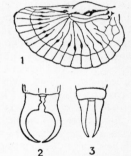

1. Hind-wing. of earwig
   expanded
w1. Fore-wings.   2. Forceps—male.
w2. Hind-wings.   3. Forceps—female.

semicircular, membranous hind-wings are tucked out of sight by dint of complicated longitudinal and transverse folding. The body is long and terminates in a pair of forceps, curved in the males but straight in the females. Metamorphosis is incomplete, the newly hatched insects approximating closely to the adult condition except that they have no wings. The eggs are laid in the soil and the mother watches over the young ones until they are able to find food and generally to shift for themselves. This is one of the few known instances of maternal solicitude shown by any other than the social insects.

Earwigs are omnivorous in diet, feeding on dead insects, carrion, roots, leaves, blossoms, and ripe fruit. Though provided with large wings, these insects are rarely seen in flight. Even when tossed in the air they will not expand their wings to break the fall. The purpose of the hind forceps is uncertain. Their chief use appears to be to pack the wings beneath the wing-cases after one of their infrequent flights. They may also be employed as offensive or defensive weapons, though observation affords little justification for this view. The curious superstition that earwigs are likely to crawl into the ears of sleeping humans and bore into the brain is wholly groundless. In the improbable event of an insect of this kind entering the human ear it would be incapable of inflicting any injury. The word earwig is generally thought to have reference to this old-time belief. More attractive is the theory that the name is derived from ear-wing, referring to the ear-like shape of the hind-wings in these insects. The earwig's habit of creeping into small crevices and holes is well known and often taken advantage of by gardeners wishing to trap the pests, which spoil his choicest blooms by nibbling the petals. Most earwigs are nocturnal, hiding under stones, loose bark, and fallen leaves, or in any other dark cranny available by day, and only emerging from their retreats to indulge in more active occupations after dusk.

SECTION V

EARWIGS

Body reddish brown with paler elytra.   Hind part
of body ending in a pair of sharp forceps which are
curved in the male, straight in the female. PL. 13.

Common Earwig, ¾ inch.
(*Forficula auricularia.*)

Common throughout the British Isles.   The eggs
are laid in winter or early spring in a crevice or hole
of some kind and watched over by the female.

Much paler than, and about twice as large as, the Common Earwig with the forceps of the male much more
slender and less curved.   **Shore Earwig,** 1½ inches.
(*Labidura riparia.*)

Locally distributed on the Hampshire coast.
Found on wet sand under seaweed.

Colour yellowish brown, otherwise like the Common
Earwig but only half its size.

Lesser Earwig, ¼–⅓ inch.
(*Labia minor.*)

Widely distributed but somewhat local.   Usually
found on or near dung heaps, hot-beds, or rotting
vegetation.   Frequently flies in sunshine.

Similar to the Common Earwig but paler in colour
and smaller.   Wingless.   The flattened bases of
the forceps are much longer in proportion to the
curved ends than in the common species.

Pale Earwig, ½ inch.
(*Forficula lesnei.*)

Locally distributed in south England.

CRICKETS AND GRASSHOPPERS

CRICKETS and grasshoppers belong to the order Orthoptera, literally straight-winged insects, in reference to their straight, longitudinal method of folding the wings. All are readily recognized by the great development of the hind-legs, in which the thighs are long, broad, and muscular, and the shanks straight and rigid. The general shape of the body shows little variation in the numerous species. The thorax is longer than broad and as wide as the bases of the fore-wings. In some species it has an extension which runs backwards almost to the end of the hind body. The fore-wings are leathery, the hind-wings thinner and transparent. The wings may extend to the

Leg of grasshopper, showing long, broad, muscular thigh and straight, thin shank.

tip of the abdomen or even beyond it, or leave a portion of the body exposed. Some forms, including one of the most common of British grasshoppers, are without functional hind-wings. In the crickets and long-horned grasshoppers the antennae are very long and slender, but in the short-horned grasshoppers they are short, not longer than the head and thorax, and stout. The British species which shows the greatest divergence from the usual type is the Mole Cricket (*Gryllotalpa gryllotalpa*), in which the fore-legs are modified to form digging implements and the general shape of the body is adapted to a subterranean existence. The familiar chirping sound, or stridulation, made by the male insects is produced either by rubbing the tip of the underside of one fore-wing over the upper surface of the other, or by friction between the underside of the fore-wing and the inside of the hind thigh. In either case the sound depends on the presence of an area in which the nervules are raised being passed over a file-like structure, causing rapid vibration.

The crickets and long-horned grasshoppers stridulate by rubbing together the tips of the elytra, while the short-horned grasshoppers bring the tip of the fore-wing across the roughened inner surface of the thigh. An auditory apparatus, or ear, is present in both sexes, either on the sides of the first abdominal segment, as in the long-horned grasshoppers and crickets, or near the base of each shank on the fore-legs, as in the short-horned grasshoppers. It consists of a membrane or tympanum, associated with special nerve centres.

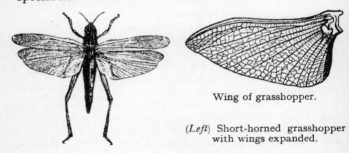

Wing of grasshopper.

(*Left*) Short-horned grasshopper with wings expanded.

Metamorphosis is incomplete. The eggs are laid in late summer in the ground, placed in position by the long ovipositor possessed by the female of all species with the exception of the Mole Cricket. This organ is conspicuous in the crickets and long-horned grasshoppers but not easily seen in the short-horned grasshoppers. The young hatch in late spring and bear a close resemblance to the adults, except that they are at first wingless. Crickets differ from grasshoppers in the possession of long, unjointed tail appendages, or cerci, which are believed to serve as sensory organs.

The great majority of these insects are vegetarian in diet. Exceptions are the Mole Cricket, which is largely carnivorous, and the House Cricket (*Gryllus domesticus*), which feeds on any fragments of either vegetable or animal food afforded by the kitchens and store cupboards in which it lives.

SECTION VI
CRICKETS AND GRASSHOPPERS

1 ⎰ Antennae long and slender.   **2**

   ⎱ Antennae short and thick.   **10**

2 ⎰ Tarsi (feet) three-jointed.   **3**

   ⎱ Tarsi four-jointed.   **5**

3 ⎰

First pair of legs very broad, shanks strongly toothed. Thorax large and domed, wider than elytra. Colour brown, covered with fine velvety down. Elytra half as long as abdomen. Wings longer than abdomen, with their ends tightly folded.

Mole Cricket, 1½–2 inches. (*Gryllotalpa gryllotalpa.*)

Locally distributed in parts of south and central England, nowhere common. The first pair of legs is modified to serve as digging tools and the insect burrows through the earth like a mole in search of the grubs on which it feeds. The eggs are laid in an underground chamber. The hind-legs are of the same pattern as those of other crickets but shorter. The Mole Cricket is nocturnal. The male produces a churring stridulation by rubbing the underside of one wing-case over the raised nervules of the other.

Not as above described.   **4**

No. 4

Head and thorax rather square in outline. When folded the right wing-case partly overlaps the left and the wings project from beneath them as long, tapering, rod-like tails. Colour pale brown speckled or finely mottled with black. Legs and long cerci hairy. Hind shanks with a double row of spines. PL. 13.

House Cricket, ¾ inch.
(*Gryllus domesticus.*)

Common in old kitchens, bakehouses, etc., where it lives in holes in walls and floors, emerging at night to feed. The male produces a shrill chirping sound by rubbing the tip of one elytron over that of the other. In hot summers the stridulation of this insect may sometimes be heard in the open. Feeds on both vegetable and animal matter.

Insect black with a band of yellow across the base of the elytra. Otherwise similar to the House Cricket, but larger. **Field Cricket,** 1 inch.
(*Gryllus campestris.*)

Locally distributed, chiefly in the south of England. Lives in holes in banks or under stones. The male chirps by day in sunshine from May to July. Feeds on grass and other herbage.

Similar to the Field Cricket but dark brown and much smaller. Elytra very short, covering about one-third of the abdomen. **Wood Cricket,** ⅓ inch.
(*Nemobius sylvestris.*)

Locally distributed in the neighbourhood of the New Forest and the Isle of Wight. Found on shady banks and in wood clearings.

5 $\Bigg\{$

Large grasshoppers—about 1½ to 2 inches long.   6

Much smaller grasshoppers.   7

6 $\Bigg\{$

Insect very large, bright green without markings. Elytra considerably longer than abdomen. Antennae and hind legs very long. PL. 13.
> **Great Green Grasshopper,** 1¾–2 inches.
> (*Tettigonia viridissima.*)

A handsome, striking-looking bush cricket found among tall grass and thick herbage in many parts of southern, eastern, and central England. Local or rare elsewhere in Britain. The male stridulates long and vigorously, usually in the late afternoon and evening of hot summer days. Despite its large size and loud song this insect is difficult to locate, for its colour harmonizes closely with that of the vegetation in which it hides.

Insect green mottled with dark brown or black on elytra and hind thighs. Thorax narrower behind than in front, with prominent keel. Hind legs very long—almost twice as long as body. Elytra barely covering abdomen.

> **Wart-biter,** 1½ inches.
> (*Decticus verrucivorus.*)

A large, stoutly built, and very handsome insect which is found only in a few localities in the south of England on grassy hillsides. The female bears a long, curved ovipositor at the end of the abdomen. The male stridulates by rubbing a file-like structure situated on the underside of the left elytron over a ridge on the upper side of the right.

7 $\Bigg\{$

Body mainly green.   8

Body mainly brown.   9

Colour deep green, finely speckled with black. Body short and rather thick. Elytra and wings absent in both sexes. The female bears a short, curved ovipositor.

Speckled Bush Cricket, ½ inch.
(*Leptophyes punctatissima.*)

Widely distributed and generally fairly common on shrubs, hedges, and trees.

Colour pale green. Body slender. Elytra and wings fully developed in both sexes. Ovipositor of female long and slightly curved.

8 ⟨

Oak Bush Cricket, ½ inch.
(*Meconema thalassina.*)

Widely distributed in England but local. Occurs mainly on oak scrub and trees.

Colour emerald green with brown markings on thorax and elytra. Body slender. Elytra as long as abdomen. Wings short. Ovipositor of female long and slightly curved.

Conocephalus dorsalis, ½ inch.

Locally distributed in the south and east of England. Usually found on rushes and reeds.

9. Insect brown, very dark in male, paler in female. Elytra reduced to round flaps (male) or almost absent (female). Wings absent in both sexes.

Brown Bush Cricket, ½ inch.
(*Pholidoptera cinerea.*)

Locally distributed in the southern half of England. Found in bushes and thickets.

10 ⟨ Antennae with clubbed, or thickened, tips. **11**

Antennae without clubbed tips. **12**

11 {

Antennae strongly clubbed with white tips. Colour uniform brown.

Red Club-horned Grasshopper, ⅝ inch.
(*Gomphocercis rufus.*)

Locally distributed on dry hillsides in southern England.

Smaller than the last species; antennae less strongly clubbed and without white tips. Colour brown, mottled with lighter and darker shades.

Spotted Club-horned Grasshopper, ¾ inch.
(*Myrmeleotettix maculatus.*)

Widely distributed and common in many parts of the British Isles. Found on commons, heaths, and in fields.

12 {

Elytra reduced to short stumps. Fore-part of thorax extending backwards as a horny shield over the whole length of the abdomen.   **13**

Thorax not as above described.   **14**

13 {

Insects brown, variegated and mottled, with black spot on each side of the thorax. Wings short.

Two-spotted Grasshopper, ½ inch or less.
(*Tetrix bipunctatus.*)

Widely distributed in Great Britain. Generally common in fields, on commons, etc.

Similar to the last species but more slender and with the hind projection of the thorax extending beyond the tip of the abdomen.

Marsh Hopper, ½ inch.
(*Tetrix subulatus.*)

Widely, though locally, distributed in marshy places.

14 {
General colour green.   **15**

General colour brown.   **16**

Upper surface dark green with longitudinal yellow stripe on elytra. Under surface yellow. Hind shanks banded with black and with stout black spines. Elytra extending beyond end of abdomen.
Bog Grasshopper, 1–1½ inches.
(*Mecostethus grossus.*)

Locally distributed in south and east England in bogs and marshes. The female is considerably larger than the male.

15 {
Colour dull olive or dark green. Elytra and wings as long as abdomen.
Dark-green Grasshopper, ½ inch.
(*Omacestus viridulus.*)

Widely distributed and common in fields and on grassy hillsides.

Similar to the last species but with white longitudinal stripe running down two-thirds of the elytra and a white spot near the tips of the wing-cases. **White-lined Grasshopper,** ⅖ inch.
(*Stenobothrus lineatus.*)

Locally distributed in south and south-east England on grassy hillsides.

16 {
Brown marked with darker shades. Elytra nearly black. Tips of palpi white. Abdomen red.
Red-bellied Grasshopper, ½ inch or more.
(*Omacestus ventralis.*)

Locally distributed in England, chiefly in the south and east. Found in fields and grassy clearings in woods.

16 ⟩ Brown, mottled darker and lighter shades, with tip of abdomen red and sometimes a variable amount of green on the hind parts of the elytra. Elytra and wings as long as abdomen. PL. 13.

Two-coloured Grasshopper, ¾ inch.
(*Chorthippus bicolor.*)

This is one of the two commonest grasshoppers of our fields. It is a very active insect, using both its long legs and its fully developed wings in making its long leaps. The male stridulates in sunshine throughout the summer, his note being a repeated short 'tiss.' In colour the species is extremely variable, hardly any two individuals being exactly alike. The female lays her eggs in the ground.

Colour similar to the last species. Elytra either very short (male) or vestigial (female). Wings reduced to mere stumps in both sexes. The coloration is extremely variable but there is a characteristic black mark at the knees.

Meadow Grasshopper, ¾ inch.
(*Chorthippus parallelus.*)

The second of our commonest grasshoppers. Abundant in meadows in almost all parts of the British Isles. The chirping of the male starts on a low note, rises rapidly, then dies away. This grasshopper is, of course, flightless.

COCKROACHES

THE cockroaches belong to the order Orthoptera, which also includes the crickets and grasshoppers. In the British Isles only three truly indigenous species occur, though several introduced forms are common as domestic pests. In these insects the head is bent beneath the thorax and is furnished with strong biting jaws. The

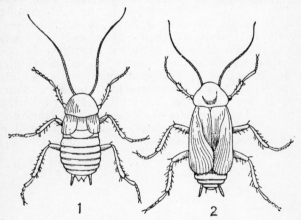

Female and male cockroach.

compound eyes are large and kidney-shaped; the antennae long and thin. The long legs enable cock-roaches to run swiftly, though their broad, flattened bodies give them a rather lethargic appearance. The hind end of the abdomen in all species bears two short, jointed appendages which, apart from other distinctive features, clearly differentiate these insects from all those of other families with which they might be confused.

The fore-wings are leathery; the hind-wings, when present, thinner and transparent. In repose these organs lie flat along the back. In some species the fore-wings are long, completely covering the abdomen, but in others a portion of the hind body is left exposed. Their length may vary in the two sexes of the same species, the

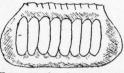

Egg capsule of cockroach.

male having longer wings than the female. Metamorphosis is incomplete. The eggs are enclosed in a horny capsule in which each egg occupies a separate chamber or pocket. This ootheca, after being carried attached to the hind end of the female's body for several days, is deposited in a crevice and, when the nymphs are ready to emerge, splits. Cockroaches are nocturnal creatures, the open-air species passing the hours of daylight under stones, leaves, or in crevices in trees; while the introduced forms, which live in buildings, remain hidden in holes in walls or under floors till darkness calls them abroad. The domestic cockroaches are omnivorous but the wild species appear to feed principally, if not exclusively, on vegetable matter.

SECTION VII

COCKROACHES

1 $\left\{\begin{array}{l}\text{Insects found indoors.} \hfill .2 \\ \\ \text{Insects found outdoors.} \hfill 3\end{array}\right.$

Body oval, dark purplish brown. Antennae long and thread-like. Head partly hidden by fore part of thorax. Elytra lying flat on back, covering about half the abdomen. End of abdomen bearing two, short, jointed appendages.

Common Cockroach (male), ¾ inch.
(*Blatta orientalis*.)

Commonly known as the 'black beetle,' an unfortunate misnomer, as this insect is neither a beetle nor really black. Common in all parts of the British Isles in kitchens, warm store-rooms, etc.

As above but with broader body and truncated extremity. Elytra and wings vestigial.

Common Cockroach (female).

2 The eggs are laid in a purse-like capsule, dark brown and nearly half an inch long, which may often be seen protruding from the hind body of the female for days before it is deposited in a warm crevice.

2 〉 This insect is not a true British native. It was
introduced from the Near East in the early seven-
teenth century and can only live in warm situations.

Larger than the Common Cockroach, and pale
reddish brown in colour. The elytra completely
cover the abdomen in both sexes.
American or Ship Cockroach, 1¼ inches.
(*Periplaneta americana*.)

Introduced from South America, now often found
in warm places on dock-sides, etc. Like the
Common Cockroach, this insect is nocturnal and
omnivorous.

Similar to above but much smaller. Colour shining
tawny brown. Crotan Bug or Shiner, ½ inch.
(*Blattella germanica*.)

Another introduced species which is now widely
distributed in Great Britain in restaurant kitchens,
bakeries, etc.

Colour brown; thorax with black centre and pale
margins. Elytra completely covering abdomen.
End of abdomen bearing two short, jointed
appendages. Head almost hidden beneath fore
part of thorax. Lapp Cockroach (male), ⅓–½ inch.
PL. 13. (*Ectobius lapponicus*.)

As above but elytra only half as long as abdomen.
Wings vestigial. Lapp Cockroach (female), ⅓–½ inch.
(*Ectobius lapponicus*.)

Locally distributed in southern England. Found
on bushes and low herbage or under stones and
3 〉 bark.

3 Colour dull yellow or pale yellowish brown.　Fore part of thorax without black central patch.　Elytra and wings as long as abdomen in both sexes.

Livid Cockroach, $\frac{1}{3}$–$\frac{1}{2}$ inch.
(*Ectobius lividus.*)

Locally distributed in the south of England, mainly in the coastal counties.　Found on low bushes or beneath dead leaves, etc.

Colour pale greyish brown with darker dots.　In the male the elytra and wings cover the abdomen, but in the female the hind-wings are vestigial and the elytra very short—covering only the first abdominal segment.　**Panzer's Cockroach,** $\frac{1}{4}$ inch or less.
(*Ectobius panzeri.*)

Locally distributed in coastal areas in south and south-east England on sand hills.

BEES, WASPS, SAWFLIES, ANTS, AND ICHNEUMON-FLIES

THE order Hymenoptera includes a large and extremely varied group of highly organized and specialized insects which rank as the most intelligent of the class. Because of their diversity it is sometimes difficult for the beginner to recognize the true relationship of several of the species. There are, however, a number of features which are common to all. The wings are membranous, transparent, and narrow; the fore-wings longer and rather broader than the hind-wings. The veins or nervules of the wings

 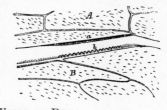

WINGS OF BEE
A. Hind edge of fore-wing with ridge and *B*. Fore edge of hind-wing with hooklets.

are few in number, thus differing from most of the other four-winged insects with which they might at first sight be confused. Even more characteristic is the peculiar manner in which the two wings on each side of the body are connected together in flight. This is effected by a series of small hooklets on the front margin of the hind-wing which catch on a fold on the hind margin of the fore-wing. The hook-and-fold arrangement cannot be seen with the naked eye but is clearly observable under a low-power microscope. The head is large, joined to the thorax by a neck, and freely movable. The mouth parts are specialized in various ways to suit the habits of the insect concerned. As a rule the mandibles are of the biting type but associated with them there is often a licking or sucking, tongue-like proboscis. This organ

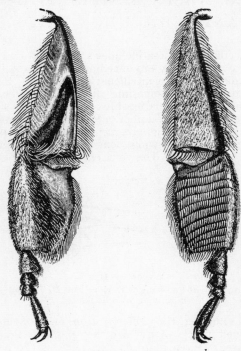

a   *b*

HIND-LEG OF HUMBLE-BEE
a. Outer side showing pollen basket.
b. Inner side, showing comb.

reaches its highest development in some bees, in which it is of considerable length and ends in a spoon-like struc-ture, enabling the insect to gain access to the nectar in deep-throated flowers. The legs are always fairly long and certain parts of them may be modified for some special purpose. In some forms the front legs are adapted for digging, in others two of the joints of the tarsus form a comb-like organ which is used to clean the antennae. In the social bees the shank of each hind-leg is broad and flat, with a fringe of long hair, and serves as a receptacle for pollen. Pollen collected on the body is brushed off by the legs and transferred to these pollen baskets.

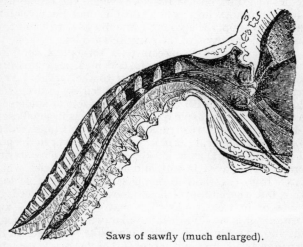

Saws of sawfly (much enlarged).

Here it accumulates till it forms the ball-like masses which are often noticed on the bees which visit garden flowers.

The females of all hymenopterous insects bear ovipositors. This may be clearly visible externally, as in several ichneumon-flies, or hidden until unsheathed and projected from the body, as in the bees and wasps. The ovipositor varies greatly in detail of structure according to the manner in which it is used. In the sawflies it takes the form of a saw, with which the insect saws slits in the tissues of plants for the reception of her eggs. In the horntails it is a boring instrument by means of which the solid wood of trees is penetrated and the eggs deposited deep in the narrow channel thus made. In the stinging bees, wasps, and ants the ovipositor becomes a sting, associated with poison glands, and may be used for aggression, as in the hunting wasps, which paralyse the insects and spiders destined as food for their larvae, or for defence, as in the social bees. The ichneumon-flies may be mentioned as examples of insects of this order in which the ovipositor is employed to place eggs on or inside the bodies of grubs, on the tissues of which the larvae feed. The involuntary host is not killed at once but lives long enough to supply the young ichneumons with fresh food until the completion of the parasite's growth.

All hymenopterous insects pass through a complete metamorphosis. The eggs are laid in a position which ensures an adequate food supply to the larvae. They may be deposited in a honey-stored cell, as in bees; in a chamber stocked with the bodies of insects or spiders, as in the hunting wasps; in a slit in a plant, as in sawflies; in a hole bored in a tree trunk, as in the horntails; on the body of a living grub, as in ichneumon-flies; or in the nest of another insect, as in cuckoo-bees and other parasitic forms. The larva is soft and legless in species which hatch from eggs laid in or on a readily available food store, but where the grub has to move about as it feeds on leaves or in tree trunks, like that of the sawflies and horntails, it is very like a caterpillar, with fully functional legs and, in some cases, with prolegs like those seen in the larvae of butterflies and moths. The pupa is quiescent, enclosed in a delicate skin but with the legs and wings separately ensheathed, resembling the pupae of beetles rather than those of butterflies and moths.

Many know bees and wasps only as social insects which live in large communities. But besides such colony builders as the humble-bees and social wasps, there are a large number of species which live solitary lives, never sharing their nests or activities with others of their kind. Among these are the Mining or Burrowing Bees, the Carpenter Bees, the so-called Nomad or Homeless Bees, and the Mason, Hunting, Digger, and Wood Wasps. A brief account of the habits of each of these types is included in the descriptive text which follows.

As an example of the manner of life of the social hymenoptera, a summary of events in the summer colony of a humble-bee may here be given. With the advent of warm spring days a female, which mated the previous summer and has lived through the winter in a state of torpor, awakens from her long sleep and is seen in fields and gardens visiting early flowers. Having collected a quantity of pollen she carries it to a previously chosen site in a hole or cavity in the ground. Here she has already constructed a waxen cell and in this receptacle her load of pollen, mixed with honey, is deposited. Next several eggs are laid in the cell and the aperture sealed over with wax. The bee now busies herself in forming a large, tub-like cell, placing it near the cell in which the eggs are hidden, and fills it with honey. She then crouches over her first cell for several days, obtaining what food she needs from the honey-filled tub near by. In about four days the eggs hatch and the soft, legless grubs begin to feed on the mess of pollen and honey by which they are surrounded. When this store is exhausted the female pierces a hole through the wall of the cell and feeds the larvae from her own mouth. When the grubs are full grown each spins a silken cocoon and pupates. The insects which arise from these pupae are small, imperfect females called workers. They are said to be imperfect because the sexual parts are imperfectly developed and they are incapable of mating. They can, however, under certain conditions, produce unfertilized eggs, from which only males develop. Soon after leaving the pupal cases these workers justify their name by helping their mother to collect food for the later broods which are already developing in newly built cells. When a sufficient number of workers has been raised the foundress of the nest rarely leaves home. Henceforth she confines herself to egg-laying; all other duties being carried out by her numerous helpers. It is for this reason that the large female humble-bees are seen in gardens only in spring. As the days lengthen the nest grows rapidly. Grubs are hatched every few days, more and more eggs are laid, and an ever-increasing army of workers appears to share the work of the community. As a safeguard against times of famine many of the older cells, and specially built waxen honey pots, are kept filled with reserves of food. These are left permanently open and attract numbers of prowling marauders which not infrequently raid and sometimes destroy the colony. Late in the season males, or drones, may appear from eggs laid by some of the workers. At the same time some of the eggs of the female, or queen, also produce males as well as perfect females. The two sexes pair during a nuptial flight, the impregnated females retiring soon after to a secluded hole or cavity to pass the winter in sleep and to become foundresses of new colonies the following spring. At the end of summer a prosperous nest of humble-bees may number three or four hundred individuals. With the onset of cold weather all die with the exception of the young impregnated females, which, as we have seen, are already safely ensconced in their winter quarters.

The history of a nest of the common wasp follows a similar course to that of the humble-bee but with several differences in detail. The young queen, or large female, on emerging from her winter sleep, constructs her first cell not on the floor of the nesting cavity but suspended from the roof. It is made not of wax but of papier mâché, formed from scrapings of wood rasped from old posts and fences by her jaws, masticated, and mixed with saliva. The foundation is laid in the form of a few cells hung from one or more small roots. This is gradually extended until a comb of some twenty or twenty-four cells has been built. An egg is laid in each cell and the whole roofed over with layers of wasp-paper. The cells are left open below and are not stored with food as in the bees. The grubs, which hatch in about a week after the eggs are laid, are fed by the queen, chiefly on animal juices. When full grown each spins a silken cocoon and pupates, the resulting imagines being small females or workers. In a day or two the workers leave the nest to collect food for the grubs and material for the enlargement of the comb. The queen now remains in the nest, spending all her energy on the production of eggs, placing each in a cell built by her assistants. As the nest grows the cavity in which it is placed is enlarged, soil being removed by the workers, who carry the particles of earth away in their jaws. A populous wasp nest consists of many tiers of cells attached to one another by slender

Nest of tree wasp with part of wall removed
to show tiers of cells.

columns of wasp-paper. Unlike the humble-bee, the wasp makes use of the same cells for two or three successive generations of eggs and grubs. Towards the end of the summer a large wasp colony will contain many thousands of individuals, made up of the female, or queen, with her large family of workers, some of which may also have contributed workers like themselves to the population. Later males and perfect females are hatched from eggs laid by the queen. After pairing the young queens hibernate but the rest of the colony perishes with the first frost.

The third group of social hymenoptera are represented by the ants. They differ from the bees and wasps in that their colonies remain active at all seasons and endure from year to year. The community consists of perfect females, males, and workers. The female, after her nuptial flight, enters the nesting chamber never to leave it. From then on her life is wholly occupied in laying. As in the bees and wasps, the sperm-cells received from the male at the time of mating are stored within her body and used to fertilize successive batches of eggs as they are passed from the ovaries. In all British ants the females and males are winged but the workers are wingless. Having mated, the female descends from her marriage flight and either re-enters the nest from which she came or finds a suitable spot in which to start a new colony. In either case, before embarking on her egg-laying career she divests herself of her wings by biting them off near their bases. Henceforth she will have no use for these organs, which might impede her movements in her underground home. Having reared a brood of small workers from her first batch of eggs, she devotes the rest of her life to the producing of more and still more eggs, her workers taking over all responsibility for the procuring of food, the rearing of the larvae, the extension and the defence and general welfare of the nest. Some time after midsummer males and perfect females are reared. These leave the nest to mate in flight. Some of the young impregnated females, perhaps the greater number, return to the original nest, for in the ant community there are many egg-laying females; not only one as in bees and wasps.

Ants, whether winged or wingless, may be distinguished from other insects by their large heads and long, thin waists, the hind segments of which bear small humps or nodes, most easily seen when the insect is examined in profile.

Besides the several kinds of hymenopterous insects dealt with in the following section, there are others which have been passed over as being too small to be likely to come to the notice of the non-specialist. Of these the most interesting are the gall wasps or gall-flies. They are responsible for the curious growths so often seen on plants of various kinds. Thus the mossy growths called robins' pincushions are caused by *Rhodites rosae*, the oak-apple by *Biorrhiza terminalis*, the marble gall by *Cynips kollari*, and the spangle gall by *Neuroterus lenticularis*, to name but a few of the most common.

These eccentric growths are caused by irritation set up in the plant's tissue as a result of the eggs being laid on or in them. As the galls grow they provide food for the grubs which live within. When mature the gall wasp bores a way out of its nursery to enjoy the life of a winged insect. The numerous pin-holes seen on the surface of old oak-apples reveal the means by which its erstwhile

Gall wasp laying egg in bud.
(Much enlarged.)

inhabitants have effected their exits. The oak-apple and robins' pincushion are examples of galls which shelter a number of developing gall wasps in their interior; while the marble gall and the spangle gall may be mentioned as among those whose cavity is occupied by but one inmate. British gall wasps, though they differ considerably in appearance in the various species, are all small, black, rather ant-like insects with slender, stalk-like waists. Several have complicated life histories involving the appearance of wingless females in one generation and winged females in the next, each form causing galls of a kind peculiar to itself. Thus the winged female which emerges from an oak-apple lays her eggs beneath the soil on the rootlets of an oak. These give rise to grubs which live and feed in root galls, in which they later pupate. The females which come from these galls are wingless. It is from their eggs, laid in the leaf buds of an oak branch, that the oak-apple grubs hatch.

SECTION VIII

ANTS, HORNTAILS, SAWFLIES, BEES, WASPS, AND ICHNEUMON-FLIES

1 {
Fore part of abdomen forming a slender pedicel or stalk, bearing hump-like protuberances, or nodes. **Ants.**  2

Abdomen not as described. 3
}

2 {
Insect dark brown with reddish-brown thorax, pedicel, and legs. Workers about ¼ inch or a little less; females and males about ⅜ inch. **Wood Ant.** (*Formica rufa.*)

Widely distributed in woods. The nest is hidden beneath a domed heap which often attains to imposing dimensions. This hillock covers a labyrinth of passages and innumerable chambers in which the populous colony is housed. In long-established settlements several mounds may be connected to the main, original habitation, the whole colony covering an area of many square yards. The Wood Ant is bold and aggressive. Intruders are met with jets of formic acid exuded from glands on the sides of the thorax of the wingless workers. These insects will also attack with their jaws. The appetite of the Wood Ant is catholic, both animal and vegetable food being taken. Insects are killed and carried to the nest, seeds are collected, and honey-dew and nectar sipped.
}

2 Similar to the Wood Ant but more ruddy brown, particularly on the head, thorax, and legs.

Blood-red Ant.
(*Formica sanguinea.*)

Unlike the last species, which this insect closely resembles in appearance, the inappropriately named Blood-red Ant does not build a domed mound above its nest. In appetite it is more strictly carnivorous, feeding largely on insects, including other ants. It also raids the nests of smaller ants and carries off cocoons, the workers emerging from these being kept as slaves.

Head, thorax, and abdomen dark brown, with lighter antennae and legs. Head long. Length of workers about $\frac{1}{8}$ inch; females and males $\frac{1}{4}$ inch.

Negro Ant.
(*Formica fusca.*)

This small, dark brown ant is common in woods and in waste places among tall herbage. It frequently occurs in shady corners in gardens. The nest is underground with no mound of any kind to indicate its position. Like the two species mentioned above, the Negro Ant keeps Aphides in the nest for their honey-dew and also visits plants to sip nectar and to 'milk' leaf-haunting plant-lice.

Ant black or blackish brown. The workers are of two kinds, large and small. The former measure about $\frac{1}{4}$ inch in length, the latter, which are the more numerous, about $\frac{1}{8}$ inch.

Black Garden Ant.
(*Acanthomyops nigra.*)

This is the small, shining black ant so often seen in gardens. The nest is either underground or in a hollow tree stump, under stones, etc. In habits

2   this species closely resembles the Negro Ant. The emergence of the young females and males from the nest preparatory to their nuptial flights is a familiar sight in July and August in most gardens.

Head and body rather light brown, legs yellowish. Size similar to that of the Black Garden Ant. PL. 59. **Yellow Ant.**
(*Acanthomyops flava.*)

Very common in fields and meadows, where it raises long mounds of earth beneath which the nests are located. This is one of the species which is most often raided by the Blood-red Ant.

3   Base of abdomen joined to thorax without constriction or waist.   **4**

Abdomen joined to thorax by waist or slender stalk.   **13**

4   Insect ½ inch or more in length.   **5**

Insect less than ½ inch in length.   **8**

5   Colour a combination of black and yellow.   **6**

Insect black.   **7**

6   Head and thorax black, abdomen yellow. Antennae long.   **Great Horntail (male),** 1 inch.
(*Sirex gigas.*)

6 As above but abdomen with broad black band across middle and long, thin ovipositor projecting beneath the hind end., PL. 59.

Great Horntail (female), 1½ inches— excluding ovipositor.

The largest of the British hymenoptera. The ovipositor of the female emerges from a sheath beneath the abdomen, its full length being about ¾ inch. This instrument is used to bore into the wood of fir-trees, in which the eggs are deposited. The larva tunnels through the wood for several years before pupating. The Great Horntail is locally distributed in districts where fir- and spruce-trees are abundant.

Body of insect many times longer than broad. Head and thorax black, abdomen blue-black, ending in a short point. Antennae long, pale brown. **Lesser Horntail**, ¾ inch. (*Sirex noctilio.*)

The ovipositor is much shorter than in the Great Horntail. Eggs are laid in the wood of pine- and fir-trees. Locally distributed in Great Britain.

Insect bee-like in general appearance but head, thorax, and abdomen shining black with yellowish-grey hair. Antennae clubbed. Fore-wings with dark margin.

Hawthorn Sawfly, ½ inch. (*Trichiosoma tibialis.*)

Fairly common on and about hawthorns. The female lays her eggs in small slits cut in the tissue of the plant. The

7 larva feeds on the leaves and

7) pupates in a brown, cylindrical case which is attached to a branch. When ready to emerge the sawfly cuts out a hinged lid and pushes its way out. These interesting little cases are waterproof and remain in position for some time after their makers have left them.

Similar to above but much larger and the antennae yellow. The thorax and head, too, are less hairy than in the Hawthorn Sawfly.

Birch Sawfly (male), $\frac{4}{5}$ inch
to (female) 1 inch.
(*Cimbex femorata.*)

A scarce and local British insect, occasionally found in birch woods.

8 { Abdomen wholly yellow. **9**

Abdomen not wholly yellow. **10**

Head black. Thorax black with yellow border. Abdomen, antennae, and legs yellow. Fore margin of fore-wings dark.

Gooseberry Sawfly (female), $\frac{1}{4}$ inch.
(*Pteronus ribesii.*)

Common in gardens and orchards where gooseberries are grown. The eggs are laid in slits cut in the young leaves. The larvae are at first green spotted with black but later become pale green without markings. In the male the abdomen is black.

Head and antennae black. Thorax and abdomen yellow. Legs yellow marked with black.

Turnip Sawfly, $\frac{1}{4}$ inch.
(*Athalia spinarum.*)

9)

9 ⎤ Common in fields and gardens where turnips are
grown. The larva is at first pale yellow or cream
with black spots on the head. Later it becomes
almost black and is known as the Nigger-worm.

Head, thorax, and antennae black. Abdomen
yellow. Front margin of fore-wings very dark.
Antennae short. **Rose Hylotoma**, ¼ inch.
(*Hylotoma rosae.*)

Common on roses. Eggs are laid in the leaves, on
which the bluish-green larvae subsequently feed.

Head and thorax black. Abdomen and legs
yellow. Antennae long.
Lyda nemoralis (**male**), ⅛ inch.

Locally distributed on and about fruit trees on
which the larvae feed. (For female *see* No. 12.)

10 ⎧ Abdomen yellow with black spot. **11**

⎨ Abdomen black with yellow or whitish markings.
12

11. Head black, thorax black with yellow front
margin. Abdomen yellow with large black spot.
Pine Sawfly, ⅛ inch.
(*Lophyrus pini.*)

Common in pine forests, where the larvae are very
destructive, feeding on the young leaves and
shoots.

12 ⎫ Head black. Thorax black edged yellow. Abdomen black with yellow base. Front edge of fore-
wings dark. Antennae and legs yellowish brown.
Apple Sawfly, ¼ inch or less.
(*Hoplocampa testudinea.*)

12 A common orchard pest. Eggs are laid in slits at the base of blossoms and the whitish larvae feed on the young fruits, into which they bore. When the apples fall the grubs bury themselves in the ground to pupate.

Head and thorax black, the latter with two small white dots. Abdomen black with conspicuous band of white below the middle. Front margin of fore-wings dark. **Rose Emphytus,** $\frac{1}{4}$ inch. (*Emphytus cinctus.*)

Common on roses, on the foliage of which the white-dotted green larvae feed.

Head and thorax black. Abdomen black with broad central band of orange. Front edge of fore-wings dark. PL. 59. **Large Larch Sawfly,** $\frac{1}{2}$ inch. (*Pteronus erichsoni.*)

Locally distributed in larch plantations. The larvae feed on the young shoots and pupate in the ground.

Head black. Thorax black, with or without yellowish markings on fore margin and centre. Abdomen with alternate bands of black and yellow, giving the insect a wasp-like appearance. Antennae long. *Lyda nemoralis* **(female),** $\frac{3}{8}$ inch.

Locally distributed on and near fruit trees, on which the larvae feed. (For male *see* No. 9.)

Head and thorax black. Abdomen black on basal half; yellow on hind half. Antennae long. Fore-wings with smoky band across middle. *Neurotoma flaviventris,* $\frac{1}{3}$ inch.

Locally common on fruit trees and hawthorns The larva is orange with black head.

13

Insects with both thorax and abdomen very hairy. **14**

Insects with thorax very hairy but abdomen not very hairy. **23**

Insects with neither thorax nor abdomen very hairy. **26**

14

Outer side of shank of hind-leg flattened, smooth, and fringed with stiff hairs, forming the 'pollen basket' in which pollen is carried. **15**

Outer side of shank of hind-leg rounded and hairy, i.e. without pollen basket. **22**

15

End of abdomen red or deep orange. **16**

End of abdomen not red or deep orange. **17**

16

Head, thorax, and legs black. Abdomen black with last three segments bright foxy red. Female ⅔ inch long; worker ⅖ inch. **Large Red-tailed Humble-bee.** (*Bombus lapidarius.*)

Common in most parts of England and Wales, becoming less abundant and more local in Scotland. The large, robustly built female is seen in May and early June. The male is similar to the worker but has a somewhat longer abdomen and the thorax is greyish yellow on the front border. The nest is built in a hole in a bank.

Similar to the last species but smaller and with the red 'tail' less bright. **Red-tailed Carder Bee.** (*Bombus derhamellus.*)

16 — Female about ⅔ inch, worker about ½ inch. Generally distributed and common in most parts of Great Britain. The nest is made on the surface of the ground and covered with moss.

Closely resembling the Large Red-tailed Humble-bee in size and general appearance but thorax banded with greyish yellow and with thin band of the same colour on the abdomen.

Early Humble-bee.
(*Bombus pratorum.*)

Widely distributed and generally common. The female appears earlier in the spring than the Large Red-tailed Humble-bee. The nest may be either in a hole or on the surface of the ground.

17 — Thorax yellowish or reddish brown. **18**

Thorax not as described. **19**

Thorax dull yellow or pale brown, sometimes with a few blackish hairs. Abdomen darker, greyish brown covered with yellowish hairs, which are thickest at the base and towards the extremity where they form a pale-coloured tail.

Common Carder Bee.
(*Bombus agrorum.*)

One of the small humble-bees, the female measuring about ½ inch in length, the males and workers somewhat less. The nest is built on the ground, usually among trees or tall undergrowth. A widely distributed and generally common species.

Thorax reddish brown with yellowish border. Abdomen deep brown banded with lighter, yellowish brown, and with pale extremity.

Moss Carder Bee.
(*Bombus muscorum.*)

18 —

18 Widely distributed and fairly common. Makes its nest in grass or moss in meadows and fields. Female and male about $\frac{3}{5}$ inch long; worker $\frac{2}{5}$ inch.

Similar to the last species but thorax uniform brown. Tip of abdomen black.

Brown Carder Bee.
(*Bombus solstitialis.*)

19 { Tip of abdomen buff. **20**

Tip of abdomen white. **21**

20. Head and thorax black, the latter with a band of dull yellow on the front margin. Abdomen black with a broad band of yellow across the middle and brownish- or yellowish-buff tail which is sometimes fringed with white. PL. 59. **Buff-tailed Humble-bee.**
(*Bombus terrestris.*)

Common and widely distributed. The nest is built underground at the end of a tunnel. This humble-bee is about the same size as the Large Red-tailed species—female over $\frac{3}{4}$ inch, male $\frac{3}{5}$ inch, worker $\frac{1}{2}$ inch.

Head and thorax black, the latter with a band of yellow on the front margin and another at the base. Abdomen black with dull yellow band on the first two segments and a white tail. Female nearly 1 inch long; male and worker about $\frac{5}{8}$ inch. PL. 14.
Large Garden Humble-bee.
(*Bombus ruderatus.*)

21 Widely distributed and generally common in England but rather local in Scotland. General appearance that of a large black bee with dull yellow collar and small white tail. Builds its nest underground.

21 ⎫ Similar to above but smaller. Female ¾ inch, male
and workers ½ inch. **Small Garden Humble-bee.**
(*Bombus hortorum.*)

Common in most parts of the British Isles.

Head black. Thorax black with yellow band on
front border. Abdomen black with broad central
yellow band and conspicuous white tail.
Small Earth Humble-bee.
(*Bombus lucorum.*)

Very like the Buff-tailed Humble-bee (No. 20),
except for the pure white tail. Common throughout the British Isles. Nest placed underground.
Female over ¾ inch long; male and worker ½ inch.

Head black. Thorax black with yellow front and
hind margins. Abdomen black with one or two
thin bands of greyish yellow. Tail white, sometimes suffused grey or yellow. Hair on body
shorter and thinner than in the other humble-bees.
Short-haired Humble-bee.
(*Bombus subterraneus.*)

Locally distributed in England, chiefly in the south
and east. Nests underground. Female about
¾ inch long, male nearly ¾ inch, worker ⅜ inch.

Head black. Thorax black with yellowish-grey
borders. Abdomen yellowish grey with two black
bands and dull white tail. Female ⅝ inch, male
and worker ½ inch. **Knapweed Carder Bee.**
(*Bombus sylvarum.*)

Common in most parts of England, local in Scotland. This bee owes its popular name to its fond-
ness for the flowers of the black knapweed. The
nest is built on the surface of the ground or in a
⎩ small, shallow tunnel.

Head and thorax black. Abdomen black with yellowish-red tail. Wings smoky. PL. 14.

Red-tailed Cuckoo-bee.
(*Psithyrus rupestris.*)

Very like the Large Red-tailed Humble-bee, for which it is very often mistaken. Like all the Cuckoo-bees it lacks pollen-baskets on the hind legs, makes no honey but lives parasitically on other bees. This species victimizes the Large Red-tailed Bee which it so closely resembles, raiding the nest in spring, killing the foundress, then living on the stores of honey and leaving its offspring to be tended by the workers of the slain female. Female over $\frac{3}{4}$ inch long; male $\frac{3}{8}$ inch. Fairly common near the nests of its victims.

22

Head black. Thorax black with band of dull yellow on front margin. Abdomen black with white tail. Wings tinged grey. Female $\frac{3}{4}$ inch long, male $\frac{3}{5}$ inch. PL. 14. **Vestal Cuckoo-bee.**
(*Psithyrus vestalis.*)

Widely distributed. Victimizes the Buff-tailed Humble-bee.

Head black. Thorax black with yellow on the fore and hind margins. Abdomen black, thinly fringed with yellow hairs at its extremity. Wings tinged brownish grey. PL. 14. **Field Cuckoo-bee.**
(*Psithyrus campestris.*)

Victimizes the Common and Moss Carder Bees and is widely distributed.

23

Thorax tawny or yellow.   24

Thorax brown or black.   25

Head black, thorax covered with reddish or tawny hair. Abdomen black with yellowish down, except at tip. PL. 60. **Tawny Burrowing Bee,** ½ inch.
(*Andrena fulva.*)

A widely distributed and generally common species which makes an early appearance in spring, when it may often be seen in gardens. Nests in burrows in the ground.

Head and thorax clad in yellowish or tawny hairs. Abdomen dark brown with fringes of pale hair on the segments. Head large, almost round. Wings slightly dusky. PL. 60. **Leaf-cutter Bee,** ⅔ inch.
(*Megachile centuncularis.*)

This is the bee which cuts the neat, circular sections from the leaves of rose bushes for the purpose

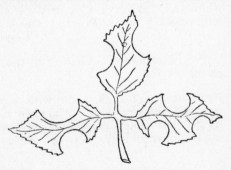

of lining her cells. Nests in a burrow. Widely distributed and generally common.

Head and thorax covered with reddish-brown hair. Abdomen dark brown and shining, with thin covering of orange down. **Red Osmia,** ½ inch.
(*Osmia rufa.*)

24

24 Common and widely distributed. This small bee bores into rotting fence posts, tree stumps, old walls, soft banks, etc., or may utilize an existing hole or crevice for nesting purposes.

Head black with white hairs. Thorax black with brownish grey hairs. Abdomen black with fringes of short white hair between the segments and a sparse covering of dusky hairs on the intervening spaces. PL. 60. **Davies's Colletes,** $\frac{1}{3}$ inch. (*Colletes daviesiana.*)

Common and widely distributed. In general appearance resembles a small hive bee. The female makes burrows in sandy banks, in which she constructs a number of cells from a secretion exuded from her mouth. These are then filled with a paste composed of pollen and nectar. This insect may often be found on composite flowers in summer.

Similar to the last species, but with head and thorax more densely covered in brown hair. On the abdomen the interspaces between the fringes of short white hairs are black and shining.

Girdled Colletes, $\frac{1}{3}$ inch. (*Colletes succincta.*)

Widely distributed in Great Britain. Often common on heaths.

Like the Girdled Colletes but much larger.

Large Colletes, $\frac{1}{2}$ inch. (*Colletes cunicularia.*)

Locally distributed in the west of England.

25 Head black with white hairs on the face. Thorax black, covered with pale brown hairs. Abdomen

25 dark brown and shining, with short orange or red hairs at the tip.

> **White-faced Burrowing Bee (female)**, ½ inch.
> (*Andrena albicans.*)

As above but hair on face pale brown. Antennae very long.

> **White-faced Burrowing Bee (male)**, ½ inch.

Widely distributed and generally common. One of the first bees to appear in spring; often seen on catkins and blackthorn blossom in March. Makes its cells in small burrows in the soil.

Head and thorax black, the latter with greyish hair. Abdomen black with broad band of reddish yellow across the middle. PL. 60.

> **Belted Burrowing Bee**, ⅓ inch.
> (*Andrena cingulata.*)

Widely distributed in fields, meadows, etc.

Hair on head and thorax black (female), or greyish brown (male), contrasting with the orange pubescence on the abdomen. PL. 60.

> **Two-coloured Osmia**, ½ inch.
> (*Osmia bicolor.*)

Locally distributed on limestone and chalky soils. The female often makes use of an empty snail shell for nesting.

Head, thorax, and abdomen black, with covering of brown hairs on the thorax. Each segment of the abdomen has a small yellow dot on each side. Head large and round. Wings slightly dusky. PL. 61. **Wool-carder Bee (female)**, ½ inch to (male), ⅔ inch.

> (*Anthidium manicatum.*)

25 Unlike all other bees, the male in this species is larger than the female. The female is remarkable for her habit of stripping the woolly hairs from plants with pubescent stems and leaves. This material she rolls into a ball which may assume such dimensions before being carried off as to be as large as the insect. The woolly hairs are used to line the burrow in which the cells are made.

26 {

Abdomen oval, joining the thorax by short stalk or pedicel.   **27**

Abdomen long and narrow, joining the thorax by long, slender stalk or pedicel.   **37**

27 {

Head, thorax, and abdomen black.

Black Wasp (sp.)

Black Wasps, of which there are many species, may be seen throughout the summer resting in the sun or moving busily among foliage or herbage and looking like small black flies. They make burrows in decaying posts, old tree stumps, plant stems, or in sandy soil, provisioning the cells with plant lice and similar small prey, on which the larvae feed. All are small; some less than $\frac{1}{4}$ inch long. The species illustrated (PL. 15) is one of the larger forms but is less than $\frac{1}{2}$ inch in length.

Abdomen yellow with brown or black bands.   **28**

Abdomen black with yellow bands.   **31**

28 {
Insect 1 inch or more in length.   **29**

Insect less than 1 inch in length.   **30**
}

29.   Head yellow marked with brown. Thorax brown. Abdomen brown at base, yellow beyond the middle with dark brown bands and small spots on the sides of the segments. Antennae and legs brown.

Hornet, 1 inch.   (*Vespa crabro.*)

The largest of British wasps. Readily distinguished from the common wasps by its larger size and brown markings. The nest is usually built in a hollow tree but may sometimes be in a hole in a bank or even in a building. In shape and structure it resembles that of the Common Wasp but is larger. The Hornet is widely but locally distributed in Britain and is not generally common.

Head yellow, with black top and facial markings. Thorax black with yellow on the sides and hind margins. Abdomen yellow with black bands, which run to a point in the middle, and black spots at the sides of the segments. Antennae black. Legs yellow with black bases. PL. 61.

Common Wasp.   (*Vespa vulgaris.*)

Very common throughout the British Isles. The nest is placed underground and consists of a comb of paper, made by masticating fragments of wood scraped from posts, etc. The female, or queen, seen in spring, is much larger than the workers which appear later. Though this insect shows so strong a liking for syrups and sweets in late summer, it is largely carnivorous, destroying large numbers of insects and their grubs. The queen wasp is about $\frac{3}{4}$ inch long, the male $\frac{5}{8}$, the worker $\frac{1}{2}$ inch.

Very similar to the Common Wasp but the middle points on the black abdominal bands are rather more pronounced. This feature is most noticeable

30 in the female. The workers of the two species are

30 ⎫ so much alike that they are very difficult to identify with certainty. **German Wasp.** (*Vespa germanica.*)

As common as the last species; similar habits.

Antennae marked with a line of yellow. Abdomen shining yellow banded with black; band on second segment thicker than the others. Side spots absent.
Tree Wasp. (*Vespa sylvestris.*)

Rather locally distributed but not uncommon. The female and worker are about the same size as in the Common Wasps, but the male is almost as large as the queen. This species suspends its nest from the branch of a tree. It is a globular or pear-shaped structure, substantial and waterproof.

Similar to the Tree Wasp but darker; the yellow being duller and the black bands thicker. **Norwegian Wasp.**
Pl. 61. (*Vespa norvegica.*)

Locally distributed but fairly common in some areas. The nest is built in a bush or shrub, sometimes in a tall hedge.

Head and thorax with slight yellow markings. Fore part of abdomen, which forms the waist, black, remainder of abdomen yellow with black bands. Legs yellow. Pl. 61.
Field Digger Wasp (female), ⅜ inch.
(male), ⅖ inch. (*Mellinus arvensis.*)

Has the general appearance of a small, rather long-waisted specimen of the Common Wasp but its mode of life is very different. The female digs a burrow deep in sandy soil and there constructs a number of cells, stocking each with several flies. On the top of each such store an egg is laid, the resulting larvae feeding on the provisions. This little wasp is widely distributed and locally common.

31 ⎧ Head black with yellow face. Thorax black with
⎩ three small yellow dots. Abdomen black with

31 bright yellow bands on the hind segments. Legs yellowish red. PL. 15. **Solidago Nomad Bee,** ⅓ inch.
(*Nomada solidaginis.*)

A small bee which looks like a wasp. The female lays her eggs in the cells of other bees, making no nest of her own. May be seen on flowers through the summer and has a special liking for the blossoms of the golden rod (*Solidago*). Widely distributed and generally fairly common.

Very similar to the last species but larger and duller in colour. PL. 15. **Gooden's Nomad Bee,** ½ inch.
(*Nomada goodeniana.*)

This species is also parasitic on other bees and is common in many parts of Great Britain.

Head black. Thorax black marked with yellow on the front margin. Abdomen shining black, narrowly barred with pale yellow or cream.
Spiny Mason Wasp, ½ inch.
(*Odynerus spinipes.*)

Widely distributed and fairly common in dry, sandy districts. The female tunnels a nesting place in a sandy bank, provisioning each cell with a number of small caterpillars that have been paralysed by stinging but not killed. On these the larvae feed.

Similar to the last but with a broader yellow band on the hind margin of the first abdominal segment.
Wall Mason Wasp, ½ inch.
(*Odynerus parietum.*)

Widely distributed and common in many parts of Great Britain. Nests in tunnels made in walls or buildings.

32 Abdomen black and orange. **33**

Abdomen not black and orange. **34**

33 Head and thorax black. Abdomen long, bright orange, or red, with two dusky bands and black

33) tip. Wing smoky with darker tips. Antennae
curled. Legs long, spiny, and black.
Banded Spider-hunting Wasp, ⅔ inch.
(*Pompilus viaticus.*)

Widely distributed and locally common on sandy
heaths. On sunny days the female may be seen
running rapidly over the ground, her long legs
assisted by upraised wings, hunting for spiders with
which to store the underground nest as provender
for the larvae. The male is somewhat smaller and
may be found on flowers.

Similar to the last species but smaller and with
broken, dusky lines instead of bands across the
reddish-yellow segments of the abdomen. PL. 15.
Lesser Red-and-black Spider Wasp, ⅖ inch.
(*Pompilus spissus.*)

Another widely distributed species which haunts
dry, sandy places. '

Head, thorax, antennae, and
legs black. Fore part of abdomen black, forming a long, very
thin stalk. Hinder part of
abdomen orange with black
extremity. Wing-tips dusky.
PL. 15. **Red-banded Sand Wasp,** ¾ inch.
(*Sphex sabulosa.*)

A striking and very active insect which digs burrows in
sandy soil and hunts caterpillars with which to store
them. Widely distributed in sandy coastal districts.

Similar to the Red-banded Sand Wasp but smaller.
More often found in inland areas.
Field Sand Wasp, ⅗ inch.
(*Sphex campestris.*)

Similar to the last species but with larger, broader
abdomen and very hairy thorax and legs.
Hairy Sand Wasp, ⅗ inch.
(*Sphex hirsuta.*)

33 Locally distributed on sandy heaths and similar places in southern England.

Head black. Thorax black with yellow front edge and a spot of the same colour near the hind border. Abdomen black with two yellow bands. Antennae long, black. Legs yellow with black bases.
Banded Ichneumon, ⅝ inch.
(*Ichneumon amatorius.*)

A fairly common species. The female lays her eggs in the bodies of caterpillars on the tissues of which the ichneumon grub feeds. The caterpillar lives long enough to pupate, then dies, the fully developed ichneumon-fly emerging from its corpse.

34 Tip of abdomen bearing a conspicuous tail-like appendage. **35**

Abdomen without tail-like appendage. **36**

Head and very long an-
tennae black. Thorax and
abdomen black with yel-
low bands. Legs yellowish
brown. Tail double, as
long as the body.
Great Black Ichneumon,
1¼ inches—excluding tail.
(*Rhyssa persuasoria.*)

The largest of British ichneumon-flies. The long
tail-like appendage is the
ovipositor with its pro-
tecting sheaths. The
female lays her eggs on the
larvae of the Great Horntail
35 (No. 6), to reach which she

35 bores several inches into the wood of fir-trees. Locally distributed in fir woods.

Head, thorax, and abdomen black. Antennae long. Legs brown. Tail as long as body.

> **Bristle-tailed Ichneumon,**
> ¾ inch—excluding ovipositor.
> (*Lissonota setosa.*)

The female of this species lays her eggs in the bodies of the goat-moth larvae which live in decaying trees. Locally distributed but not uncommon where it occurs.

Similar to above but much smaller. Female with ovipositor twice as long as the body.

> **Small Bristle-tail,** ¼ inch.
> (*Lissonota sulphurifera.*)

The female lays her eggs in the caterpillars of some of the Clearwing moths.

Head, antennae, and abdomen black. Legs reddish brown. Tail short and stout.

> **Red-legged Pimpla,** ⅖ inch.
> (*Pimpla rufata.*)

Widely distributed and common in many parts of the British Isles. The eggs are laid in the caterpillars of the large white butterfly.

Head, long, slender antennae, abdomen, and legs dully yellow or pale orange. Hind part of abdomen curved downwards and flattened from side to side. Pl 13.

> **Yellow Ophion,** ¾ inch.
> (*Ophion luteus.*)

36

36) A widely distributed and generally common insect
which often enters lighted rooms, sometimes in
large numbers. Its eggs are laid in the bodies of
caterpillars of several kinds.

Similar to the Yellow Ophion but more slender.
Head and antennae black. Thorax and tip of
abdomen dusky or greyish black.

Slender Paniscus, ½ inch.
(*Paniscus virgatus.*)

Fairly common in many parts of Great Britain.
The female lays her eggs on the skin of the caterpillars of small moths.

N.B. The males of the ichneumon-flies described in
No. 35 are, of course, all tailless.

DRAGONFLIES

THERE is little likelihood of a dragonfly being mistaken for any other kind of insect. Though the species vary considerably in size and much in coloration all resemble one another closely in general shape. Characteristic features are the large, broad head with huge compound eyes, long body, four large, netted wings in which the fore and hind pair are of equal length, and the minute, bristle-like antennae. In the males the long abdomen ends in a pair of claspers. These are used to hold the female, either by the head or neck, during mating. This operation takes place during flight, the paired insects flying tandem fashion.

Fertilization is effected by the female bending her abdomen forward until the tip is brought into contact with the underside of the male's second abdominal segment, on which a mass of spermatozoa has previously been deposited. In some species the male retains his hold on the female till the eggs have been laid, in others the sexes separate soon after pairing. The eggs are laid in water and the nymphs are aquatic. Dragonfly nymphs are long-bodied, large-headed creatures with rather long legs. They are remarkable for the extraordinary development of the labium or lower lip. This forms a large, roughly triangular process which is hinged and capable of rapid move-ment. Normally it is hidden beneath the head, but when prey, in the form of an insect, small worm, water snail, or tadpole, comes within reach, the mask, as it is called, is shot forwards, the victim

Dragonfly larva, showing mask.

impaled on the two sharp teeth on its fore corners, brought back to the strong jaws, and devoured. These nymphs are active and voracious at all stages of their development. Respiration is carried out partly through spiracles which open on certain of the thoracic segments but mainly by means of gill-like structures concealed in the hind part of the body. When ready for its final transformation the nymph creeps from the water up the stem of a water plant or reed and becomes quiescent. Soon the skin along the back splits and the imago pulls itself out. When finally released it remains for a time resting on the nymphal skin to enable the cuticle to dry and harden and the abdomen and wings to expand.

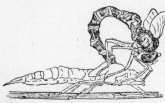

Dragonfly releasing itself from nymphal skin.

There are over forty species of British dragonflies. All are predatory, hunting insects of all kinds on the wing and sometimes dipping down to snatch a victim from a plant or the water surface. All three pairs of legs are directed forwards and are used not for walking but to capture prey and in alighting and holding to leaves or stems when the insect settles.

Although some of the larger dragonflies are known in some rural localities as horse-stingers, these insects are devoid of any means of stinging or otherwise harming any warm-blooded animal.

SECTION IX
DRAGONFLIES

1 {
Large dragonflies with robust bodies and eyes which meet at the centre of the head. Hind-wings broader at bases than fore-wings. PL. 62. **2**

Smaller, delicately built dragonflies with very slender bodies. Eyes not meeting at centre of head. Hind-wings not broader at bases than fore-wings. PL. 62. **15**
}

2 {
Abdomen broad and flattened, with tapering or rounded tip. **3**

Not as above described. **4**
}

3 {
Eyes and thorax brown. Abdomen tapering; reddish brown with yellow spots on the sides. Hind-wings with large brown patch at bases. All wings with dark brown spot near middle. Length of head and body 2 inches.
Four-spotted Libellula.
(*Libellula quadrimaculata.*)

Widely distributed and locally common in many parts of Great Britain in spring and summer. Has strong, rapid, darting flight.

Wings with dark bases but without central spot. Abdomen not tapering. Head and thorax brown. Abdomen blue with yellow spots on side margins (male), or tawny brown with yellow side spots (female and immature male). Length of head and body 2 inches. **Flat-bodied Libellula.**
(*Libellula depressa.*)

Locally common in the southern half of England, but rare or absent elsewhere in Great Britain.
}

4 $\left\{\begin{array}{l} \text{Abdomen black or black and yellow.} \qquad \textbf{5} \\[1em] \text{Abdomen other than black or black and yellow.} \quad \textbf{6} \end{array}\right.$

5 $\left\{\vphantom{\begin{array}{l}1\\2\\3\\4\\5\\6\\7\\8\\9\\10\\11\\12\\13\\14\\15\\16\\17\\18\\19\\20\\21\\22\end{array}}\right.$

Eyes green. Thorax black and yellow. Abdomen black with yellow bands. Length of head and body about 3 inches. PL. 62
Great Black-and-yellow Dragonfly.
(*Cordulegaster boltonii.*)

Locally distributed in England, Wales, and Scotland; sometimes fairly abundant in favoured areas from June to mid September.

Eyes blue (male) or pale brown (female). Thorax dark brown marked with pale green or yellow, covered with velvety pile. Abdomen black or blackish brown marked with short streaks or spots of blue (male), or yellow (female). Length of head and body about 2 inches. **Hairy Dragonfly.**
(*Brachyton pratense.*)

Locally distributed in England, from the south coast to Yorkshire, and Ireland.

Eyes brown. Thorax and abdomen black. Wings clear. Length of head and body about 1½ inches.
Black Sympetrum (male).
(*Sympetrum danaë.*)

Eyes brown. Thorax black spotted with yellow. Abdomen yellow or yellowish brown with blackish base, tip, and sides. Length about 1½ inches.
Black Sympetrum (female).

Locally common in Great Britain from July to October. Usually found near water or on swampy ground.

6 ⎰ Abdomen dark brown or yellow.   **7**

  ⎱ Abdomen other than dark brown or yellow.   **8**

7 ⎰ Eyes blue (male) or green (female). Thorax dark brown streaked with blue and yellow. Abdomen dark brown marked with bright blue (male) or yellowish green (female). Front edges of wings golden yellow. Length of head and body about 2¾ inches.   **Common Aeshna.**
(*Aeshna juncea.*)

Widely distributed and generally common from July to September.

Similar to above but thorax pale green (male) or yellow (female), striped with brown. Length of head and body about 2¾ inches.
    Southern Aeshna.
    (*Aeshna cyanea.*)

Common in many parts of the southern half of England but scarce or absent elsewhere in Britain. Flies over water and nearby country from June to October.

8 ⎰ Abdomen tawny or light brown.   **9**

  ⎱ Abdomen other than tawny or light brown.   **10**

9 ⎰ Eyes blue (male) or pale brown (female). Body tawny brown; sides of thorax yellow. Abdomen showing a few small blue or yellow spots. Length of head and body nearly 3 inches. **Brown Aeshna.**
    (*Aeshna grandis.*)

Locally common in the southern half of England, rare elsewhere in Great Britain. Flies from July to September. Sometimes seen far from water.

9 — Eyes brown.   Thorax yellowish brown striped and edged with cream.   Abdomen pale brown.   Fore edges of wings yellow.   Length of head and body about 1⅖ inches.   **Keeled Orthetrum (female).**
(*Orthetrum caerulescens.*)

Locally distributed in the southern and midland counties of England and in Ireland.   Rare elsewhere in the British Isles.   Usually seen over still water or in marshy places from June to early September.   (For male *see* No. 11.)

Eyes brown.   Thorax yellowish brown on top, yellow at sides.   Abdomen yellowish brown.   Wings without yellow fore edges.   Length of head and body about 1½ inches.
Common Sympetrum (female).
(*Sympetrum striolatum.*)

Widely distributed and common in many parts of Great Britain.   Flies over pools, fields, and roadsides from July to October.
(For male *see* No. 14.)

10 — Abdomen blue.   **11**

Abdomen not blue.   **12**

Eyes blue.   Thorax green or greenish blue.   Abdomen azure blue with black stripe down centre and black lines down the sides.   Length of head and body about 3 inches.
Emperor Dragonfly (male).
(*Anax imperator.*)

A large and brilliant insect which is locally distributed and usually scarce in southern England.   Rare further north; absent from Scotland and Ireland.   Usually seen in strong, soaring flight over or near

11 — water.   (For female *see* No. 13.)

11 }
Eyes blue. Thorax dark brown marked with two cream stripes. Abdomen pale blue. Length of head and body about 1⅝ inches.
Keeled Orthetrum (male).
(*Orthetrum caerulescens.*)

Locally distributed in the south and midland counties of England and in Ireland. Rare elsewhere in Britain. (For female *see* No. 9.)

12 {
Abdomen green. **13**

Abdomen red. **14**

13 {
Eyes and thorax green. Abdomen green with black stripe down centre and black lines along the sides. Length of head and body about 3 inches.
Emperor Dragonfly (female).
(*Anax imperator.*)

Locally distributed, usually scarce, in southern England. Rare further north; absent from Scotland and Ireland. On the wing in strong, soaring flight over or near water from June to August.
(For male *see* No. 11.)

Eyes green. Thorax and abdomen hairy, bronzy green, the latter marked with yellow on the basal segments. Wing-bases yellow. Length of head and body about 2 inches. **Downy Emerald.**
(*Cordulia aenea.*)

Locally distributed in south and south-east England. Rare or absent elsewhere in Great Britain. Flies from late May to late July.

14.
Eyes red. Thorax pale brown; red at sides. Abdomen bright red. Length of head and body about 1½ inches. **Common Sympetrum (male).**
(*Sympetrum striolatum.*)

14.   Widely distributed and common in many parts of Great Britain. Flies over pools, meadows, fields, and roadsides from July to October.

(For female see No. 9.)

15
{ Abdomen blue.   **16**

      Abdomen other than blue.   **19**

16
{ Legs white.   **17**

      Legs not white.   **18**

17   Legs pure white. Eyes greenish blue. Thorax black striped with blue. Abdomen greenish blue streaked with black. Length of head and body about 1½ inches. **White-legged Damsel-fly (male).**

(Platycnemis pennipes.)

Locally common in southern England, scarce or absent elsewhere in Great Britain. Flies near streams and rivers from June to August.

(For female see No. 21.)

Head and body deep metallic blue. Wings dark iridescent brown. Length of head and body nearly 2 inches. **Demoiselle Agrion (male).**

(Agrion virgo.)

Widely but locally distributed in Great Britain, most common in southern England, Wales, and Ireland. Flies over streams and rivers from June to August.   (For female see No. 22.)

Very similar to the last species but the brown pigment on the wings is confined to a large patch or band on the centre of each; the basal and apical portions being clear. Length of head and body about 1¾ inches. **Banded Agrion (male).**

18

(Agrion splendens.)

244

18 Locally common in the southern half of England, Wales, and Ireland. Scarce or absent elsewhere in Britain. Flies over pools, streams, and meadows from late May through the summer.

(For female *see* No. 22.)

Eyes blue. Thorax blue with black front border and central band. Abdomen bright pale blue with a black spot or streak on most of the segments. Wings clear. Length of head and body about 1¼ inches. **Common Blue Damsel-fly (male).**
(*Enallagma cyathigerum.*)

Common in many parts of Great Britain in open country, as well as near lakes, rivers, and marshes, from early June to late August.

(For female *see* No. 22.)

Similar to the last species but thorax black with blue at the sides. Black markings on the abdomen thicker than in the Blue Damsel-fly. Length of head and body about 1¼ inches.
Common Coenagrion (male).
(*Coenagrion puella.*)

Common in many parts of England; more local elsewhere. May be seen flying, often in large numbers, over or near water from June to late August. (For female *see* No. 24.)

19
{ Abdomen green.   **20**
{ Abdomen not green.   **23**

20
{ Legs white.   **21**
{ Legs not white.   **22**

21.   Legs pure white. Eyes pale green. Thorax black striped and edged yellowish green. Abdomen yellowish green with short streak of black on most of the segments. Length of head and body about 1¼ inches.   **White-legged Damsel-fly (female)**
(*Platycnemis pennipes*.)

Locally common in southern England. Scarce or absent elsewhere in Great Britain. Flies near streams and rivers from June to August.
(For male *see* No. 17.)

Eyes red brown. Thorax and abdomen metallic green. Wings suffused pale brown. Length of head and body about 2 inches.
Demoiselle Agrion (female).
(*Agrion virgo*.)

Widely but locally distributed in Great Britain, most common in southern England, Wales, and Ireland. Flies over streams and rivers from June to August.   (For male *see* No. 18.)

Very similar to the last species but with clear, colourless wings.   **Banded Agrion (female).**
(*Agrion splendens*.)

Locally common in the southern half of England, Wales, and Ireland. Scarce or absent elsewhere. Flies over pools, streams, and meadows from late May through the summer.   (For male *see* No. 18.)

Eyes dark blue (male) or brown (female). Thorax metallic green with yellow on the basal half. Abdomen metallic green, sometimes powdered blue on sides (adult male). Length of head and body about 1¼ inches.   **Green Lestes.**
22   (*Lestes sponsa*.)

22 〉 Locally distributed over the British Isles. Common in some parts of England near ponds, streams, and marshes. Flies in July and August.

Eyes, thorax, and abdomen greyish green. Thorax striped with black on the centre and sides. Abdominal segments streaked with black. Length of head and body about 1¼ inches.
Common Blue Damsel-fly (female).
(*Enallagma cyathigerum.*)

Common in most parts of the British Isles in open country as well as near rivers, lakes, and marshy ground. Flies from early June to late August.
(For male *see* No. 18.)

23 { Abdomen black.   **24**

{ Abdomen red.   **25**

Eyes red. Thorax red (male) or black and green (female). Abdomen black with green at the segment joints; sometimes powdered blue at base and tip. Length of head and body about 1¼ inches.
Red-eyed Damsel-fly.
(*Erythromma naias.*)

Locally distributed in the southern half of England, nowhere common. Frequents still water and flies in June and July.

Eyes green. Thorax black striped with pale green or blue on the centre and sides. Abdomen black with greenish tinge; tip blue. Length of head and body about 1¼ inches.   **Common Ischnura.**
(*Ischnura elegans.*)

24 〉 Widely distributed and common in most parts of the British Isles. Flies over and near ponds, lakes, and slow streams from early June to the end of August.

24 Eyes brownish green. Thorax black edged pale green at segment joints and along sides. Length of head and body about 1¼ inches.

Common Coenagrion (female).
(*Coenagrion puella.*)

Common in many parts of England; more local elsewhere in Great Britain. Flies over or near water, often in large numbers, from June to late August. (For male *see* No. 18.)

Eyes red (male) or pale brown (female). Thorax black edged red. Abdomen red with bronzy black on the hind segments. Legs black. Length of head and body about 1½ inches.

Large Red Damsel-fly.
(*Pyrrhosoma nymphula.*)

Widely distributed and common in many parts of Great Britain. Flies from early May to late August over or near pools, streams, marshes, and rivers.

25 Similar to the last species but smaller and with red legs. In the male the abdomen is wholly red, but in the female the joints of the segments are black, and some of the hind segments are marked with bronzy black. The eyes are red in both sexes. Length about 1¼ inches. **Small Red Damsel-fly.**
(*Ceriagrion tenellum.*)

Locally distributed, usually scarce, in some southern and eastern counties of England and in Wales. Flies from June to the end of August over reed-grown pools and marshes.

SECTION X

MAYFLIES, ALDER-FLIES, CADDIS-FLIES, STONE-FLIES, SNAKE-FLIES, SCORPION-FLIES, AND LACEWING-FLIES

THE insects included in the following section are so diverse, both in structure and habits, that no general description can be given here. The characteristics of the different orders to which they belong are, therefore, described separately in the portions of text devoted to each.

1 {
Fore-wings longer than hind-wings. **2**

Fore-wings and hind-wings of about equal length. **5**
}

2 {
Antennae very short. Extremity of abdomen bearing two or three long, tail-like filaments. **3**

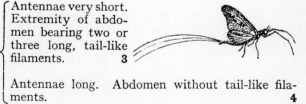

Antennae long. Abdomen without tail-like filaments. **4**
}

3   Body dull yellow except for part of the thorax and a line down each side of the abdomen, which are black. Tip of abdomen bearing three long, jointed filaments. Wings glistening; showing a close network of brown veins. At rest the wings are folded together high over the body as in butterflies. **Antennae minute.** Legs very slender. PL. 63.
Mayfly. (*Ephemera vulgata*.)

3. This is one of the large British mayflies, measuring about 1½ inches across the outspread wings. The mayfly nymph is aquatic, living in ponds, streams, and rivers, some species favouring still water, others more rapid currents. It is a rather shrimp-like creature with long tail processes which serve as breathing organs. When fully grown it creeps from the water and, bursting through the nymphal skin, emerges as a winged insect, but differing from the perfect mayfly in its duller wings, shorter legs, and tail filaments. Shortly after it undergoes another moult which transforms it into the final adult form. Having at length achieved maturity the mayfly rises into the air to mate. Its life as a winged insect is brief, lasting from a few hours to a day or two. During this time no food is taken, the mouth

Nymph of mayfly.

parts being atrophied. In contrast to the very short life of the perfect insect, the aquatic nymphal stage may extend over a year or more. Mayflies usually rise to mate about sundown, large numbers often swarming in the air together. The mated females drop their eggs in disk-shaped masses into the water while on the wing. There are over forty British species of mayflies, varying in size from 1½ inches to less than ¼ inch across the outspread wings. All resemble one another closely in life history and habits.

4. Body black, minutely marked with reddish brown. Wings semi-transparent, yellowish brown with conspicuous black veins. At rest the wings are

4. folded obliquely on the sides of the body. Head broad, antennae long. Length of head and body ¾ inch. **Alder-fly.**
(*Sialis lutarius.*)

A rather dingy-looking fly which may be found resting on tree trunks and posts near water or making short flights among herbage. The larva is aquatic, living in ponds or slow muddy streams. It is carnivorous, with broad head furnished with large, pointed jaws, slender legs, and seven pairs of breathing appendages along the sides of the abdomen. The abdomen tapers to a slender, fringed tail. When fully grown it leaves the water to bury itself in the earth to pupate.

5. ⎰ Hind-wings appreciably broader than fore-wings. **6**
⎱ Hind-wings not appreciably broader than fore-wings. **9**

6. ⎰ Wings hairy, large, and broad. General appearance of insect moth-like. **7**
⎱ Wings not hairy. Appearance of insect not moth-like. **8**

7. Wings sombre brown in colour. Body and wings densely covered with brown or brownish grey hair.

At rest the wings are closed along the sides of the body. Fore-wings narrower than hind-wings. Flight weak and fluttering. PL. 63. **Caddis-fly.**
(Order Trichoptera.)

7   The caddis-flies are often mistaken for moths, to which they bear a strong superficial resemblance. They are mostly nocturnal. The chief difference is that the wings are covered with hairs, not scales as in the moths, and the mouth parts are adapted for lapping. The larva is aquatic, soft-bodied, and cylindrical, with the head and first three body segments horny. The legs are moderately long and the abdomen bears a series of small, tubular filaments which extract air from the water in which

Some types of cases made by caddis-fly larvae.

the grub lives. The most striking peculiarity of the larvae of caddis-flies is their practice of forming cases from grains of sand, small stones, snail shells, fragments of twigs, leaves, etc., in which the soft hind body is sheltered. The case is held in position by two strong hooks which are borne on the last abdominal segment of the grub. The materials of which the cases are made are held together by fine silk threads exuded from spinnerets near the mouth. As the larva grows the case is extended to cover the larger body. When the grub is fully grown it spins a network of silk across the aperture and pupates within this shelter. The majority of caddis-worms seem to be vegetarian, feeding on

7. water-plants, but some species are carnivorous, devouring small water snails, tadpoles, water worms, etc. When the nymph is ready to emerge it bites its way out of the case, rises to the surface of the water, and creeps to dry land up the stem of a water-plant. Shortly afterwards the skin bursts and the caddis-fly is liberated. There are a very large number of British caddis-flies, varying in size from 2 inches to $\frac{1}{4}$ inch across the outspread wings.

Wings narrow and membranous, longer than the rather thick body. The three segments of the thorax separate and distinct. Fore-wings narrower than the hind-wings. At rest the wings are folded flat on the back. Head broad, antennae long. Flight slow and laboured. Colour blackish brown with yellow streak on centre of thorax and head. Abdomen bearing two long, jointed appendages, almost as long as the antennae. Length of body and head about $\frac{3}{4}$ inch. PL. 63.

Stone-fly. (*Perla bicaudata.*)

Stone-flies occur near water, flying weakly in sunshine or creeping on water-plants, tree trunks, or stones. The nymphs are aquatic, living in lakes, streams, and rivers, usually in hilly or mountainous districts, where they may be found hiding under submerged stones or in small chambers in the banks. In shape they resemble the adult fly except that they are wingless. They breathe by means of tufts of gill filaments situated at the bases

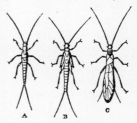

STONE-FLY
A. and B. Nymphs.
C. Perfect insect.

of the legs and tail appendages, or cerci, and feed
8 on any small prey they can capture. The perfect

8 insect takes no food and lives a very short time, but the nymphal life extends over a year or more.

Similar to the above but yellowish brown with black eyes and green-tinted wings. PL. 63.
Green Stone-fly. (*Chloroperla viridis.*)

Resembling the Stone-fly in shape but smaller and with very small, inconspicuous cerci. Colour of body mottled brown. **Willow-fly,** ½ inch.
(*Nemoura variegata.*)

A common species which may be found near ponds as well as by streams and rivers.

9 Thorax very long and attenuated, so that the head appears to be set on a long, slender neck. **10**

Thorax not as described above. **11**

10 Wings large and netted, with an opaque spot near the tip of each. Thorax long, thin, and neck-like, bearing the large, oval head. Eyes small but prominent. At rest the wings lie along the sides of the body. Legs and antennae long. In the female the tip of the abdomen bears a long, sharp ovipositor. General colour greenish black, with dull brassy sheen and a few yellow spots. Legs yellow. Length of head and body about ½ inch. PL. 63.
Snake-fly. (*Rhaphidia ophiopsis.*)

This interesting and curiously shaped fly occurs locally in wooded districts, where it may be seen resting or crawling on tree trunks, foliage, and blossoms. The long, slender prothorax is freely movable on the hind segments and its frequent movement gives the insect a very peculiar appearance. Snake-flies, of which there are four British species, all very much alike, are carnivorous, feeding on small insects. The larva is long and

10. cylindrical, with large horny head and prothorax. It lives under the bark of dead trees and in rotting wood, feeding on insects. The pupa is at first inactive but later leaves the pupal case and crawls about, again becoming quiescent prior to completing its metamorphosis. None of the British species is common.

11 { Wings spotted with brown.   **12**
    { Wings without spots.   **13**

12. Wings long and rather narrow; transparent with brown veins, all four with several well-defined dark brown spots. Antennae and legs long. Head produced into a long, beak-like process at the apex of which is the mouth. Body long and narrow. Abdomen tapering towards the tip which in the male bears a pair of forceps-like processes. Colour black with a few yellow spots. In the male the tip of the abdomen is reddish yellow. Legs yellow. Length of head and body $\frac{2}{3}$ inch. Pl 63.   **Scorpion-fly.**
                                      (*Panorpa communis.*)

Takes its name from the habit of the male insect of curling the abdomen upwards, thus showing the terminal forceps. Despite this terrorizing attitude the Scorpion-fly is quite harmless. It is fairly common on herbage by the sides of ditches, ponds, etc., where it feeds on small insects. Eggs are laid in the soil in which the caterpillar-like larva lives and eventually pupates.

13 { Body slender, delicate green. Wings large, transparent, and tinged with green. At rest they are folded roof-like over the body. Antennae long. Eyes shining gold. Length of head and body about $\frac{1}{2}$ inch. Pl. 63.

Green Lacewing.
(*Chrysopa perla.*)

13 | A widely distributed and common insect which
may be seen fluttering over plants both in gardens
and open country, or in rooms in the evening, which
it enters attracted by lights. The beauty of the
shining golden eyes, which fades shortly after death,
has earned for this insect the name Golden-eye.
Its title of Stink-fly refers to the unpleasant odour
exhaled by the fly when held in a closed hand.

Lacewing with egg and larva.

The oval eggs are supported on thin, hair-like,
foot-stalks on the leaves of plants. The larva is
carnivorous, impaling its prey, consisting of various
kinds of aphides or green-fly, on its sharp jaws and
sucking the juices through the hollow channels
with which these highly specialized organs are
perforated. When fully grown the larva spins a
cocoon of white silk in which to pupate.

Similar in shape to the Green Lacewing but with
brown body. Wings clear, without green tint.

Brown Lacewing.
(*Hemerobius concinnus.*)

There are several British species of both green and
brown lacewings but their differences are of a kind
which can be determined only by close anatomical
examination. All resemble one another in habits.
The Brown Lacewing mentioned above, though
less often noticed than the Green Lacewing, is
widely distributed and generally common.

TWO-WINGED FLIES

THE word fly as generally used is about as ambiguous as a
word can be. The term is frequently applied to any kind
of flying insect other than those not at once recognizable
as a bee, a wasp, or a dragonfly. Strictly, however, flies
are sharply differentiated from all other types of insects
by the presence of only one pair of functional wings.
The organs used for flying are the fore-wings. The hind-
wings are vestigial, represented by tiny structures called

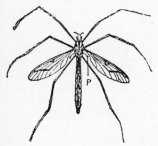

Crane-fly, showing halteres (P).

Head of house-fly showing
compound eye-masses and
trunk-like proboscis with
dilated end.

halteres or balancers, because their purpose appears to be
to enable an insect to maintain its balance in the air.
Each consists of a slender stalk bearing a minute round
or pear-shaped knob at the end. In most flies the
balancers are too small to be visible to the naked eye, but
in the larger crane-flies they may be plainly seen. The
true flies belong to the appropriately named order
Diptera. Over six thousand species occur in the British
Isles. Their chief characteristics, apart from the possession of but one pair of wings, are a large head, in which
the compound eyes occupy most of the surface, and

mouth parts adapted for sucking, often associated with a piercing proboscis. All the other regions of the body vary considerably with the manner of life of the species concerned. The antennae may be long, slender, and many-jointed, or very short, thick, and with but three joints. In the blow-flies and their relatives these organs are of the latter type and hang down, close pressed against the front of the head, so that their presence may remain unsuspected until the head of the fly is carefully examined through a strong lens.

The great variation shown by dipterous insects is sufficiently exemplified by such well-known flies as the crane-flies and mosquitoes on the one hand and the house-fly, blow-fly, and bee-fly on the other. In one group the parts of the body are long and narrow, the legs very long and excessively thin, while in the other the head, thorax, and abdomen are all short and stout, the legs of only moderate length and not particularly slender. The habits of flies are as variable as is their shape. Some feed on blood sucked from the larger mammals, others are predacious, capturing other insects. Many are vegetarian, either piercing the cuticle of plants and imbibing the juices or sipping nectar from flowers. Yet others feed on the liquids emanating from decaying

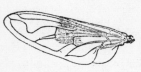

Wing of fly.

animal or vegetable matter. The wings are thin, membranous, and transparent. In a few species, like the bee-fly (*Bombylius major*), a portion of the wings may be clouded with pigment, or spotted with brown as in some of the crane-flies and mosquitoes, but no true fly has wholly opaque wings.

Metamorphosis is complete. From eggs laid on or in plants, animals, decaying matter, or water, legless grubs hatch. These may be headless, like the maggots of the house-fly, blow-fly, dung-flies, and many others, or provided with a distinct head as in the larvae of gnats. The maggot is a peculiar type of grub which is specialized for living among soft food masses. The fore part is narrow and pointed, the hind end being much broader, truncated, and with two large spiracles on its posterior surface. This arrangement enables these wriggling creatures to feed with the whole body buried in rotting, often semi-liquid, material, leaving only the broad tail end

A   B

(A) Maggot and (B) pupa case of blow-fly.

exposed to the air. The pupa may be free, as in the active, aquatic, tadpole-like pupa of the gnat, or enclosed in a barrel-shaped case composed of the hardened larval skin, as in the blow-flies. In the latter case a curious provision is made to enable the perfect insect to escape from the closed puparium. When the fly is ready to emerge a small inflated bladder is protruded from the front of the head. This presses strongly against the top of the barrel and causes the walls to rupture, a small lid being forced upwards to release the fly.

SECTION XI

TWO-WINGED FLIES

1 ⎰ Body long and narrow.
⎹ Legs very long, slender, and
⎹ fragile.　　　　　　　**2**

⎹ Not as described above.　　　　　　　**7**

2 ⎰ Legs excessively long, fragile, and thread-like.　End
⎹ of abdomen blunt and somewhat swollen (male)
⎹ or sharply pointed (female).　Hind-wings repre-
⎹ sented by small organs, each consisting of a slender
⎹ stalk bearing a round knob, clearly visible beyond
⎹ the outspread fore-wings.　　　　**Crane-flies.　3**

⎹ Legs long but not excessively so.　Antennae
⎹ plumose (male) or long with short hairs at the
⎹ joints.　Head with piercing proboscis.
⎹ 　　　　　　　**Gnats and Mosquitoes.　6**

3 ⎰ Wings clear.　　　　　　　**4**

⎹ Wings spotted or blotched.　　　　　　　**5**

4 ⎰ Insect large.　Head and body greyish brown.
⎹ Wings clear.　Legs hairlike and very long.
⎹ 　　　　**Common Crane-fly** or **Daddy-long-legs.**
⎹ 　　　　　　　(*Tipula oleracea.*)

⎹ A familiar insect in fields, meadows, and other
⎹ grassy places.　Often enters houses.　The larva is

260

4 equally well known as the leather-jacket, a destructive pest which lives in the soil, feeding on the roots of grasses and other plants. The long, fragile legs of the Crane-flies are used for alighting and holding on to grasses. They are of little use for walking and are readily shed.

Rather smaller than the Daddy-long-legs and with the yellow abdomen marked with a row of short black bands or stripes. **Banded Crane-fly.**
(*Pachyrhina maculata.*)

More locally distributed than the Daddy-long-legs but not uncommon in meadows and fields in many parts of the British Isles.

Larger than the Daddy-long-legs and with wings blotched with brown. **Large Crane-fly.**
(*Pedicia rivosa.*)

Less generally common than the Daddy-long-legs. Usually found in damp meadows or by river sides.

Less than half the size of the Common Crane-fly with reddish-brown body and several dark spots on the wings.

5
Marsh Crane-fly.
(*Ptychoptera paludosa.*)

Common on marshy ground.

Larger and less slender than the last species (length of head and body about ¾ inch). Wings tinged yellow, with one large brown blotch near the apex of each. **Ornate Crane-fly.**
(*Ctenophora ornata.*)

Fairly common in fields and meadows.

Wings without spots. When the insect is at rest the body is held in horizontal position, often with the hind pair of legs raised.

Common Gnat or **Mosquito.**
(*Culex pipiens.*)

Too well known to need detailed description. The female has a long, sharp proboscis with which the skin of her victims is punctured and through which their blood is sucked. In the male the proboscis is smaller and weaker. He is not a blood-sucker. Such food as he takes consists of the juices of plants. The larva is aquatic, with large head and thorax, and long, more slender abdomen bearing a breathing tube, or siphon, on the eighth segment. The pupa looks like a diminutive tadpole and is also aquatic. Both may be found in rain-water barrels, static water tanks, ditches, ponds, and streams. The swollen fore body of the pupa bears a pair of trumpet-shaped breathing tubes. The very different positions of their breathing apparatus causes the larva and pupa to assume opposite attitudes at the water surface. The larva hangs tail upwards from the surface film, the pupa head upwards. *Culex pipiens* is the commonest British gnat but there are several others, differing very little in general form.

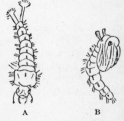

A   B

6 Many suck human blood.   Larva and pupa of gnat.

6 ⎞ Wings spotted with brown.   When the insect is at
rest the body is held slanting upwards from head to
tip of abdomen.   **Spangled-winged Mosquito.**
(*Anopheles maculipennis.*)

This is the commonest of the Anopheline mosquitoes and is notorious as being a transmitting
agent of malaria.   All mosquitoes of this type are
characterized by the inclined position of the body
when at rest.   Both larva and pupa are aquatic,
but the larva, unlike that of *Culex*, has no breathing
tube, respiration being effected through spiracles
on the upper surface of the eighth abdominal segment.   For that reason when taking in air it lies
with the body parallel to the water surface, not
head downwards like the gnat larva.

Insect much larger than the Common Gnat, with
abdomen and legs banded with white.
Ringed Mosquito.
(*Theobaldia annulata.*)

This is the largest of British mosquitoes, being
about half as large again as the Common Gnat and
Spangled-wing.   The female attacks humans as
well as other warm-blooded animals.   Though
less generally abundant than the gnat, it is widely
distributed in Britain and active in warm spells
at all seasons.

About the same size as the Common Gnat.   Wings
unspotted.   Thorax with two lines on the front
portion.   Abdomen with scanty golden yellow
hairs.   **Two-striped Mosquito.**
(*Anopheles bifurcatus.*)

6 } Considerably smaller than gnat. Thorax marked with grey. Palpi banded. Wings clouded dusky grey. **Dark-winged Mosquito.** (*Anopheles plumbeus.*)

Both these mosquitoes are common and widely distributed and frequently attack humans.

7 {
Whole body very hairy. Fly robust, rotund; resembling a small humble-bee. **8**

Abdomen hairy but fly not resembling a humble-bee in shape. **17**

Abdomen not hairy. **20**

8 {
Insect over ¾ inch long. **9**

Insect considerably less than ¾ inch long. **10**

9. Abdomen long and thick. Head and thorax blackish. Abdomen yellow with black on the fore half and some black spots on the hind segment. Legs black. General appearance that of a long-bodied humble-bee. PL. 16. **Great Robber-fly,** ⅞ inch. (*Laphria flava.*)

Locally distributed and uncommon. A carnivorous insect which preys on beetles, flies, and ants of many kinds.

10 {
Front edge or base of wings densely clouded with dark brown. **11**

Wings not as described. **12**

11 }
Body stout and globose, thickly covered with long, tawny brown hair paling to golden yellow on the sides of the abdomen. Head with long, pointed proboscis—about ⅓ inch in length—held stiffly in front of the insect. PL. 64. **Bee-fly,** ½ inch. (*Bombylius major.*)

11 Widely distributed and generally common. Often visits gardens. Despite its formidable appearance, this fly is quite harmless, its long, lance-like proboscis being used to suck nectar from deep-throated flowers. The larva lives as a parasite in the nests of several kinds of solitary bees, at first feeding on the stores of pollen in the cells of its hosts and later devouring the bee grubs.

Considerably smaller than the last species. General colour of body black; the fore part of the thorax and the abdomen tinged yellow. Wings densely clouded with black on the basal halves, otherwise clear. **Black-and-white Bee-fly,** ⅓ inch.
(*Anthrax semiatra.*)

May be seen about flowers in dry, sunny places or basking on stones, etc. Locally common.

Similar to the last species but with the dark clouding extending to the basal two-thirds of the wings and with small clear spots on the dark areas.
Windowed Bee-fly, ⅓ inch.
(*Anthrax fenestralis.*)

The larva of this fly is parasitic on the grubs of other insects. A not uncommon, though somewhat local, insect, which visits flowers and flies in sunshine.

12 Body of fly black. **13**

Body of fly not wholly black. **14**

13. Thorax broader than head. Abdomen broad, almost circular in outline. Head reddish yellow, all other parts black. Body covered with stiff black hairs which are spiny on the legs. Bases and edges of wings yellowish. **Black Spiny Fly.**
(*Echinomyia grossa.*)

13. A large, robustly built fly as large as a humble-bee. The larva is parasitic on caterpillars of butterflies and moths and on beetle grubs. The eggs are laid on plants from which the newly hatched, very active larvae reach the bodies of nearby caterpillars, boring into the interior of their victims and feeding on their tissues. Locally distributed but not uncommon.

14 { Fly black, with yellow, red, or white markings. **15**

Colour not as described. **16**

Head, thorax, and hind part of abdomen black. Fore half of abdomen white. Wings showing a dark patch in the middle. **White-belted Hover-fly.** (*Volucella pellucens.*)

All the hover-flies frequent flowers for the nectar on which they feed. They owe their popular name to their habit of hovering on rapidly beating wings over blossoms, then darting away to another possible source of food. The White-belted, or Pellucid, Hover-fly lays its eggs in the nests of wasps, the larvae feeding on the remnants of food and detritus left in the used cells, thus acting as scavengers to their hosts. The wasps appear to recognize their services and leave the intruders unmolested. This hover-fly is widely distributed and fairly common. It takes the name Pellucid from the semi-transparent white belt on the abdomen.

Head, thorax, and abdomen black with a bright red or orange tail. Wings showing dark transverse wavy lines. **Red-tailed Hover-fly.** (*Volucella bombylans.*)

15 The adult insect frequents flowers and is generally fairly common. The larva lives in the nests of humble-bees, acting as scavenger in much the same

15 way as does the grub of the last species in wasps' nests.

Head and thorax blackish brown. Abdomen black with white tip. **White-tailed Drone-fly.**
(*Eristalis intricaria.*)

When seen at rest on a flower this fly bears a close resemblance to a small humble-bee. The larva lives in stagnant water, breathing by means of a long, telescopic siphon on the end of the abdomen.
(*See* Drone-fly, No. 24.)

Head and body dark brown. Abdomen yellow with a dark brown band near the base. **Narcissus-fly.**
(*Merodon equestris.*)

This fly derives its popular name from the partiality shown by its larvae for narcissus bulbs, from which it eats the centres, thereby wreaking havoc in gardens in which it occurs.

Head brown. Thorax golden-yellow with brown patch in centre. Abdomen golden yellow with one broad and one narrow band of brown. Fore edge of wings yellow. *Arctophia mussitans.*

A large, brown-banded, golden yellow hover-fly. Not uncommon in summer about flowers. Its larva preys on other insects.

Head brown. Thorax and abdomen golden yellow. Legs brown with yellow hairs. Some darker, brownish hairs usually occur on the central part of the thorax and on the sides of the abdomen.
Criorrhina floccosa.

Another of the hover-flies. The general appearance is that of a golden-yellow, hairy, humble-bee
16 without any special markings.

16 〉 Head greyish brown.　Thorax blackish brown with the fore part covered with greyish yellow hairs. Abdomen greyish yellow with a broad patch of brown across the middle.　Wings rather dusky.

Ox Warble-fly.
(*Hypoderma bovis.*)

This and the closely related *Hypoderma lineatum* are found where cattle are grazed in late spring and summer.　The female lays her eggs on the hairs of the grazing beasts, usually on the flanks or legs. The larva hatches in a few days and bores into its victim's skin, moving and feeding in the tissues for several months.　Eventually it reaches the back, where it pierces the hide to enable its spiracles, or breathing pores, borne on the tip of the body, to reach the air.　The presence of these larvae beneath the skin causes swellings or 'warbles' to appear along the back of the affected beast.　When fully grown the larvae drop to the ground and pupate.

17 ⎰ Fly wholly black.　　　　　　　　　　　　**18**

⎱ Fly not wholly black.　　　　　　　　　　**19**

18.　Fly about the size of a Blow-fly.　Body and legs covered with black hairs.　Legs long; carried in a loose bundle when the insect is in flight.

St. Mark's Fly.
(*Bibio marci.*)

Owes its name to its appearing on or about St. Mark's Day, 25th April.　Common by hedgerows, in woods, and in fields.　In the male the head is broad and almost round, with the compound eyes so large that they meet in the middle.　Close examination shows that each eye is formed of two

18.   portions, an upper and a lower. The head of the
female is longer than broad and the eyes are
noticeably smaller. The larva feeds on the roots
of grass.

19 {

Fly brown covered on head, thorax, abdomen, and
legs with yellow hair.   **Yellow Dung-fly.**
                               (*Scatophaga stercoraria.*)

Common on fresh cattle dung throughout the
summer. The female is less hairy than the male.
Eggs are laid in dung, in which the larvae feed.
This fly appears to be partially carnivorous as it
may occasionally be seen preying on smaller flies.

A long, slender fly with ashy grey, hairy body
chequered with black, and pale brownish wings.
Head with long beak-like proboscis, carried vertically downwards. PL. 64. **Tesselated Empis,** ⅓ inch
                               (*Empis tesselat/*

Common near woods and hedgerows, where the
female may be seen hawking for small flying
insects, which are impaled on her long, sharp
proboscis. The male feeds on nectar and sometimes visits gardens. The larva is carnivorous.
It lives under dead leaves, moss, etc.

20 {

Abdomen long and narrow.   **21**

Abdomen not long and narrow.   **22**

21 {

A large and striking-looking insect nearly an inch
in length. Head brown with yellow markings.
Thorax fulvous, hairy. Abdomen black on basal
half, remainder bright yellow, ending in a short tail.
Legs brown. Wings pale brown with dark spot on
the hind margins.   **Hornet-fly.**
                               (*Asilus crabroniformis.*)

21 ⎱ Locally distributed in southern England. The female is larger than the male. An active, predatory fly which preys on other insects of all kinds, including bees, wasps, beetles, dragonflies, grasshoppers, etc. Despite its popular name it has little resemblance to the Hornet but is not unlike the Great Horntail. This is the largest of British robber-flies, of which there are some twenty species. All are characterized by their large bulging eyes, long legs, and horny, beak-like proboscises. All prey on other insects, seizing their victims in the forelegs and sucking their juices through the long 'beak.'

Eyes dark brown. Body pale greyish brown with darker markings. Abdomen with blackish tip, somewhat tapering. *Philonicus albiceps.*

An example of the smaller kinds of robber-flies, measuring about ⅔ inch in length. The larvae live in the soil and are predatory. This species is widely distributed and generally common.

Head and thorax blackish. Abdomen yellow with a row of black spots down the centre. Legs long, yellowish brown. Wings with brown spot.
PL. 16. **Snipe-fly, ¾ inch.**
(*Leptis scolopacea.*)

Common in fields. Looks somewhat like a stoutly built crane-fly but has thicker and shorter legs. The Snipe-fly is carnivorous, preying on other insects both in its adult and larval state.

Similar to above but with abdomen banded alternately with black and yellow. Wings clouded— not spotted. **Ibis-fly.**
(*Atherix ibis.*)

21 This fly is found in meadows and by stream sides. The larva is aquatic. The eggs are dropped as the females fly above the water, often in swarms.

22

Insect showing general resemblance to a bee. **23**

General appearance wasp-like. **25**

General appearance neither bee- nor wasp-like. **28**

23

Abdomen almost as broad as long, flattened and square in outline except for a small projection at the tip. Thorax narrower than abdomen. Antennae strongly elbowed. Colour black tinged yellow, with yellow markings on the head and three short yellow streaks on the sides of the abdomen. Wings dusky. **Chameleon-fly,** ½ inch. (*Stratiomys chamaeleon.*)

Common on umbelliferous flowers, usually in damp situations. The larva is long and rather flattened; broadest in the middle, tapering to the tail. It is aquatic, hanging head downwards with its tail breaking the water surface.

Not as above described. **24**

24

Head and thorax dark brown. Abdomen dark brown, with two large patches of dull orange near its base. Legs brown. Wings tinged yellowish brown. PL. 64. **Drone-fly.** (*Eristalis tenax.*)

Bears a strong resemblance to the hive-bee, for which it is often mistaken as it flies about flowers in late summer. It may also be seen crawling leisurely on windows indoors. The larva is known as the rat-tailed maggot. It lives in stagnant water, resting on the mud at the bottom and

24 ⎫ stretching its long, telescopic tail—which is a breathing tube—to the surface to bring the respiratory pores in contact with air. This curious organ may be extended to a length several times that of the larva's body. The adult insect feeds on nectar.

Head brown. Thorax yellowish brown with darker longitudinal stripes. Abdomen yellow, banded transversely with dull brown.

Helophilus pendulus.

A pretty hover-fly, generally distributed and often seen hovering over flowers in gardens. The larva is rat-tailed and aquatic, similar to that of the Drone-fly (above).

Head brown. Thorax blackish brown. Abdomen with alternate bands of blackish brown and yellow. Legs yellowish brown. *Sericomyia borealis.*

Another hover-fly which in the larval state lives in muddy water.

Head brown. Thorax greyish brown marked with greyish yellow. Abdomen dull yellow with three dark brown transverse bands and a central longitudinal stripe. *Myriatropa florea.*

The larva of this hover-fly lives in rotting wood.

Head and thorax brown. Abdomen orange or reddish brown, with dark brown longitudinal stripe down the centre. Legs brown. Wings dusky with yellowish edges. Hair on sides and tip of abdomen and on legs spiny. **Brown Spiny Fly.**
(*Echinomyia fera.*)

Closely related to the Black Spiny Fly (No. 13) and ⎭ of similar habits.

24 ⎱ Fly similar in size, shape, and colour to the hive bee. Usually seen where horses are grazed or stabled.

Horse Bot-fly.
(*Gastrophilus equi.*)

The female lays her eggs on the hair of horses and asses. The larvae are conveyed by the licking tongue of the affected beast into its mouth, from which they make their way to the stomach or intestines. When full

Larvae of horse bot-fly in stomach of horse.

grown the grub is voided with its host's excrement and pupates in the ground.

Similar to the Horse Bot-fly but found about sheep pastures. The eggs hatch in the body of the female insect. The newly born larvae are deposited in the nostrils of sheep, whence they move to the frontal sinuses of the head. PL. 64.

Sheep Bot-fly.

25 ⎰ Abdomen black, marked with pale yellow. **26**

⎱ Abdomen deep yellow with dark bands. **27**

Head dark brown. Thorax black. Abdomen black with three short, curved transverse streaks of pale yellow on each side. PL. 16.

Black-and-yellow Hover-fly, ½ inch.
(*Catabomba pyrastri.*)

26 ⎰

26 〉 One of the commonest of the hover-flies. Frequently seen in gardens, hovering over flowers or darting with sight-baffling rapidity from plant to plant. The larva, which is flattened and maggot-like, lives on leaves, feeding on aphides.

Similar to the last species but the streaks on the abdomen are straight, forming thin, interrupted bands. *Chrysotoxum festivum.*

Head broader than thorax. Abdomen long, narrow at base, broadening towards the end. General colour black, with three thin bands of pale yellow on the abdomen. Legs dusky yellow.
Yellow-legged Conops, ⅔ inch.
(*Conops flavipes.*)

Bears a strong resemblance to some of the solitary wasps. Much less active than the hover-flies. The adult insect frequents flowers and is not uncommon. The eggs are laid on the hairy covering of bees and wasps, the larva boring into the body of its host and feeding on its blood

Head broader than thorax. Abdomen long; narrow at base, broader towards the hind end. Head, thorax, and base of abdomen blackish. Remainder of abdomen yellow, with three thin black bands. **Four-banded Conops,** ⅔ inch.
(*Conops quadrifasciata.*)

27 〈 Similar in habits to the Yellow-legged Conops (No. 26).

Head and thorax blackish brown. Abdomen broad at base, rounded at end; yellow banded with blackish brown, the first two bands being connected by a central spot. **Currant Hover-fly,** ⅖ inch.
(*Syrphus ribesii.*)

Widely distributed and generally common. The larva lives on leaves, feeding on aphides.

28 {
Insects as large as the Blow-fly.   **29**

Insects smaller than the Blow-fly.   **32**
}

29 {
Abdomen metallic blue, green, or black.   **30**

Abdomen not as above.   **31**
}

Head reddish brown.   Body dull blue with black hairs.   **Blow-fly or Bluebottle.**
(*Calliphora vomitoria.*)

A very well-known fly, everywhere abundant. The female lays her eggs in carrion or in any meat to which she can gain access. The larva is limbless and headless, with spiracles, or breathing pores, at the broad, hind end. Pupation occurs in the hardened larval skin, which forms a barrel-shaped case, the perfect insect emerging from its cradle by breaking through the top by means of a peculiar inflatable bladder on the front of the head.

Similar to the Blow-fly but much brighter metallic blue.   **Bright Bluebottle.**
(*Cynomya mortuorum.*)

Similar to the Blow-fly but somewhat smaller and with darker brown head and darker, shining blue abdomen.   **Azure-fly.**
(*Protocalliphora azurea.*)

This fly lays its eggs in birds' nests, the maggots feeding on the newly hatched birds.

Thorax and abdomen shining metallic green, sometimes with bronze sheen.   **Green Bottle.**
30   (*Lucilia caesar.*)

30

A very common fly which, unlike the Blow-fly. rarely enters houses. It feeds on flesh of all kinds and has a special liking for fish.

Head dark brown. All other parts glistening black with conspicuous orange wing-bases. **Noon-fly.**
(*Mesembrina meridiana.*)

A widely distributed, large, and handsome fly which may often be seen sunning itself on posts, walls, etc. The female lays her eggs in dung, in which the larvae feed.

Insect about the size of a Blow-fly. Head brown. Thorax striped grey and black. Abdomen chequered black and grey.

Chequered Flesh-fly.
(*Sarcophaga carnaria.*)

Often seen basking in sunshine on walls, paths, and stones. As its name suggests, this fly feeds on decaying animal matter. The eggs hatch within the body of the female, the larvae being born in a fully active condition.

Large, stoutly built fly with broad head, grey-striped thorax, and greyish-brown abdomen. Eyes shine with metallic markings when examined closely. Flies with a deep humming sound.
PL. 16. **Great Horse-fly,** $\frac{9}{10}$ inch.
(*Tabanus sudeticus.*)

Occurs in fields and by hedgerows and woods in summer. The female is a blood-sucker, piercing the skins of horses and cattle with her strong proboscis. In the male the proboscis is smaller and weaker, the food of this sex being confined to nectar and plant juices. The larva is carnivorous,

31 feeding on small worms and grubs in damp soil.

31 Similar to the last species but somewhat smaller and greyer.   **Grey Horse-fly,** ¾ inch.
(*Tabanus bromius.*)

Commoner than the Great Horse-fly but of similar habits.   There are several other horse-flies met with in Great Britain.   All resemble one another closely both in appearance and habits, though differing in size.   The Great Horse-fly is the largest.

Fly about the size of a small Blow-fly and of similar shape.   General colour yellowish grey.   Thorax with darker marks in the centre and near the hind margin.   Abdomen with obscure spots and lines between the segments.   Body covered with short, golden hairs.   At rest the wings overlap one another like scissor blades.   **Cluster-fly.**
(*Pollenia rudis.*)

A fly which, though in no way conspicuous in form or colour, sometimes arrests attention by its habit of congregating in swarms in late autumn and early winter in buildings and lofts.   This clustering is a prelude to a kind of communal hibernation.   The larvae are parasitic on earthworms, the bodies of which they enter on hatching from eggs laid in the ground.

Fly intermediate in size between the Blow-fly and the House-fly.   General colour dusty grey with blackish legs ringed with dull yellow and small white dots on the facial region.   Antennae black. Wings clouded and mottled with brown.

Rain-fly or Clegg, ⅔ inch.
(*Haematopota pluvialis.*)

Common in fields, meadows, woods, and about
32 hedgerows.   The female is a blood-sucker, piercing

32) the skin of cattle, horses, and humans with her
sharp proboscis and inflicting considerable after-
pain. Most visitors to the countryside have
suffered from the attacks of this dusty-grey fly,
which approaches noiselessly—without the humming sound which heralds the larger Horse-flies.
The larva resembles that of the Horse-flies, is
carnivorous, and lives in damp soil.

Similar to the Clegg but rather smaller. Characterized by its brilliant eyes, which are golden green
spotted with purple. This brilliance disappears soon
after the fly is killed. **Gold-eye.**
(*Chrysops caecutiens.*)

Common in meadows and fields in summer. Like
the Clegg, the female attacks both man and
cattle.

Insect closely resembling the House-fly but
slightly smaller, with sharp-pointed proboscis,
carried straight forward in front of the head.
Pl. 64. **Sharp-nosed Fly.**
(*Stomoxys calcitrans.*)

Frequently mistaken for the House-fly. It is
common in dwelling rooms as well as out of doors in
late summer and autumn, making its presence
known by its sharp 'bite.' Its close resemblance
to the House-fly has given rise to the legend that
towards the end of summer that insect changes its
habits and becomes a 'biting fly.' The eggs of the
Sharp-nosed Fly are laid in manure heaps.

Fly resembling House-fly in general appearance but
larger—about half as large again as that common
domestic nuisance—and greyer, with a dusty look.
Stable-fly.
(*Cyrtoneura stabulans.*)

32 } Common in stables and about dung. Sometimes
enters houses. Its sharp proboscis inflicts a sharp
prick on human flesh, though it usually attacks
horses.

Similar to the House-fly but rather larger. Has the
habit of congregating in numbers in buildings in
autumn. **Autumn-fly.**
(*Musca autumnalis.*)

Usually mistaken for the House-fly but differs in its
habit of coming together in large numbers to
hibernate. Breeds in dung.

SECTION XII

WINGLESS INSECTS

IN foregoing sections mention has been made of insects of various kinds, one or both sexes of which are without wings. There are a few others which deserve attention here for, though not generally common, they may be encountered occasionally and a desire felt to identify them. It is not thought necessary to include very small insects, whose shape and structure can be determined only by the aid of a lens or microscope, or such types as fleas and lice, the general appearance of which is well known but whose detailed study is for the specialist.

1 { Abdomen long and tapering.   2
    { Abdomen short and broad.   3

Head small. Antennae very long and many-jointed. Thorax large and broad, composed of three well defined, separate segments. Abdomen long, tapering, with three long, tail-like appendages. Colour silvery. Length about ½ inch.

Silver-fish.
(*Lepisma saccharina.*)

2 Common in warm store-cupboards, where it feeds on sugar, starch, and other dry provisions, in the absence of which it will eat the dry paste behind old wall-paper. The body is covered with silver scales of the same type as those which occur on the

2 ⎫ wings of butterflies and moths. The young closely
⎪ resemble their parents. This very active and slippery
⎪ little insect is not found out of doors in Britain.
⎪ It was probably originally introduced to these
⎪ islands from a warmer country.

⎪ Similar to the Silver-fish but somewhat smaller and
⎪ with longer antennae and tail appendages. The
⎪ latter organs are as long as the head and body; the
⎪ former nearly twice as long. **Fire-brat.**
⎪ (*Thermobia domestica.*)

⎪ Less common than the Silver-fish but sometimes
⎪ found in bakehouses and restaurant kitchens,
⎪ feeding on flour.

⎪ Similar to the Silver-fish in general shape but more
⎪ slender and mottled metallic brown. Occurs
⎪ locally under seaweed on rocky shores. The
⎪ central tail appendage is much longer than the
⎪ lateral ones. **Bronze-fish.**
⎪ (*Petrobius maritimus.*)

⎪ These three insects belong to the order Thysanura
⎪ or Bristle-tails. The other British representatives
⎪ of the order are small, dull-coloured, obscure insects
⎪ which inhabit damp situations beneath dead leaves
⎪ in woods, under stones, or on hillsides. Little is
⎩ known of their habits.

3. Insect flattened. Colour greyish brown. Head
sunk into the fore margin of the thorax; furnished
with a beak-like proboscis. Antennae very short,
consisting of one joint with a small terminal tuft
of bristles. Abdomen joined to thorax by a narrow
waist and broadening abruptly to the hind
extremity so that it has a pear-shaped form. Legs,
short and stout with strong claws. Body covered
with hairs. PL. 64. **Sheep-ked** or **Sheep-tick.**
(*Melophagus ovinus.*)

3. This remarkable insect is a wingless fly, belonging to the order Diptera (Section XI). It lives under the wool of sheep, sucking the blood of its host. The female gives birth to a single larva at a time, which pupates almost immediately. In a few weeks the fully developed ked emerges, the whole life history being passed beneath the sheep's fleece. Other closely related species of wingless, degenerate flies victimize other beasts and many kinds of birds. The Forest-fly (*Hippobosca equina*) is a pest on ponies in the New Forest. Unlike the Sheep-ked this insect is winged. The Deer-fly (*Lipoptena cervi*), too, has wings in early life but casts them after mating, when it lives as a wingless parasite under the coat of the red deer.

INDEX

Scientific names of insects are given only when
there is no generally recognized English name.
The figures in square brackets refer to plates.

INDEX

INDEX

INDEX

INDEX

INDEX

INDEX

INDEX